Toward Multilateral C

VÖLKERRECHT EUROPARECHT UND INTERNATIONALES WIRTSCHAFTSRECHT

Herausgegeben von Peter Hilpold und August Reinisch

Band 4

PETER LANG
Frankfurt am Main · Berlin · Bern · Bruxelles · New York · Oxford · Wien

Daniela Kröll

Toward Multilateral Competition Law?

After Cancún: Reevaluating the Case for Additional International Competition Rules Under Special Consideration of the WTO Agreement

PETER LANG
Internationaler Verlag der Wissenschaften

Bibliographic Information published by the Deutsche Nationalbibliothek
The Deutsche Nationalbibliothek lists this publication in the Deutsche Nationalbibliografie; detailed bibliographic data is available in the internet at <http://www.d-nb.de>.

Printed with financial support of
Leopold-Franzens-Universität Innsbruck.

ISSN 1862-457X
ISBN 978-3-631-56120-1
US-ISBN 0-8204-8779-1

www.peterlang.de

"The challenge is to rise above horizontal thinking and to appreciate the gains to be derived from a global perspective, both in terms of aggregate economic welfare and in terms of the smooth and peaceful workings of the world system, while respecting national law as much as possible"[1].

---

[1] E. M. Fox, *National Law, Global Markets, and Hartford: Eyes Wide Shut,* in: 68 Antitrust Law Journal 2000, 81.

CONTENTS

Abstract

Competition policy has a more prominent role than ever. More and more countries are adopting domestic competition laws in order to reap the maximum benefits from competition within their jurisdiction. However, competition increasingly occurs in a global market place. The trans-national business activities of private market participants may have negative implications for both traditional domestic competition policy and international trade policy.

This book analyses the case for supplementing the existing legal framework with additional international competition rules from a private as well as a state's perspective, and takes into account the Doha Development Agenda and the failed Cancún Ministerial Conference. For the purpose of this analysis, special consideration is given to the WTO Agreement and economic development. The author argues that neither a requirement to adopt a competition law nor substantive harmonization is required to further link trade and competition so as to reduce potential welfare losses.

Chapter I provides an introduction to the economic principles underlying competition law, the aims of competition policy and a high-level summary of the prevailing approaches of competition policy implementation and their divergences.

Chapter II briefly analyses the implications of the internationalisation of competition in a global market place.

Chapter III provides an in-depth analysis of the case for international competition rules from a competition policy perspective. Starting from the implications for private market participants as opposed to those coming about at state level, the analysis also covers existing approaches and their shortcomings.

Chapter IV examines the case for complementary international competition rules from a trade policy perspective. Starting with the relationship of trade and competition policy, the existing legal instruments addressing competition in the WTO Agreement are presented, followed by a critical re-evaluation of traditional arguments in favour of additional WTO competition rules. Subsequently, the results of the relevant Ministerial Conferences and their major stumbling blocks will be considered.

In **Chapter V**, the author considers more recent perspectives in the discussion and identifies potential new incentives for a relaunch of negotiations on competition policy. Thereafter, the author advances her approach for the inclusion of an additional set of competition rules in the WTO Agreement.

This book aims to provide a comprehensive overview of the current status of the discussion on the case for additional international competition rules, and is intended to suit both the advanced reader and any reader not yet familiar with this topic. It considers both competition policy as well as trade policy, and also illustrates a possible solution for a set of international competition rules within the ambit of the WTO.

I. Introduction

Traditional competition law and policy have evolved in a national context in order to *(i)* promote efficiency, liberty, equal opportunities, consumer welfare and the proper functioning of price mechanisms, and *(ii)* to protect competitors and consumers against *private* abuses of market power[2]. Thus, the concept of free competition depends on the legal protection of individual autonomy with regard to economic freedom (e.g. freedom of contract, individual property rights, contract law), but requires supplementary regulation of certain "market imperfections", like market power, external effects or the influence of public goods[3]. The distinction between "competitive" and "anti-competitive" behaviour will, besides economic rationales, depend to a large extent on individual policy goals and the institutional framework provided for the enforcement of the respective rules, although there is growing consensus on certain "hardcore restrictions", such as price fixing agreements or certain types of abuses of market power. Two main approaches to competition policy can be distinguished. First, the "protection of competition approach" emphasizes the enforcement of predictable competition rules in order to prevent "anti-competitive conduct". Second, the "wealth-maximizing approach" places more of a result-oriented and utilitarian focus on general welfare considerations[4].

Therefore, *private* anti-competitive behaviour limiting competition and, thereby, affecting efficiency and consumer welfare has traditionally been targeted by domestic competition law instruments[5]. However, in light of today's global market and international economic interdependence, market participants are increasingly engaging in trans-national activity. Consequently, restrictive business practices have assumed an international dimension.

For the individual competitor, this brings about implications mainly relating to *competition policy*. These implications refer to *(i)* an extension of the underlying business case and *(ii)* to aggravated compliance with the applicable competition law instruments. Thus, from an individual competitor's perspective, a single transaction might invoke competition law implications under various jurisdictions with notable different approaches to competition law as illustrated above. This may trigger conflict of laws issues and aggravate compliance with the various competition law instruments possibly applying for a particular international transaction in the affected jurisdictions.

However, global competition and international restrictive business practices may equally result in implications at the individual *state level*. Domestic com-

---

2 Compare also E.-U. Petersmann, *Proposals for Negotiating International Competition Rules in the Gatt-WTO World Trade And Legal System*, in: 49(II./III.) Aussenwirtschaft 1994, 232 et sqq.

3 E.-U. Petersmann, *ibid.*

4 E.-U. Petersmann, *ibid.*

5 Compare J. Epstein, *The Other Side of Harmony: Can Trade and Competition Laws Work Together in the International Marketplace?* 17 American University International Law Review 2002, 345.

petition law is *de iure* aimed at and limited to the protection of domestic markets or competitors. Thus, from a *competition policy perspective,* an international dimension in competition and restrictive practices may bring about *(i)* the incapability of efficient enforcement due to the limited reach of domestic competition law, and *(ii)* frictions in inter-governmental relationships or diplomacy due to alleged infringement of national sovereignty where a state tries to overcome the legal limitations with recourse to the effects doctrine.

As a third dimension at the state level, the (deliberate or incidental) non-application of domestic competition law to situations with an international dimension must be considered. From a competition policy perspective, the toleration of certain domestic anti-competitive business practices by one state may result in immediate welfare losses for another state affected by the non-avenged international restrictive business practice, or even global welfare in case the relevant geographic market is a worldwide one.

This toleration of international welfare losses links up with the question if *trade policy* is also affected by domestic competition policy and private practices. In particular, an individual state's competition policy could be regarded as infringing its agreed obligations in multilateral intergovernmental trade agreements, e.g. by nullifying or impairing the individual concessions granted under the GATT[6]. For example, concerns have been raised as to whether domestic application of competition law could foreclose market access for or result in discrimination against potential foreign competitors. When these effects come about due to purely public action or through a combination of private and public action, a state will beyond doubt have autonomous responsibility for foreclosing effects via other Member States[7].

Purely private practices may also hamper market access for foreign competitors and, thus, deprive these foreign competitors from the alleged benefits of the liberalisation of trade. Nevertheless, multilateral trading agreements are concluded among governments and only create direct inter-state obligations. Can governments infringe their obligations as agreed in multilateral trading agreements such as the GATT through their domestic approaches to competition policy? Can purely private restrictions replace governmental restrictions to trade? Is private behaviour being addressed at all in the GATT, and if so, are the existing legal instruments sufficient? Is there a need for international competition rules? Which situations should be addressed by such rules?

---

6 Compare WTO Case *Japan – Measures affecting Consumer Photographic Film and Paper,* WTO/DS44/R, commented for example at: D. K. Tarullo, *Norms and Institutions in Global Competition Policy,* in: (94) The American Journal of International Law 2000, 484. See in particular the discussion concerning governmental involvement in a private business practice at para. 10.204 in the decision. In comparison see the argumentation in the GATT case *EEC – Payments and Subsidies Paid to Processors and Producers of Oilseeds and Related Animal-Feed Proteins,* 37th Supp. BISD 86, adopted on January 25, 1990, at para. 148.

7 For many see M.-C. Malaguti, *Restrictive Business Practices in International Trade and the Role of the World Trade Organization,* in: 32(3) Journal of World Trade 1998, 119.

Trade law and policy operate in an international context and concentrate on the liberalisation of *governmental* measures restricting or distorting trade through market access barriers or other distortions. This traditional focus on governmental measures is based on the general assumption that such measures must be regarded as more invasive barriers to international trade than private access barriers and distortions[8]. In this regard, it is worth noting that the GATT rules were elaborated under the expectation that they would be supplemented by additional competition rules as foreseen in chapter V of the 1948 Havana Charter for an International Trade Organization, and would guarantee import and export competition based on the theory of comparative advantage and on "sales in the ordinary course of trade under fully competitive conditions", as postulated by Article VII:2 GATT.

Thus, as early as 1948, the proposed International Trade Organization's Charter contained nine articles dealing with restrictive business practices, obligating Member States to "take appropriate measures" and to "co-operate with the Organization in order to prevent, on the part of private or commercial public enterprises, business practices affecting international trade which constrain competition, limit access to markets, or foster monopolistic control, whenever such practices have harmful effects on the expansion of production or trade and interfere with the achievement of any of the other objectives set forth in Article 1 [*Remark:* of the Charter]"[9]. These provisions would have required members to prevent business practices affecting international trade which restrained competition, limited access to markets or fostered monopolistic control[10].

The Charter listed the following practices as the main practices considered detrimental to Trade Policy or the other objectives of the Charter as set forth in its Article 1[11]:

1. *Price fixing or agreements on terms and conditions of supply of a product;*
2. *Agreements to exclude suppliers or allocating markets between suppliers;*
3. *Discrimination against particular enterprises;*
4. *Limiting production or fixing production quotas;*
5. *Agreements preventing the development of particular technologies;*
6. *Unjustified or unlawful extensions of patent or intellectual property rights;*

---

8 E.-U. Petersmann, *ibid.*

9 *Havana Charter for an International Trade Organization ("ITO-Charter"),* Article 46 para 1, available at: http://www.wto.org/english/docs_e/legal_e/havana_e.pdf (09.08.2005).

10 Compare Jackson/Davey/Sykes, *ibid.*, 1118.

11 *ITO Charter,* Article 46 para. 3, available at: http://www.wto.org/english/docs_e/legal_e/havana_e.pdf (09.08.2005).

7. *Any other business practice held to be restrictive of competition by the Members.*

In addition, Members would have been permitted under the Charter to file a complaint with the organization on the basis that another Member had failed to deal with a situation related to competition[12].

However, the Havana Charter never entered into force[13]. Therefore, apart from fragmentary provisions addressing competition in the Marrakesh Agreement Establishing the World Trade Organisation (hereafter "WTO Agreement") which shall be addressed below, it is only in other free trade areas[14] and customs unions[15] that trade rules have been supplemented by formal and sophisticated competition rules in order to *(i)* guarantee the full benefits of trade liberalisation, and *(ii)* prevent these benefits from being undermined by private restraints of competition[16].

Given the overall success of worldwide trade liberalisation and the constant growth in trans-national private business activity, many authors have argued that trade and competition policies increasingly overlap[17]. It has been argued, for instance, that the more government-mandated trade barriers were lowered, the greater the incentive for private market actors to create their own barriers[18], as they would be subject to increased competition from abroad.

In line with these developments in Academia, a broader concept of competition, covering *both governmental and private* distortions, has been adopted in

---

12 *Ibid.*, Article 46 para. 2.

13 Its failure has been ascribed to the reluctance of the United States Congress to ratify it due to fears concerning a loss of sovereignty. Compare, S. Bilal/M. Olarreaga, *Competition Policy and the WTO: Is there a need for a multilateral agreement?* European Institute of Public Administration Working Paper 98/W/02, available at: http://www.eipa.nl/Publications/Summaries/1997_2000/WorkingPapers/98w02.pdf (04.06.2005).

14 E.g. NAFTA, EFTA, EEA.

15 E.g. the EC.

16 E.-U. Petersmann, *ibid*, 235.

17 For many, see J. H. Jackson, *Alternative Approaches for Implementing Competition Rules in International Economic Relations*, in 49(II/III) Aussenwirtschaft 1994, 177 et sqq.; E.-U. Petersmann, *Proposals For Negotiating International Competition Rules In The GATT-WTO World Trade And Legal System*, in 49(II/III) Aussenwirtschaft 1994, 231 et sqq.; R. D. Anderson/P. Holmes, *Competition Policy and the Future of the Multilateral Trading System*, in 2002 Journal of International Economic Law, 531 et sqq.; I. G. Bercero/S. D. Amarasinha, *Moving the Trade and Competition Debate Forward*, in 2001 Journal of International Economic Law, 481 et sqq; A. D. Mitchell, *Broadening the Vision of Trade Liberalisation. International Competition Law and the WTO*, in 24(3) Journal of World Competition 2001, 343 et sqq.; J. F. Bellis, *Anti-competitive Practices and the WTO: The Elusive Search for New World Trade Rules*, in *Bronckers, M./Quick, R. (eds.)*, New Directions in International Economic Law. Essays in Honour of John H. Jackson, 2000, at 361 et sqq.; M. J. Trebilcock, *Competition Policy and Trade Policy. Mediating the Interface*, in 30(4) Journal of World Trade 1996, 72 et sqq.; A. Mattoo/A. Subramanian, *Multilateral Rules on Competition Policy – A Possible Way Forward*, in 31(5) Journal of World Trade 1997, 95 et sqq.; *P. Lloyd/G. Sampson, Competition and Trade Policy: Identifying the Issues after the Uruguay Round*, in: Lloyd, P. J. (ed.) *International Trade Opening and the Formation of the Global Economy: Selected Essays of P. J. Lloyd* (1999), at pp. 435-459; R. Pitofsky, *Competition Policy in a Global Economy – Today and Tomorrow*, in 1999 Journal of International Economic Law, 403 et sqq.

18 R. E. Hudec, *A WTO Perspective on Private Anti-Competitive Behaviour in World Markets*, 34(1) New England Law Review 1999, 80.

younger regional free trade area and customs union agreements and, to some extent, the 1994 Agreement establishing the new World Trade Organization. Nevertheless, conflicts between trade and competition policies have purportedly led to an increasing number of international disputes and unilateral trade restrictions in return for anticompetitive practices from abroad[19].

Recently, the discussion about the interrelationship between trade and competition policy has been re-institutionalised within the ambit of the WTO by the 1996 Singapore Ministerial Declaration[20] and, subsequently, by the 2001 Doha Ministerial Declaration[21]. The Singapore Declaration established the WTO Working Group on the Interaction of Trade and Competition Policy (WGTCP), whose mandate covered the examination of the interaction between trade and competition policy in light of private anticompetitive practices so as to evaluate the need for negotiations on additional competition rules within the WTO framework. Therefore, the Doha Ministerial Declaration was already building on a recognized case for a multilateral framework to enhance the contribution of competition policy to international trade, and mandated the WGTCP to clarify core principles such as transparency, non-discrimination and procedural fairness, and hard-core cartels as well as voluntary co-operation. Notably, the Doha Declaration brought an additional aspect to the discussion. It focused explicitly on the contribution of competition policy to development, and, therefore, put developing countries' needs at the centre of attention. In particular, it mandated negotiations on technical assistance and capacity building so as to progressively reinforce competition institutions in developing countries on a flexible basis. An emphasis was also placed on co-operation with other intergovernmental organizations and regional and bilateral channels for strengthened assistance. Accordingly, the WTO Member States agreed that negotiations on WTO competition law would start after the following Ministerial Conference in Cancún[22].

The European Union originally had always been a major proponent of an additional multilateral WTO agreement on competition. This can be explained by the particular importance competition policy has been afforded in the European Common Market. The original EC Commission's proposal was centred on the adoption of the following elements[23]:

1. *Core principles and common rules relating to the adoption of a competition law and its enforcement;*

---

19 E.-U. Petersmann, *ibid.*

20 For the text of the Singapore Ministerial Declaration refer to Footnote 328.

21 For the text of the Doha Ministerial Declaration refer to Footnote 330.

22 *Doha Ministerial Declararation,* at para. 23, available at: http://www.wto.org/english/thewto_e/minist/min01_emindecl_e.htm (18.09.2004).

23 Compare EC Commission, *Communication from the Commission to the Council and to the European Parliament: The EU Approach to the WTO Millenium Round,* 1 March 1999, available at: http://trade-info.cec.eu.int/doclib/cfm/doclib_section.cfm?order=date&sec=182&lev=2&sta=21&-en=52&page=2 (02.10.2005), at 11 et sqq.

2. *Common approaches on anticompetitive practices with a significant impact on international trade and investment;*
3. *Provisions on international co-operation;*
4. *Dispute settlement to ensure compliance of domestic competition laws; and enforcement with the provisions agreed multilaterally.*

The 1998 Report on Trade and Competition Policy issued by the WGTCP entailed broad consensus on the relationship of trade and competition policy and identified three major types of international restraints on competition. In light of these results, the WTO General Council gave new directions to the ongoing discussion[24]. In particular, the WGTCP was instructed to research *(i)* the relationship of fundamental WTO principles and competition policy, *(ii)* approaches to promoting co-operation and communication and *(iii)* the contribution of competition policy to the achievement the objectives of the WTO. In relation to these directions, the European Union adapted its original proposal. By the time of the 2003 Cancún Ministerial Conference, the EU proposal consisted of the following three major elements[25] which had also been implemented in the Doha Ministerial Declaration[26]:

1. *Definition of core principles of domestic competition policy, including enforcement mechanisms, the fundamental WTO principles of transparency, non-discrimination, procedural justice and a prohibition of hardcore cartels,*
2. *Promotion of international co-operation between enforcement authorities; and*
3. *Support for the implementation of competition structures in developing countries through capacity building.*

However, the discussion on competition policy in the context of the WTO Agreement has been adjourned for an indefinite period by the "fiasco"[27] of the WTO Cancún Ministerial Conference of September 2003. In Cancún, the initiatives on competition policy and investment, the most controversial Singapore issues, were dropped off the agenda so as to break the deadlock of negotiations. However, this did not bring about the expected result, as the Cancún Ministerial Conference subsequently failed completely.

---

[24] Compare J. Drexl, *International Competition Policy after Cancún: Placing a Singapore Issue on the WTO Development Agenda*, in: 27(3) Journal of World Competition 2004, at 431.

[25] European Commission, *Communication of 21 September 2000 from the European Community and its Member States to the WTO Working Group*, WT/WGTCP/W/152, 25 September 2000, available at: http://docsonline.wto.org/gen_search.asp?language=1 (02.10.2005).

[26] *Ministerial Declaration of 20 November 2001 ("Doha Declaration")*, WT/MIN(01)/DEC/1, 20 November 2001, No. 23-25, available at:
http://www.wto.org/english/thewto_e/minist/min01_emindecl_e.htm (18.09.2004).

[27] S. Cho, *A Bridge Too Far: The Fall of the Fifth WTO Ministerial Conference in Cancún and the Future of Trade Constitution*, in: 7(2) Journal of International Economic Law 2004, 219 et sqq.

Arguably, these developments were the result of an increasing rift between developed and developing countries[28] on core labour standards, investment and competition since the Singapore Ministerial Declaration, which had already culminated at the Seattle Conference in 1999. The events at the Seattle Conference had resulted from discussions concerning the continuous maintenance of high trade barriers on imports of primary labour intensive goods such as agricultural and products and textiles, on which developing countries generally hold a comparative advantage[29]. The Doha Development Agenda brought momentary hope, centred on the priority of development in any new trade agreement. Still, that hope could not outweigh certain inherent ambiguities about the Doha Declaration. In particular, the question of funding of the ambitious technical assistance programme was and remains unclear, and so is the legal nature of the Doha Declaration[30]. A new US farm bill introducing US $180 billion in subsidies and the European Union's failure to reform its Common Agricultural Policy led to the further disappointment of developing countries on the route to Cancún. At the same time, developed countries may have felt deprived of reciprocal concessions from developing countries after the WTO TRIPS Council's decision on then Implementation of paragraph 6 of the Doha Declaration on the TRIPS Agreement and public health[31].

At Cancún, the political sensitivity of the Singapore and Doha issues and a lack of preparation brought about the collapse of the Conference[32]. Nevertheless, the diametrical split of North and South over competition policy was only one issue among others. The essence of the resistance on the part of the developing countries was their fear that the linkage of competition policy to trade could undermine their specific comparative advantage and act as disguised discrimination[33]. From a legal point of view, however, the Doha Declaration first remained the mandate for future work on competition policy[34]. The Ministerial Statement concluding the Cancún Conference reaffirmed the Doha Declaration as a whole[35]. Consequently, the understanding that Doha can and should be saved[36] or at least rehabilitated appeared to be appropriate then.

---

28 S. Cho, *ibid.*, 221 et sqq.

29 S. Cho, *ibid.*, at 223. *Cho* is citing to a World Bank Policy Research Paper on *Globalization, Growth and Poverty: Building an Inclusive World Economy* (2002) 9, 53, according to which this "development deficit" results in costs of about $100 billion per year, which is twice the amount of total foreign aid received from developed countries.

30 In the Declaration, it is referred to as "work program". Arguably, this document would not be enforceable under the DSU which only applies to "covered agreements", compare Article 1 para. 1 of the *Understanding on Rules and Procedures Governing the Settlement of Disputes.* See also S. Cho, *ibid.*, 226 in this regard.

31 S. Cho, *ibid.*, 234.

32 S. Cho, *ibid.*

33 S. Cho, *ibid.*, 231.

34 J. Drexl, *International Competition Policy after Cancún: Placing a Singapore Issue on the Development Agenda*, in: 27(3) Journal of World Competition 2004, at 421.

35 Ministerial Statement of 14 September 2003, WT/MIN(03)/20, 23 September 2003, No. 6, available at: http://www.wto.org/english/thewto_e/minist_e/min03_e/min03_20_e.doc (12.08.2005).

36 S. Cho, *ibid.*, 219.

In light of these developments, the European Union gave up the single undertaking approach in favour of a plurilateral approach[37], so that negotiations would occur selectively. This was not, however, the approach favoured by developing countries, which expressed that they would not only reject negotiations on any of the Singapore issues, but also any plurilateral approach in respect of any multilateral issue like competition policy[38]. They also argued that such approach would be prevented by the consensus requirement of Art. X:9 of the WTO Agreement.

Subsequently, however, the adoption of the "July Package" on 1 August 2004 formally excluded the issue of competition policy from the Work Programme. In this decision, the Council agreed that "no work towards negotiations on [...] these issues will take place within the WTO during the Doha Round"[39]. This exclusion of competition policy was implicitly re-affirmed in the Hong Kong Ministerial Declaration of 18 December 2005[40].

In light of the above, the political appraisal of the case for international competition rules within the WTO is characterized by hardened positions and emotional debate. Although subject to extensive institutionalised academic research and discussion in the past, the case for additional international competition rules merits a comprehensive and objective re-evaluation in light of the developments at the WTO. In re-evaluating, the author will not focus on the numerous alternative proposals for international competition rules advanced by Academia. The author will rather focus on the underlying justifications and rationales for additional international competition rules from both a competition policy and a trade policy perspective. Furthermore, the Doha Declaration and the *status quo* of institutionalised discussion within the WTO as well as possible solutions will be considered.

To this end, the author will first introduce the non-familiar reader to traditional domestic competition policy and competition law. After having discussed the underlying policy considerations, the commonalities and differences among existing domestic competition laws will be considered. The competition laws of the United States and the European Union will primarily serve as examples for this purpose.

Second, the author will assess the case for additional international competition rules from a competition policy perspective. For this purpose, the author will

---

37 J. Drexl, *ibid.*

38 *Joint Communication from Bangladesh (on behalf of the LDC group) et al.*, WT/GC/W/522, 12 December 2003, available at:
http://www.wto.org/english/thewto_e/gcounc_e/gcounc_e.htm (17.08.2005).

39 General Council to the WTO, *Decision adopted by the General Council on 1 August 2004 ("July Package")*, WT/L/579, 2 August 2004, at para. 1 (g), available at:
http://www.wto.org/english/tratop_e/dda_e/draft_text_gc_dg_31july04_e.htm (01.11.2006).

40 Hong Kong Ministerial Declaration of 18 December 2005, WT/MIN(05)/DEC, 22 December 2005, available at:
http://www.wto.org/English/thewto_e/minist_e/min05_e/final_text_e.htm (01.11.2006).

first discuss the impact of the liberalisation and integration of world markets which occurred since World War II on competition and competition policy. Thereafter, the author will assess the resulting implications from both an individual competitor's as well as from a national government's and legislator's perspective. Having established a case for international competition rules from a competition policy perspective, the author will consider existing approaches and their shortcomings.

Third, the author will discuss the case for additional international competition rules from a trade policy perspective. After examining the interface between Trade and Competition Policy, the author will consider existing competition law instruments in the WTO Agreement and their shortcomings. Thereafter, the author will assess the case in favour of additional international competition rules within the ambit of the WTO in light of traditional arguments. The author will also consider the course and results of past negotiation efforts as well as their major stumbling blocks.

Finally, the author will analyze recent perspectives so as to identify new incentives for a relaunch of negotiations. In light of the results of this analysis, the author will then advance her approach for additional WTO competition rules. This approach does not impose any obligation to adopt a competition law or to harmonise existing substantive competition rules. Rather, the advanced approach attempts to focus on the needs of developing countries in that it builds on a system of enforceable exemptions and exceptions together with soft law instruments, specifies the principle of non-discrimination, formulates the prohibition of restrictive practices affecting export markets, foresees the obligation of cooperation and administrative assistance and institutionalises technical assistance and capacity building.

II. An Introduction to Traditional Domestic Competition Policy and Competition Law

A. Why Regulate Competition?

The problem of how to most efficiently allocate national resources has always challenged national governments. The solution to this problem will depend on a state's individual economic and political choices.

According to liberal economic theory, the allocation of resources in free market economies should ideally be determined solely by supply and demand, without any state intervention being necessary[41]. In the ideal situation of perfect competition, consumer welfare would be maximized without any need for additional rules. This situation is utopian, however, for it has already been recognized by *Adam Smith*[42] in the eighteenth century that firms operating within the same product market are likely to conspire to fix prices. Firms are tempted to collude in a way profitable to them, by distorting competition to the detriment of consumer welfare. This has also been demonstrated by means of the Nash Equilibrium which is commonly known as the "prisoners' dilemma"[43]. According to this concept, there will always be an economic incentive for market operators to ally and fix prices, as either party will be able to charge higher prices and, consequently, accrue higher profits. At the same time, competition can be distorted by one dominant player on a certain market, who will be able to act independently from the forces of supply and demand. Therefore, national legislators have traditionally created rules to steer and control the market actors in order to preserve the competitiveness of the market by ensuring a mostly undistorted interplay of supply and demand and in order to, thereby, achieve economic efficiency.

Notwithstanding those economic rationales, competition law and policy are also used by legislators to achieve certain other goals, such as the preservation of liberty, fair competition by protecting individual competitors or other sociopolitical motives.

This becomes especially apparent when taking EC Competition Law as an example, which arguably "serves two masters"[44]. Apart from economic efficiency considerations, EC Competition Law has been dominated by the Internal Market objective and market integration goals. The EC authorities and the Commission in particular, have taken a harsh approach against business practices impeding these goals. Their approach is visible in their attitude toward vertical

---

41 For many, compare A. Jones/B. Sufrin, *EC Competition Law. Text, Cases and Materials* (2001), 3.

42 Adam Smith, *The Wealth of Nations*, 1776 (reprinted 1979).

43 S. Bishop/M. Walker, *The Economics of EC Competition Law: Concepts, Application and Measurement* (1999), 23.

44 A. Jones/B. Sufrin, *ibid.*, 32 et sqq.

restraints[45]. The EC approach is traditionally much stricter than the more economic-based approach toward vertical restraints in the US, where in 1977 the Supreme Court recognized that vertical restraints might promote intra-brand competition by allowing the manufacturer to achieve certain efficiencies in the distribution of his products[46]. In addition to market integration considerations, public policy considerations have influenced EC Competition Law. This influence has recently been amplified by Reg 1/2003[47] which provides for direct application of Art 81(3) EC[48] by national competition authorities. Accordingly, national public policy goals can be considered in the application of EC law[49].

In the following section, the author will provide more detailed definitions of "competition", "competition law" and "competition policy". Additionally, some underlying basic economic principles will be explained in order to lay down a comprehensive analysis of both aims and subject matter of competition policy.

B. Economic Principles

Competition is generally considered beneficial for consumer welfare. It enhances individual liberty and welfare[50] in various ways[51]. First, competition may serve as an important information mechanism, as markets reveal consumer preferences and information on supply and demand. Second, competition may contribute to the allocation of scarce resources and the co-ordination of supply and demand corresponding to the maximization of free choice, thus satisfying consumer preferences and respecting individual responsibility. Third, competition may serve as a mechanism for income distribution by rewarding productivity and innovation. Thus, "competition" is the means promulgated by the supporters of a free market economy of how to achieve a more efficient allocation of resources[52]. But what exactly does "competition" mean?

---

45 Compare for example Case 56&58/64 *Consten & Grundig v Commission* [1966] ECR 299.

46 Compare the US Supreme Court's decision in *Continental TV Inc v. GTE Slyvania Inc* 433 US 36 (1977).

47 OJ L 1, 4.1.2003.

48 For references to EC Treaty articles as they stand after 1 May 1999, the author uses the abbreviation "EC". For references to Treaty articles as they stood before 1 May 1999, the author uses the abbreviation "EC-Treaty". See *Informative Note on the citation of articles of the Treaties in the publications of the Court of Justice and the Court of First Instance,* available at: http://curia.europa.eu/en/content/juris/noteinfo.htm (07.10.2006)

49 According to G. Monti, the CFI has endorsed a rather wide scope for possible justifications under Art 81(3) EC in *Métropole* (Cases T-528/93, T-543/93 and T-546/93, [1996] ECR II-649, para 118): "[...] the Commission is entitled to base itself on considerations connected with the pursuit of the public interest in order to grant exemption under Art 81(3)". Compare G. Monti, *Article 81 and Public Policy,* 39(5) Common Market Law Review 2002, 1057 et sqq.

50 Unless specified otherwise, the author uses the term "welfare" in the sense of "welfare economics".

51 E.-U. Petersmann, *International Competition Rules for Governments and for Private Business,* 30(3) Journal of World Trade 1996, 7.

52 J. Vickers/D. Hay, *The Economics of Market Dominance,* in: Vickers, D./Hay, D. (eds.), *The Economics of Market Dominance,* 1987, 2.

In economic theory, "competition" is often referred to as rivalry among market actors. This definition is of course a very general one, and may be redefined depending on various schools of economic theory. According to the neo-classical approach[53], for example, competition policy regulates the marketplace through legal rules in order to guarantee efficiency, whereby society's economic welfare is maximized by the efficient deployment of the existing resources. In comparison, according to the ordo-liberal tradition, the process of competition also expresses economic freedom in that it is seen as a process whereby market actors participate in the economy without being unduly constrained by private or public power[54].

This concept of efficient resource allocation is linked with the consumer's impact on demand, which is influenced by the relationship between price and supply. This influence can be measured by certain instruments of economic theory. The price elasticity of demand measures the extent to which a price raise will influence demand. If demand is inelastic, consumers will still buy the product at a higher price (e.g. petrol will always be in demand), if it is elastic, demand for the product might fall. By comparison, the cross-elasticity of demand measures how much the demand for a certain product increases if the price for another product is raised. It is positive, if the price increase for one product leads to an increase in demand for another one[55]. By deciding on a personal reservation price for a certain product, the consumer can influence demand, and thereby indirectly steer the supplier's price conduct. This theory is however based on the general assumption within welfare economics that firms will act rationally, and will always try to maximize profits. Legitimately, the accuracy of this assumption has been criticized[56], since a firm's behaviour is subject to numerous factors, and decisions might not always be taken for profit maximization purposes only. Instead, decisions might be concerned with corporate survival, individual growth or strategic goals.

The author shall in the following briefly explain the concepts of perfect competition, monopoly and oligopoly.

1. Perfect competition[57]

Under conditions of perfect competition, a large number of buyers and sellers would trade homogenous goods in an environment where all parties would have perfect information and could freely enter and exit the market. As a result,

---

[53] This definition has been promulgated in particular by R. Posner, see for example his arguments in *Antitrust Law*[2], 2000, 29.

[54] This approach has been argued to apply in particular to EC competition law, compare *G. Monti*, Article 81 EC and Public Policy, 1059.

[55] At the same time this implies that those two products are substitute products and therefore part of the same product market, which is crucial for the purposes of market definition.

[56] Compare J. E. Parkinson, *Corporate Power and Responsibility*, 1993, Chapters 2 et sqq.

[57] Compare A. Jones/B. Sufrin, *ibid.*, 8 et sqq.

a single seller would be insignificant in relation to the market as a whole, and could never bear any influence on prices. Consumer welfare would be maximized due to the economic efficiency that would prevail. Economic efficiency presupposes both allocative and productive efficiency:

- Allocative efficiency is referring to the hypothesis that the output equals the quantity valued by society. The supplier will expand output until market price and marginal costs[58] coincide. Every consumer willing to purchase this product at its costs of production will be able to buy it. Under the assumption that the supplier will act rationally to maximize profits, the supplier will produce neither more nor less.
- Productive efficiency means that goods are produced at the lowest possible costs. On a perfectly competitive market, sellers would be price-takers, and would be forced never to sell above marginal costs. Otherwise, they would lose their customers to other competitors, make losses and would eventually be forced to leave the market. Consequently, due to the perfect information prevailing on a perfectly competitive market, any techniques to reduce costs would be copied by competitors. This constant downward pressure on costs would result from the fact that cost-reduction would be the only means to increase profits and to remain on the market. Thus, cost reductions would be passed on to the consumer and the market price would be constantly lowered.

The hypothetical state of economic efficiency is also referred to as "Pareto Optimal". It describes a situation where no market player could be made better off without another one being worse off at the same time.

2. *Monopoly*[59]

On the other end of the spectrum, there is monopoly. Monopoly describes a situation where there is only one seller for many buyers. This may be so due to natural, legal or other barriers for potential competitors to enter that specific product market. According to economic theory, this seller is not constrained by other competitors and will price as high as it possibly can. Consequently, the monopoly charges more than the competitive price. Nevertheless, the monopolist remains restrained by cross elasticity of demand: a consumer might switch to another product if the price for the monopolist's product exceeds the consumer's individual reservation price.

The main concern with regard to monopolies is their economic inefficiency. If the monopolist chose to sell just one single unit, it might receive an extremely high price for that unit, but at the same time it is unlikely that the monopolist

---

58 Marginal costs are the extra costs needed to produce one extra unit of the product.

59 Compare A. Jones/B. Sufrin, *ibid.*, 10 et sqq.

will be able to cover its costs. Therefore, the monopolist will intend to produce more units. However, it will have to lower the price for each additional unit. Its marginal revenue is the extra amount obtained by selling one extra unit, but as it has to lower the price, the marginal revenue will be less than the selling price. Therefore, the monopolist will sell units only until the point where the marginal revenue equals the marginal costs. As the monopolist's marginal revenue will be below the market price, it will supply fewer units than it would on a competitive market. Accordingly, the prices on a monopolistic market will be higher than on a competitive market, and that output will be restricted. This means that those consumers who would have paid the competitive price for the monopolist's product are deprived of it. This phenomenon has been referred to as the "deadweight loss of monopoly". The monopolist cannot turn the loss of consumer surplus into profit.

As the monopolistic price will always exceed marginal costs while the competitive price will not, the monopoly pricing leads to a transfer in wealth from consumer to producer. As a result, a loss to consumer welfare and efficiency as a whole will occur. Although the income of society as a whole does not change, monopoly pricing results in a redistribution of income and also in a misallocation of resources and is therefore considered detrimental.

3. *Oligopoly*[60]

Oligopoly is another type of market structure, situated in between perfect competition and monopoly. On an oligopolistic market, there are only few leading competitors. Given this typical structure, competitors are likely to be aware of each other's existence and behaviour in the market. This mutual awareness results in a tendency for collusion on oligopolistic markets. However, this is not necessarily true, as oligopolistic markets can be characterized by fierce competition. The "prisoners' dilemma" phenomenon[61] is strongly linked to oligopolistic market structures. Therefore, oligopolies have traditionally attracted considerable attention of legislators. The problem is that oligopolistic market structures may not necessarily result in collusion, but likely will. The legislator is challenged to create efficient instruments flexible enough to distinguish between efficient and inefficient oligopolies. Due to the small number of market actors, they may recognize their interdependence and also the possibility to increase profit by jointly setting prices at profit-maximizing level without any need for explicit communication. Given that kind of market structure, it may also be difficult for the authorities to establish the minimum degree of interac-

[60] Compare A. Jones/B. Sufrin, *ibid.*, 681 et sqq.

[61] See Chapter II.A. for more details on Prisoner Dilemma.

tion that is necessary for concertation to be established if there is no proof of explicit collusion[62].

C. The Aims of Competition Policy

Traditionally, competition policy has been a national regulatory instrument addressed toward private market actors, by which governments of individual states adhering to the principles of a free market economy have tried to steer the process of competition by embedding it into a legal framework. At first sight, it may appear ironic that competition law seeks to control and interfere with the freedom of conduct of market actors while at the same time promoting free competition. Nevertheless, the welfare gain through the maximization of efficiency inherent in free competition appears to justify state intervention[63]. Basically, competition policy defines the specific legal environment for an unfettered process of competition in order to maximize general "welfare" through the promotion of economic efficiency and consumer welfare[64].

In this regard, however, the question is the definition of "welfare". For an answer, economical, political and institutional aspects have to be considered:

1. Economic aspects

For western market economies, the economic goals and principles behind individual laws will bear many commonalities. Nevertheless, different schools of thought exist.

For example, the Harvard School[65] has established the Structure-Conduct-Performance Paradigm. According to this theory, the structure of the market determines the firm's conduct which in turn determines market performance. Given the resulting belief that certain industry structures will lead to a certain economic performance, e.g. that highly concentrated industries can only produce poor output due to reduced output and monopoly prices, this school has been convinced that competition is about structural remedies rather than behav-

---

62 That this may not always be easy to achieve can be seen from the EC Commission's problems in proving tacit collusion, e.g. *Wood Pulp* [1993] ECR I-1307, [1993] 4 CLMR 407, para. 251. In that case, the ECJ held it was necessary to economically analyze the prevailing market structures in detail and to evaluate the evidence carefully. The Commission is therefore not able to rely on parallel market behaviour as a proof of concertation where any plausible explanation is provided for such conduct.

63 In this regard, the author is referring to developed countries with an established tradition of free market economy only.

64 E.-U. Petersmann, *Legal, Economic and Political Objectives of National and International Competition Policies: Constitutional Functions of WTO "Linking Principles" for Trade and Competition*, 34(1) New England Law Review 1999, 150 et sqq.

65 The Harvard School has been influenced to a large extent by E. S. Mason's work at Harvard University in the 1930s, compare A. Jones/B. Sufrin, *ibid.*, 20.

ioural remedies. Under this school of thought, US antitrust law has been marked by an extremely interventionist enforcement policy in the 1960s.

In comparison, the Chicago School[66], although criticized for its static and theoretical approach and for concentrating too much on long-term effects, is said to have produced "a revolution in antitrust thinking"[67]. It has advocated that allocative efficiency should be the sole goal of antitrust legislation. This approach is optimistic with regard to the market's ability to correct and achieve efficiency by itself.

Today, there is general consensus that economics will help to define the problems at issue, but not the concrete answers. Modern Industrial Organization theory stresses the effect of a firm's strategic conduct in different market situations, e.g. that a firm may try to strategically deter entry for its competitors.

2. *Political aspects*

Although the basic economic goals and principles are rather homogenous for western industrial states, divergent competition policy goals may nevertheless be recognized. In particular, the perception of "welfare" is still a very individual one and depends to a large extent on a state's individual political choices.

Looking at the competition policy goals prevailing in the United States, Germany or Japan it may be seen that they are very much directed toward the abatement of economic power curtailing the economic freedom of other market participants[68]. In comparison, EC competition policy has traditionally been used as an instrument to realize the political goals inherent to the Treaty of Rome, one of which was the creation of the Single Market[69]. EC competition policy aims at the protection of individual competitors, of small and medium-sized enterprises, of consumers in a "non-technical" sense and of cooperation to enhance European technology. Its goal is to keep markets open rather than the protection of competition and consumer welfare in general[70]. This is in line with the ordoliberal approach underlying EC competition policy[71]. Certainly, the economic rationales behind EC competition policy have sometimes had to stand back behind other considerations, such as to ensure market access for all market actors across member states or to prevent market segmentation through vertical agreements. The ECJ has repeatedly held that the competition rules must be read in the context of the wider ambitions of the Community as laid down in Art 2 and 3 of the Treaty and has defined the aim of EC competition

---

66 The Chicago School was led by Milton Friedman in the USA in the 1970s and 1980s.
67 A. Jones/B. Sufrin, *ibid.*, 20.
68 H. Wins, *Eine internationale Wettbewerbsordnung als Ergänzung zum GATT*, 2000, 24 et sqq.
69 A. Jones/B. Sufrin, *ibid.*, 30.
70 A. Jones/B. Sufrin, *ibid.*, 34.
71 Compare comments in Chapter II.A. above.

policy as the achievement of "workable competition"[72]. The author considers the ECJ's interpretation mandatory, given the mentioned explicit references in the Treaty. Those articles of the Treaty itself will in the end only consolidated political choice of the member states and show again the individual nature of competition policy. For example, Art 81(3) EC requires an assessment as to whether an agreement "contributes to improving the production or distribution of goods or to promoting technical or economic progress while at the same time allowing consumers a fair share of the resulting benefit".

Another sign of the individuality in the aims of competition policy is the fact that the underlying policy goals often change in the course of time. Once more, this can be illustrated by looking at EC competition policy. In recent years, the nature of the European Union has changed. Not only has this been illustrated by the Treaty amendments since Maastricht in 1992, but also by the political agenda prevailing today. Apart from purely integrationist motives, social considerations have repeatedly occurred thereon, and the scope of community protection has been expanded toward the concept of "citizenship"[73]. At the same time, recent EC case law has expanded the original scope of EC law on establishment and services as purely "economic" activities to public services such as health, welfare and education[74]. In line with those policy shifts, changes have also been reflected in the case law based on the Articles 81 et sqq. of the Treaty. In this case law, other considerations have been valued in addition to the core aims of EC competition policy of economic freedom, market integration and efficiency[75]. For example, the ECJ stated in Art 81(3) decisions that an agreement may have a beneficial effect on employment, since it improves the general conditions of production[76]. Industrial policy has also been considered in light of structural problems or of the strengthening of the Community's industry on the global market[77]. Moreover, environmental policy considerations have been used by the Community authorities to justify an exemption under Art 81(3) EC[78]. In addition, consumer protection has been given a wider meaning than just economic interests[79]. This wider meaning embraces health and safety

[72] Compare for example Case 26/76, *Metro v. Commission (No 1)* [1977] ECR 1875, [1978] 2 CMLR 1, para 20, where the ECJ created the concept of "workable competition", " [...] that is to say the degree of competition necessary to ensure the observance of the basic requirements and the attainment of the objectives of the Treaty, in particular the creation of a single market achieving conditions similar to those of a domestic market."

[73] Compare Art 17 EC. Compare also P. Craig/G. de Búrca, *EU Law. Text, Cases and Materials* (2003), 755 et sqq., Case C-85/96, *Maria Martinez Sala v. Freistaat Bayern* [1998] ECR I-2691, Case C-184/99 *Rudy Grzelczyk v. Centre Public d'Aide Sociale d'Ottignes-Louvain-la-Neuve (CPAS)* [2001] ECR I-6193.

[74] Compare for example C-157/99, *Geraets-Smits v. Stichting Ziekenfonds, Peerboom v. Stichting CZ Groep Zorgverzekeringen* [2001] ECR I-5473, *Case 340/89*, Vlassopoulou v. Ministerium für Justiz, Bundes und Europaangelegenheiten Baden-Württemberg [1991] ECR 2357, Case C-238/98, *Hocsman v. Ministre de l'Emploi [2000] ECR I-6623.*

[75] G. Monti, *ibid.*, 1057 et sqq.

[76] Compare Case 26/76 *Metro I* [1977] ECR 1875 para 43.

[77] For example, compare *BPCL/ICI* [1984] OJ L212/1 para 37.

[78] Case *DSD* [2001] OJ L319/1.

[79] See Article 153(1) EC.

considerations or the right to information has also found expression in competition matters[80].

Most interestingly, in comparison to the divergent policy goals prevailing in western industrialised countries, the differences relating to competition policy goals are less pronounced for developing countries or transformation countries. In those countries, the competition policy goals rather feature a certain degree of homogeneity[81].

With regard to developing countries, there used to be a general interest in manufacturers' protection, which was based on the general assumption that due to small market sizes, monopolistic or oligopolistic market structures had to be accepted. Only since the collapse of socialistic planned economies and the development of consumerism has a rethinking occurred in this regard. Thus, the distrust in the automatic control inherent in market mechanisms has declined and consumer protection and the control of restrictive business practices are being emphasized for the process of re-enacting or reformation of competition laws. At the same time, certain aspects of development politics like regional promotion, export advancements or the control of domestic production capacities will usually still be contained in those laws.

For transformation countries, on the other hand, the privatisation of former state monopolies and deregulation of prices are primarily emphasized. As a reformation process usually entails political and administrative opposition, young competition authorities often act as an intermediary between government and administrative bodies. Therefore, the common policy goals of transformation countries are the creation of free markets and an economic environment amiable to small and medium-sized undertakings. In particular, protection against the abuse of power of former state undertakings and conditions beneficial to (foreign) trade and investment are sought.

Thus, competition policy clearly reflects individual political choices and is being used to control very different policy goals.

3. Institutional aspects

In addition to being influenced by economics and political aspects, competition policy is also influenced by institutional structures. More specifically, enforcement will always imply a certain amount of discretion and, therefore, must be seen as an indirect policy instrument. This amount will differ depending on the institution that enforces competition rules. As two basic types, administrative

[80] Case *Asahi* [1994] OJ L 354/87 paras 24-26.

[81] Compare H. Wins, *Eine internationale Wettbewerbsordnung als Ergänzung zum GATT*, 2000, 24 et sqq.

and judicial enforcement procedures can be distinguished for competition matters[82].

The first approach has *inter alia* been chosen by the United Kingdom, Denmark, Switzerland and the European Union. The characteristic feature inherent in administrative procedures is the amount of discretion the authorities have in their application of the respective set of substantive competition rules, which also implies the admissibility of the "rule of reason". Moreover, administrative authorities are generally free to take up proceedings in a certain case, except for where special thresholds are postulated by law[83]. Nevertheless, there is a certain risk of non-competition related influences and also of a lack of transparency inherent in the administrative decision-making process. For example, decisions of the EC Commission's Directorate Competition are closely examined by Legal Service. However, decisions must be approved by the Board of Commissioners, which can overrule the Competition Commissioner's vote.

The second approach has particularly influenced the United States' enforcement tradition. Competition authorities or private parties file an action, and the court must initiate proceedings unless *de minimis* rules apply or unless the claim is unfounded. Substantive discretion is characterized by the "Rule of Law". Arguably, courts are more politically independent than administrative authorities. Consequently, one would expect a reduced risk of non-competition related factors influencing the decision-making process.

The foregoing considerations have played an important role in the discussion of certain recent changes under European law with regard to enforcement. According to EC Regulation 1/2003, Article 81 EC has to be directly applied by national courts and competition authorities in the Member States since May 1, 2004. There is a large degree of administrative or policy discretion inherent in the application of Art 81(3) EC[84]. Given the fact that the ECJ has considered itself incompetent to assess the complex economic facts involved in earlier case law[85], it could be argued that national courts are even less apt to balance the various interests involved. Therefore, one might share the view that national courts might not be capable of making the policy decisions at the European level[86]. Yet, this line of argument was eased by the ECJ's judgment in *Tetra Laval*[87] where it held that while it recognized that the Commission had a margin of discretion with regard to economic matters, the EC Courts would not re-

[82] Compare H. Wins, *Eine internationale Wettbewerbsordnung als Ergänzung zum GATT*, 2000, 33 et sqq.
[83] For example, under the EC Merger Regulation, there are certain thresholds with regard to turnover that trigger the Community authorities' competence, compare Art. 1 of EC Regulation 4064/89 [OJ 1990, No. L257/13] as amended by Council Regulation (EC) No 1310/97 of 30 June 1997 [OJ 1997, No. L180/1].
[84] Compare R. Wesseling, *The Commission White Paper on Modernisation of E.C. Antitrust Law: Unspoken Consequences and Incomplete Treatment of Alternative Options*, ECLR 1999, 420 et sqq.
[85] Cases 56 and 58/64 *Consten and Grundig v. Commission* [1966] ECR 341, Case T-17/93 *Matra Hachette v. Commission* [1994] ECR II-595.
[86] Compare R. Wesseling, *ibid.*
[87] *Tetra Laval BV. v. Commission*, Case C-12/03 P, [2005] OJ C82/02, at para. 39.

frain from reviewing the Commission's interpretation and assessment of information of an economic nature.

In a constitutional state, judges are by definition independent state organs which are personally and materially free in their individual decision-taking. At EU level, the EC Commission applies the same legal text through its Commissioners. Although they, too, are independent in their decision taking the final decision will be taken by the College of Commissioners by simple majority. It is apparent that a single judge might not necessarily appreciate the circumstances of a certain case in the same way as an interdisciplinary body of many. Also, national interests might be valued differently.

As for the United States, a combination of administrative and court proceedings has been adopted in competition matters. However, the Department of Justice and the Federal Trade Commission as administrative bodies have as their main functions procedural initiative rights as well as party rights for court proceedings. Thus, the main decision-making authority remains with the competent courts.

It is therefore established that the institutional composition may bear an influence on the application and enforcement of competition law, and may, thereby, indirectly also impact competition policy at the national or regional level. It will be demonstrated below that institutional aspects significantly influence the discussion on competition policy at the international level.

In the following, a brief analysis of the differences in individual substantive competition laws will be carried out.

D. Domestic Competition Law Addressing Private Market Actors – Commonalities and Differences

Competition law is the means by which competition policy considerations are being transformed into domestic law by national legislators. Competition laws are based on the general premise that while free market behaviour is desirable, some interference with the market is necessary to maintain competitive pressures, to promote competition amongst producers and to achieve an efficient allocation of resources. "Efficiency" in this context refers on the one hand to productive efficiency in that the cheapest producers undersell and replace less efficient competitors. On the other, it refers to allocative efficiency in that consumers' values and choice will direct production[88].

[88] A. D. Mitchell, *Broadening the Vision of Trade Liberalisation. International Competition Law and the WTO*, in 24(3) Journal of World Competition 2001, 345.

The United States was the first country to attempt general statutory control of restrictive or anticompetitive business practices in 1890[89]. Since World War II, most developed countries and many developing countries have enacted comparable legal instruments. Currently, about 90 states have competition rules in place.[90] Also, there are regional competition law systems in addition to domestic laws. For example, the European Union has elaborated its own regional competition regime effective in its member states[91].

The main regulatory techniques to pursue the goals described above are the following:

1. *Control of existing monopoly or other market power and its possible abuse;*
2. *Prevention of restrictive horizontal agreements between competitors;*
3. *Prevention of restrictive vertical agreements;*
4. *Control of oligopolistic markets;*
5. *Prevention of mergers which would lead to a concentration in market power.*

1. Control of existing monopoly or other market power and its possible abuse

Monopolies are considered detrimental due to economic inefficiency. Statutory monopolies can be established for the utilities and transport markets, for example. Natural monopolies emerge where markets allow for large economies of scale[92] and where it is therefore impossible for a second producer to maintain efficient production. For example, this may be the case for utilities requiring a network of pipes or cables.

However, despite the lack of monopoly in terms of a single producer, a sufficient degree of market power can be equally detrimental to the welfare of an economy. Market power is considered critical if a firm can raise prices above competitive level and keep them there[93]. This is why the abuse of market power

[89] J. Jackson/W. Davey/A Sykes, *Legal Problems of International Economic Relations. Cases, Materials and Text*, 2002, 1107.

[90] Countries which have adopted corresponding regulations are usually pursuing a free market economy approach, compare F. Amato, *International Antitrust: What Future?* In: 24(4) Journal of World Competition 2001, 451.

[91] In the following, the author will make reference to the EU approach in the context of "national competition law". Albeit formally incorrect, this approach is considered justified due to the *sui generis* nature of the European Union and also for the purposes of subsequent analysis.

[92] Economies of Scale are factors which cause the average cost of producing a certain commodity to fall the more of it is produced. If they are large, a firm will need to invest a lot before making a profit.

[93] Compare A. Jones/B. Sufrin, *ibid.*, 14.

tends to be similarly sanctioned by legislators like the abuse of monopolistic market power.

Although national legislators may deliberate similar rationales, their individual implementations may differ to a considerable extent. This is especially true for the approaches toward monopoly power or a dominant position pursued in the EU and the US, respectively[94]. The competition laws of both the US and the EC impose comparable restraints upon the exercise of monopoly power. Both legislators prohibit predatory pricing or tie-ins. Nevertheless, there are striking differences as to the standard of behaviour that must be met before sanctions are imposed. Arguably, the United States is much more reluctant to restrict behaviour of firms with market power than the European Union, who is acting on the assumption that dominant undertakings have a special responsibility toward their competitors and must act accordingly.

According to the case law of the US Supreme Court, the offence of monopoly under Article 2 of the Sherman Act[95] has two elements, the possession of monopoly power in the relevant market and the wilful acquisition or maintenance of that power. However, offensive monopoly power is clearly distinguished from growth or development as a consequence of a superior product, business acumen or historic accident[96]. The Supreme Court has explicitly stated that "the successful competitor, having been urged to compete, must not be turned upon when he wins"[97]. Consequently, the US legislator and jurisprudence do not condemn monopoly power *per se*.

In contrast, the EC Competition Law condemns the reaping of competitive awards under Art 82 EC[98]. Also, the EC competition authorities stress a form of strict liability, in that the abuse of monopoly power may arise without any intention being necessary to commit an abuse. Accordingly, the ECJ has repeat-

---

94 Compare P. Jebsen/R. Stevens, *Assumptions, Goals and Dominant Undertakings: The Regulation of Competition Under Article 86 of the European Union,* (1995-96) Antitrust Law Journal 443, 487-491.

95 Article 2 of the Sherman Act, 15 U.S.C. s. 2, reads as follows: "Every person who shall monopolize, or attempt to monopolize, or combine or conspire with any other person or persons, to monopolize any part of the trade or commerce among the several States, or with foreign nations, shall be deemed guilty of a felony, and, on conviction thereof, shall be punished by fine not exceeding $10,000,000 if a corporation, or, if any other person, $350,000, or by imprisonment not exceeding three years, or by both said punishments, in the discretion of the court."

96 *United States v. Grinnell Corp.*, 384 US 563, 570-71 (1966).

97 *United States v. Aluminum Co. of America,* 389 US 49 (1967).

98 Article 82 EC reads as follows: "Any abuse by one or more undertakings of a dominant position within the common market or in a substantial part of it shall be prohibited as incompatible with the common market in so far as it may affect trade between Member States. Such abuse may, in particular, consist in: *(a)* directly or indirectly imposing unfair purchase or selling prices or other unfair trading conditions; *(b)* limiting production, markets or technical development to the prejudice of consumers; *(c)* applying dissimilar conditions to equivalent transactions with other trading parties, thereby placing them at a competitive disadvantage; *(d)* making the conclusion of contracts subject to acceptance by the other parties of supplementary obligations which, by their nature or according to commercial usage, have no connection with the subject of such contracts."

edly held that the concept of abuse is an objective one[99]. The ECJ infers a special responsibility of dominant firms from their market power[100]. Their behaviour will be scrutinized in detail where this undertaking has a dominant position by which it can influence the market structure. Behaviour will be regarded an abuse if the degree of competition on that market is weakened solely because of the firm's presence, and if the firm hinders the maintenance of the prevailing degree or the growth of competition through recourse to methods other than those prevailing under normal competition.

2. *Prevention of restrictive horizontal agreements between competitors*

National legislators tend to sanction behaviour directed at a detrimental restriction of competition. The term "detrimental" merits further clarification. Any agreement between competitors could *per definitionem* be regarded as restricting competition, as it will always affect the parties' capacity to act. Therefore, in order not to block all economic activity, legislators will usually tie the prohibition to other variables. Mostly, the prohibition is formulated as a general ban of restrictions of competition by object or effect. In addition, however, certain agreements or practices will usually be excluded from the scope of that general prohibition.

The United States was the first jurisdiction that adopted a "modern" competition law[101]. The Sherman Act was adopted in 1890 as a means to "combat the power of trusts"[102]. Stocks held of competing companies had then often been transferred to trustees, so as to control the activities of those competing companies by lessening competition through the trustees. Section 1 of the Sherman Act provides that "every contract, combination in the form of trust or otherwise, or conspiracy, in restraint of trade or commerce among the several States, or with foreign nations, is hereby declared to be illegal. Every person who shall make any contract or engage in any combination or conspiracy hereby declared to be illegal shall be deemed to be guilty of a felony."

From a policy point of view, it is interesting to note that this piece of legislation was originally adopted as a very "neutral" instrument[103]. During the subsequent decades, however, the policy goals underlying the Act's application have changed in light of the economic developments in the United States, such as the

99 Compare for example Case 85/76 *Hoffmann-La Roche & Co AG v. Commission* [1979] ECR 461, [1979] 3 CMLR 211.

100 Thus, the ECJ appears to have created the concept of "superdominance". Compare for example Cases C-395 & 396/96, *Compagnie Maritime Belge Transporst SA v. Commission* [2000] 4 CMLR 1076, paras. 113-121, and Opinion of Fennelly AG, and para. 136. Compare further A. Jones/B. Sufrin, *ibid.*, 235 et sqq.

101 Compare A. Jones/B. Sufrin, *ibid.*, 18 et sqq.

102 Compare A. Jones/B. Sufrin, *ibid.*, 19.

103 A. Jones/B. Sufrin, *ibid.*, 19 et sqq.

Depression of the 1930s. Also, economic scientific research[104] and certain schools of thought have shaped the scope of the Act. Under the Harvard School of the 1950s, the Act was applied in a rather interventionist manner so as to protect small businesses against large firms on the presumed fragile market. Thereafter, the Chicago School assumed the market to be able to correct and achieve efficiency itself. Allocative efficiency was deemed to be the sole pursuit of antitrust, and the consumer was more put into perspective[105].

Today, the Act is applied by American courts in a way that emphasizes rigorous economic analysis[106]. At the same time, Section 1 has been construed by American courts to mean that competition must not be restrained unreasonably. Some contracts are considered as illegal *per se*, for example price-fixing agreements among competitors. However, the majority of agreements are deemed to come under the "rule of reason". Agreements are examined in their legal and economic context:[107] Courts have to weigh an agreement's pro- and anti-competitive effects against each other[108].

Under EC law, Article 81(1) EC prohibits "agreements, decisions by associations of undertakings and concerted practices which may affect trade between Member States and which have as their object or effect the prevention, restriction or distortion of competition within the common market".

This prohibition is directed toward all kinds of concertation of independent market actors, and has been applied by the European competition authorities in a rather rigid and extensive mode.

In comparison to the US approach, there is no consistently applied "rule of reason". However, there is consistent jurisprudence with regard to the requirement of an appreciable effect[109]. Moreover, the European legislator has postulated a legal exemption from this universal prohibition in Article 81(3) EC. According to that provision, paragraph 1 of Article 81 EC may be declared inapplicable if the agreement, decision of associations of undertakings or concerted practice "contribute to improving the production or distribution of goods or to promot-

---

[104] For example, the concept of "workable competition" was of fundamental influence for the emerging legal practice, compare J. M. Clark, *Toward a Concept of Workable Competition,* 30 American Economic Review (1940), 241-56.

[105] A. Jones/B. Sufrin, *ibid.,* 25.

[106] A. Jones/B. Sufrin, *ibid.,* 26.

[107] A. Jones/B. Sufrin, *ibid.,* 142 et sqq.

[108] Under EC law, on the other hand, the applicability of a rule of reason has been extremely controversial. The Commission has consistently denied the necessity of a rule of reason under Article 81, and has in turn been vastly criticized for disregarding economic necessities. A recent example could be the decision in Case T-112/99 *Métropole television (M6) and others v. Commission* [2001] 5 CMLR 1236. In contrast, however, the ECJ has been willing to adopt a more economics-based approach. For example, compare Cases T-374, 375, 384 & 388/94, *European Night Services v. Commission* [1998] ECR II-3141; Case C-309/99 *Wouters and Others v. Algemene Raad van de Nederlands Orde van Advocaten* [2002] 4 CMLR 27.

[109] In this regard, compare Case 5/69, *Völk v. Vervaecke* [1969] ECR 295, 302, where the ECJ held that even where an agreement has as its object the prevention, restriction or distortion of competition must have an appreciable effect in order to be caught be the prohibition.

ing technical progress, while allowing consumers a fair share of the resulting benefit", and which does not "impose [...] restrictions which are not indispensable to the attainment of these objectives; afford such undertakings the possibility of eliminating competition in respect of a substantial part of the products in question". Specifications of that latter provision were postulated by means of secondary EU legislation (e.g. "Block Exemption Regulations") or soft law instruments[110].

Nevertheless, the application of Article 81(3) EC has been extremely controversial in the past. The Commission has been criticized for placing too much emphasis on Article 81(3) EC. Critics argued the Commission should take up the signals repeatedly issued by the European Courts, which have pursued a more economics-based approach. In particular, the requirement to take account of the economic context of an agreement and the actual conditions prevailing on the market (including potential competition) has been stressed[111]. Yet, the Commission has rather applied Article 81(1) EC extensively and completed its assessment under Article 81(3) EC. This led to practical problems. For example, it is difficult for undertakings to draft agreements in a way that would not preclude the block exemption regulation's applicability. Also, given the Commission's former monopoly to exempt, it was been particularly troublesome that the Commission appeared incapable to deal with its workload satisfactorily. Undertakings had to settle for "comfort letters" in most cases. Those letters were informal administrative documents, not binding on national courts. In addition, procedures usually involved unacceptably long periods of time[112]. These problems in the application of Article 81 EC have not necessarily been diminished by Regulation 1/2003, but rather substituted[113].

3. Prevention of restrictive vertical agreements

Agreements concluded between non-competitors are called vertical agreements. Staying with the previous examples of US and EC law, differences in national approaches can be illustrated very clearly.

110 For example, Commission Notice on agreements of minor importance [OJ 2001/C 368/07]; Commission Guidelines on the applicability of Article 81 of the EC Treaty to horizontal cooperation [OJ 2001, No. C3/02].

111 Compare the decisions in Cases T-374, 375, 384 & 388/94, *European Night Services v. Commission* [1998] ECR II-3141; Case C-250/92, *Gøttrup-Klim Grovvareforening and Others v. Dansk Landbrugs Grovvareselskab AmbA (DLG)* [1994] ECR I-5641, [1996] 4 CMLR 191.

112 For example, Commission Regulation 2659/2000 on the application of Article 81(3) of the Treaty to categories of research and development agreements [OJ 2000, No L304/7] was alleged to be difficult to apply in practice, compare A. Jones/B. Sufrin, *ibid.*, 181.

113 After Regulation 1/2003, firms are now expected to self-assess themselves the compatibility of their agreements with Article 81 EC, as a consequence of the Commission's monopoly of exemption being lifted and a new system of direct application of Article 81 EC being introduced. Critics argued that this would mean increased uncertainty and higher costs for undertakings involved. Also, they argued that there would be considerable uncertainty with regard to case allocation and to the notion of trade between Member States being affected. Compare, for example, A. Jones/B. Sufrin, *ibid.*, 1031 et. sqq., R. Wesseling, *ibid.*

Under US law, Section 1 of the Sherman Act equally applies to vertical agreements. However, the analysis of vertical restraints has given rise to considerable debate. Although only considering selective practices as *per* se infringements of Section 1 of the Sherman Act since 1911[114], the Supreme Court extended the *per se* rule to any vertical restraint by the 1970s. This sterner attitude was first expressed in 1967, when the Supreme Court held that "under the Sherman Act, it is unreasonable without more for a manufacturer to seek to restrict and confine areas or persons with whom an article may be traded after the manufacturer has parted with dominion over it [...] Such restraints are so obviously destructive of competition that their mere existence is enough"[115]. This attitude of the Supreme Court was harshly criticized by economists, and in particular those from the Chicago School. The arguments raised against this case law put much emphasis on the benefits for competition resulting from vertical restraints. It was put forward that a manufacturer did not have the same motives in imposing resale price maintenance as distributors had in forming a cartel, and the manufacturer had no interest in creating a monopoly profit for its distributors. In light of these arguments, the decision in *Schwinn* was accused to be based on an "erroneous economic assumption"[116].

Since that decision, US jurisprudence has been reversed. By 1977, the Supreme Court had recognized that vertical restraints, and especially those restricting only intra-brand competition, might be able to promote inter-brand competition[117]. In *Continental TV Inc v. GTE Slyvania Inc*[118], the Supreme Court held that the scope of *per se* illegality should be limited for vertical restraints, and that the rule of reason approach should be applied to all vertical restraints not relating to prices. The economic reasoning behind the ruling was the understanding that vertical restraints would potentially reduce intra-brand competition among sellers of the same brand while at the same time stimulating inter-brand competition by allowing the manufacturer to achieve certain efficiencies in the distribution process. Moreover, consumers would be protected from excessive prices or service through *(i)* competition from sellers of other brands and *(ii)* because of each individual manufacturer's interest in maintaining as much intra-brand competition as is consistent with efficient distribution.[119]

From that point in time, US courts have applied the rule of reason to vertical restraints and have consistently declined to find an infringement unless the firm who had imposed the restraint had market power. The underlying rationale was that a firm without market power cannot afford to behave independently from

[114] *Dr Miles Medical Co v. John D Park & Sons Co,* 220 US 373 (1911).
[115] *United States v. Arnold Schwinn & Co,* 338 US 365.
[116] Compare R. H. Bork, *The Antitrust Paradoxon: A Policy at War with Itself,* 1993, 32-33.
[117] A. Jones/B. Sufrin, *ibid.,* 495 et sqq.
[118] Case *Continental TV Inc v. GTE Slyvania Inc* 433 US 36 (1977).
[119] E. Gelhorn/W.E. Kovacic, *Antitrust Law and Economics*[4], 312 et sqq.

the preferences of its consumers[120]. By the 1980s, US legal practice generally considered vertical restraints were innocuous for competition[121]. Despite this perception being upheld in general, current US legal practice will always weigh the restraint against a business justification. For example, non-price restraints may be regarded as anti-competitive if they are used to raise competitors' costs, as a barrier to entry, or if they might promote tacit collusion[122].

Under EC competition law, the treatment of vertical agreements has also been subject to intense debate. Article 81 EC equally applies to vertical restraints[123]. In the light of the Single Market objective, EC authorities have taken an "extremely strict and interventionist approach"[124] toward vertical agreements[125]. One of the main reasons for that approach was the tendency of such agreements to incorporate territorial restraints, and thus, to interfere with the creation of a Single Market. The Commission argued that the removal of non-tariff barriers was not sufficient for the full development of parallel trade, arbitrage and changes in distribution across the EC territory. It argued that it was crucial for successful economic integration that producers, distributors and consumers would find it profitable to make use of the new market situation, and that producers and distributors would not be allowed to introduce practices contrary to integration[126].

In this debate on the treatment of vertical agreements under EC competition law, the concerns put forward[127] with regard to intra-brand competition were, firstly, that territorial restrictions might lead to the division of markets along national borders and limit the consumers' ability to purchase goods and services in other Member States. Secondly, vertical restraints might reinforce horizontal agreements and, thereby, lead to higher prices and weaker inter-brand competition. Also, the legitimacy of the "free-rider"-argument[128], which has commonly been used to justify intra-brand restrictions like resale price maintenance and exclusive or selective distribution, has been doubted and considered overstated. With regard to the latter practices, consumers might be deprived of price dis-

---

[120] Compare the decision in *Valey Liquors Inc v. Renfield Importers Ltd*, 678 F.2d 742 (7th Cir. 1982), 745.

[121] A. Jones/B. Sufrin, *ibid.*, 497.

[122] Compare, for example, the speech of C. A. Varney at the ALI-ABA Eleventh Annual Advanced Course, *Product Distribution and Marketing", Vertical Restraints Enforcement at the FTC*, 1996, available at: http://www.ftc.gov/speeches/varney/varnmg.htm (30.04.2004).

[123] Compare decisions in Case 56/65 *Société Technique Minière v. Maschinenbau Ulm GmbH* [1966] ECR 235; Case 56&58/64 *Consten & Grundig v Commission* [1966] ECR 299.

[124] A. Jones/B. Sufrin, *ibid.*, 98 et sqq.

[125] Compare, for example, the decisions in Case 56/65 *Société Technique Minière v. Maschinenbau Ulm GmbH* [1966] ECR 235; Case 56&58/64 *Consten & Grundig v Commission* [1966] ECR 299.

[126] Compare EC Commission, *Green Paper on vertical restraints in competition policy*, COM(96) 721, para, 78.

[127] W. S. Comanor, *Vertical price-fixing, vertical market restrictions, and the new antitrust policy*, 98 Harvard Law Review (1985) 983 et. sqq.; For a good summary of the Commission's concerns, see EC Commission, *Guidelines on Vertical Restraints* [2000] OJ C291/1.

[128] "Free-riding" has been explained in the context of competition law as the practice to sell goods at low prices by keeping down one's costs, while at the same time leaving the expenses of promoting and advertising the goods to others; compare A. Jones/B. Sufrin, *ibid.*, 1078.

counts, as retailers engaging in significant price discounts would be eliminated from the market. In addition, vertical agreements could be used to reduce price competition between manufacturers. Selective distribution systems could be used by the manufacturer to increase prices by reducing intra-brand competition. These increased prices might in turn encourage the manufacturer's competitors to raise their prices, and inter-brand competition may be reduced. Thus, selective distribution systems have been deemed to be akin to tacit collusion[129]. The foreclosure of markets has been another important aspect. Vertical restraints were regarded to affect and stifle inter-brand competition, in that obligations not to deal with competing goods would create barriers to entry and foreclose the market to competitors. The Commission broadly summarized those concerns into four groups, *(i)* a single branding group, *(ii)* a limited distribution group, *(iii)* a resale price maintenance group, and *(iv)* a market partitioning group[130].

Using the above arguments, the EC Commission has pursued a very hostile stance over vertical restraints and has condemned all practices excluding the possibility of parallel trade[131]. This practice has been subject to vast criticism. Critics argued that due to the overbroad application of Article 81(1) EC on part of the Commission in combination with an inadequate analysis of economic factors has created "extraordinary legal uncertainty"[132]. More precisely, the Commission was accused to have failed to consider adequately whether a given vertical restraint harms competition in the consumer welfare sense of economics with regard to its effect on price or output. Also, despite its importance for a comprehensive analysis, market power would hardly ever be examined. The Commission's approach was criticized for its emphasis on economic freedom of individual market actors, putting aside consumer welfare and efficiency considerations. Moreover, the Commission's approach was also criticized for being incongruent with the Community Courts' decisions, which have featured certain concessions of economic justifications for vertical restraints. Although the ECJ had also been extremely interventionist in earlier days[133], and had been criticized for its equation of restraints on conduct with restrictions of competition without properly analyzing the underlying market structure and the impact of distribution agreements on it[134], this attitude has changed in recent years. An

129 S. Bishop/M. Walker, *ibid.*, para. 4.35.

130 See EC Commission, *Guidelines on Vertical Restraints,* ibid., para. 104.

131 See in particular Case T-41/96, *Bayer AG v. Commission,* [1996] 5 CMLR 416.

132 See the analysis of B. E. Hawk, *System Failure: Vertical Restraints and EC Competition Law,* 32 CMLR (1995), 974-986.

133 Compare Case 56&58/64 *Consten & Grundig v Commission* [1966] ECR 299, where the ECJ held despite the alleged economic necessity of the envisaged agreement to prevent free-riding and to prevent an incentive to distribute by providing for absolute territorial protection, that clauses resulting in the isolation of a national market and/or maintaining national markets would always distort competition and constitute an infringement of Article 81(1) EC.

134 D. Deacon, *Vertical Restraints under EU Competition Law: New Directions* [1995] Fordham Corporate Law Institute 307, paras. 16 and 18.

important change had already been signalled in the Court's decision in *STM*[135], where the ECJ held that it was necessary to look at the concrete effect of an agreement. In *Delimitis*[136] the ECJ held that exclusive purchasing agreements did not appreciably restrict competition and would therefore not fall under Article 81(1) EC unless they had the effect of foreclosing market access to competitors. The Commission, however, has only applied a severely limited version of the *Delimitis*-Test in subsequent cases[137]. Another point of criticism with regard to vertical restraints was directed against the legal uncertainty purportedly created through the overbroad application of Article 81(1) EC and the unconvincing subsumption under formalized categories under the respective Block Exemption Regulations[138].

This last point of criticism, at least, must be considered as partly overcome. In light of the immanent criticism concerning the Community authorities' approach toward vertical restraints and the recognition that the existing block exemption regulations were not working, the Commission adopted a new regime by introducing the new "umbrella-style"[139] Block Exemption Regulation for vertical agreements. This Block Exemption Regulation provides for a general presumption of legality for all distribution agreements where the market share of the undertakings concerned does not exceed 30%[140]. This new regime acknowledges a more economics-based approach, as expressed in the related Guidelines issued by the Commission[141]. For example, the Commission states that it will adopt an economic approach based on the effects on the market, and proceeds that vertical agreements have to be analysed in their legal and economic context. Also, it recognizes that vertical restraints are generally less harmful than horizontal ones, and provides for the possibility of exemption even in cases where the market share threshold of 30% is exceeded[142]. Those developments certainly reflect the reduced political necessity of drastic measures after the achievement of the Single Market in 1992.

From the above, the author concludes that different policy considerations may influence the national judiciary's approach toward certain categories of restrictions on competition. Similar kinds of restraints may provoke diametrical out-

---

135 Case 56/65 *Société Technique Minière v. Maschinenbau Ulm GmbH* [1966] ECR 235.

136 Case C-234/89 *Delimitis v. Henninger Bräu* [1991] ECR I-935.

137 Compare *Schöller Lebensmittel GmbH*, OJ 1993, L 183/1; *Langnese-Iglo GmbH*, OJ 993, L 183/19.

138 B. E. Hawk, *ibid.*, 984 et sqq.

139 Before Regulation 2790/1999, four different block exemption regulations applied to four different categories of distribution agreements for exclusive distribution agreements, exclusive purchasing agreements, franchising agreements and motor vehicle distribution agreements, respectively. Arguably, adherence to their terms often entailed practical difficulties, and the parties' freedom of contract was strongly curtailed. In this regard, compare A. Jones/B. Sufrin, *ibid.*, 527 et sqq.

140 EC Commission, *Commission Regulation (EC) No 2790/1999 on the application of Article 81 (3) of the Treaty to categories of vertical agreements and concerted practices* [OJ 1999 No L336/21].

141 EC Commission, *Commission Notice – Guidelines on Vertical Restraints* OJ 2000 C291/1.

142 EC Commission, *Guidelines on Vertical Restraints*, ibid., paras. 7, 100 and 120.

comes, depending on the actual individual economic goals underlying the legislative process.

4. *Control of oligopolistic markets*

Oligopolistic market structures are prone to coordination among market actors. The characteristic problem of such market structures lies in the difficulty to establish and prove concertation. Due to their small number and the transparency prevailing in an oligopolistic market, the individual players in an oligopolistic market do not need to communicate explicitly in order to be aware of each others' market strategy[143]. They may align each others' conduct in a way to respond to the market. Recognizing their interdependence, they may conjointly raise their prices to a profit-maximizing level without explicit communication. Therefore, oligopolistic markets are inclined to cartelization[144].

For cases of concertation that mount to an agreement, the rules for agreements will apply. Classic cartels are usually operated by fixing prices, imposing quotas (quantitative restrictions) or sharing markets among its members. Those practices are generally viewed as "hard-core" restrictions, and are widely condemned. Difficulties may, however, arise for national authorities in the assessment whether a concerted practice can be established. The respective practice under EC competition law may provide a vivid example of how the inherent problems in that assessment may be addressed.

Once again, the EC competition authorities have pursued a very restrictive approach, given the "safety-net" character[145] of the concept of concerted practices. Subsuming concerted practices under Article 81 EC, the ECJ has defined the term "concerted practice" as "co-ordination substituting practical cooperation between undertakings for the risks of competition"[146]. Although the ECJ accepted that the concept of a concerted practice required, in addition to concertation, "subsequent conduct on the market, and a relationship of cause and effect between the two", it also clarified that once there was evidence of concertation, it was for the undertakings at issue to establish that there was no subsequent conduct on the market after concertation. Although economic operators must be free to adapt themselves intelligently to the existing and anticipated conduct of their competitors, they must not influence the conduct of an actual or potential competitor or disclose the course of the conduct they have adopted for themselves[147].

---

143 A. Jones/B. Sufrin, *ibid.*, 663.

144 Compare A. Jones/B. Sufrin, *ibid.*, 663 et sqq.

145 *Ibid.*, 658.

146 Cases 48, 49, 51-7/69, *ICI v. Commission* [1972] ECR 619.

147 Case C-199/92P, *Hüls AG v. Commission* [1999] 5 CMLR 1016, paras. 160 et sqq.

An important issue is the minimum extent of interaction required for the establishment of concertation. Therefore, it is important for market actors to know whether parallel behaviour or conscious parallelism may be regarded as prohibited. The ECJ has chosen the approach of a general exclusion of tacit coordination of the ambit of Article 81 EC. Nevertheless, the ECJ has also clarified that parallel behaviour may furnish proof of explicit collusion if the behaviour cannot be plausibly explained otherwise by the conditions prevailing on the respective market[148].

The question of how to treat oligopolistic market structures under competition law will to a considerable degree depend on the individual executing authority's discretion. The outcome in individual cases may however also depend on the applicable procedural rules, such as the rules relating to the burden of proof[149]. Procedural differences may, therefore, amplify differences within national substantive rules.

5. *Prevention of mergers which would lead to a concentration in market power*

A merger occurs where two or more previously independent economic entities unite. Mergers can come about horizontally between market actors operating at the same level of economy. Alternatively, they can occur between market actors at different levels of production. The most common economic rationale for a vertical merger is to secure an outlet or an supply of raw materials. Alternatively, mergers may occur between undertakings on different product markets. Such conglomerate mergers do not have any impact on market power, but may constitute a way to reduce economic risk or to expand into another market.

The purpose behind merger control is the ability of national competition authorities to act as a regulator with regard to market structure. Mergers usually imply substantial impact on an individual company's ability to act freely, in that the previously unhindered capacity of at least one market actor may be lost. This results in more permanent and lasting changes to the conditions of the market prevailing than from agreements. Consequently, mergers may raise severe competition concerns[150].

More precisely, horizontal mergers in particular may imply the acquisition or the strengthening of market power and an increase in the market price of the product at issue. Even if dominance or the acquisition of market power may not

---

[148] Compare the ECJ's judgement in Cases C-89, 104, 114, 116-117, 125-129/85 *Re Wood Pulp Cartel: Ahlström Oy v. Commission (Wood Pulp II)* [1993] ECR I-1307.

[149] It is interesting to note that the EC Courts have restrained the Commission in its freedom of appraisal, in that the Commission must adduce sufficient evidence to corroborate any allegations with regard to concerted practices: Case C-199/92 P, *Hüls AG v. Commission*, ibid.; Cases T-68 and 77-78/89, *Società Italiana Vetro SpA v. Commission [1992] ECR II-1403.*

[150] Compare A. Jones/B. Sufrin, *ibid.*, 701 et sqq.

always be the underlying motive of the transaction it may nevertheless be its effect. Mergers may also bring about collective dominance. The concentration thereby created or enforced may facilitate collusion on an already concentrated market. With regard to vertical mergers, the most common fear is the inherent risk of market foreclosure or the foreclosure of a particular source of supply to competitors. Albeit, vertical mergers are considered less harmful in some jurisdictions as they will hardly ever imply an increase of market power[151]. Finally, a common concern with regard to conglomerate mergers is the risk of leverage in that an undertaking dominant in one market could use its market power for tying or for predatory pricing through cross-subsidizing. Also, the potential competition could be reduced.

Apart from these possible negative effects of mergers, however, such transactions may also have positive effects, like efficiency. Moreover, cross-border mergers may promote market integrationist goals. In addition, mergers are generally a possible expression of the freedom to sell a business and must therefore be considered crucial to any business owner, without which few people would take the risk to set up a business. In addition, mergers can be a way to prevent a firm's liquidation in the case of bankruptcy[152].

The illustrated inherent effects of mergers have been weighed differently in the various national jurisdictions. Moreover, although a merger will by definition always entail a unification of the decision-making processes of formerly independent undertakings', the underlying contractual framework can be designed in various forms. National legislators may deploy different definitions for the prerequisites required for a commercial transaction to constitute a merger as well as the associated legal consequences. Therefore, the outcome of merger-related proceedings may differ depending on national legal implementation, although certain similarities in substantive evaluation may be observed. Once again, this will be illustrated by a comparison of the individual approaches prevailing in the United States and in the European Union. Notably, a certain degree of convergence of merger standards in the US and the EU has developed through the last decades.

First, under European law, the ECJ'S decision in *Kali*[153] and the CFI's decision in *Gencor*[154] laid down the requirement of a detailed microeconomic analysis to determine the concrete potential for coordinated behaviour in the market at issue for European competition authorities. This EU approach corresponds to the one deployed in the US since *General Dynamics*[155].

---

[151] For example, this approach has been chosen in the United States.

[152] Compare A. Jones/B. Sufrin, *ibid.*, 700 et sqq. for an overview of motives and drawbacks of mergers.

[153] Cases C-68/94 & C-30/95 *France v. Commission & Société Commerciale des Potasses et de l'Azote (SCPA) v. Commission*, [1998] ECR I-1375, [1998] 4 CMLR 829.

[154] Case T-102/96 *Gencor v. Commission* [1999] ECR II-7153.

[155] *United States v. General Dynamics Corp.*, 415 US 486 (1974), compare *J. Wilson*, ibid., 194.

Second, the substantive test applied in the EU has moved toward a "substantial lessening of competition" test as applied in the US[156]. Lately, this trend has been confirmed through the new wording of the substantive test as formulated in the revised EC Merger Regulation adopted in 2004[157].

Third, the test applied in the US to define market concentration is the *Herfindahl-Hirschmann Index*. In order to measure concentration, the squares of the market shares of the undertakings at issue are added together[158]. In the EU, this method had not been adopted in the former Merger Regulation 4064/89. Rather, the Commission had referred to its general notice on market definition[159]. The notice takes account of econometric and quantitative tests for the definition of the relevant market, but it does not lay down a uniform method for the quantification of market concentration. EU authorities would generally define markets more narrowly and apply a lower market-share threshold for a finding of substantial market power[160]. Yet, in the new Guidelines on the assessment of horizontal mergers under the Council Regulation on the Control of Concentrations between Undertakings[161] (referring to the Merger Regulation 139/2004[162]) the Commission now explicitly refers to the *Herfindahl-Hirschmann Index* for its assessment of concentration[163].

Fourth, rapprochement also occurred with regard to the efficiency defence. In the United States, merger analysis does not end with the determination that the merger would have anticompetitive effects. Rather, the efficiencies created are weighed against possible anticompetitive effects. The US Merger Guidelines provide for the admissibility of the defence where the efficiencies are merger-specific, come about in the same market as any anti-competitive effects, are verifiable and measurable, and where the efficiencies also outweigh any potential harm to consumers[164]. Thus, consumer benefits, such as economies of scale, integration of production facilities, enhanced research and development poten-

---

[156] See W. J. Kolalsky, *Conglomerate Mergers and Range Effects: It's a Long Way from Chicago to Brussels,* 23 Address before the George Mason University Symposium, Washington, D.C. (9 November 2001), http://www.usdoj.gov/atr/public/speeches/9536.htm (29.05.2005).

[157] The new test under the Council Regulation (EC) No 139/2004 of 20 January 2004 on the control of concentrations between undertakings [OJ 2004, No. L24/1] reads as follows: "A concentration which would significantly impede effective competition, in the common market or in a substantial part of it, in particular by the creation or strengthening of a dominant position, shall be declared incompatible with the common market", see Article 2 para. 3 of the Regulation. Arguably, this wording now clearly covers all anti-competitive post merger scenarios, including oligopolies, see EC Commission, *Merger Overview,* available at: http://europa.eu.int/comm/competition/publications/special/3_merger.pdf (13.01.2005).

[158] Compare A. Jones/B. Sufrin, *ibid.*, 704.

[159] EC Commission, *Commission Notice on the definition of relevant market for the purposes of Community competition law* [OJ 1997, No. C372/5].

[160] J. Wilson, *ibid.*, 192 et sqq., referring to William E. Kovacic's analysis in: *Merger Enforcement in Transition: Antitrust Controls on Acquisitions in Emerging Economies,* 1998 (66) U. Cin. L. Rev. 1075, 1086.

[161] [2004] OJ C31/03.

[162] EC Council Regulation (EC) No 139/2004 on the control of concentrations between undertakings [OJ 2004, No. L24/1].

[163] [2004] OJ C31/03, paras. 16 et sqq.

[164] 1997 US Merger Guidelines, para. 4.

tial, plant specialisation or a reduction in production costs are considered by the DoJ/FTC as possible benefits of mergers[165]. In comparison, European authorities would not admit efficiencies as a possible means of justification, but would consider them in the overall assessment of the significant impediment of effective competition under the former Merger Regulation 4064/89[166]. The applicable test was "the creation or strengthening of a dominant position", which, according to the Commission, did not legally permit any justification by means of an efficiency defence[167]. For example, the Commission argued in *Aérospatiale-Alenia/de Havilland*[168] that any advantages had to accrue to consumers and that the concentration would be harmful to consumers due to the creation of a dominant position. The Commission's assessment of efficiency considerations was, however, rated insufficient by the Court of First Instance in its decisions in *Airtours*[169], *Schneider*[170] and *Tetra Laval*[171] in 2002[172]. In light of this adjudication, the wording of the new Guidelines on the assessment of horizontal mergers under the Council Regulation on the Control of Concentrations between Undertakings now provides for considerable similarities to the US Merger Guidelines with regard to the admissibility of an efficiency defence[173].

Despite this established degree of substantive convergence of merger standards in the US and the EU, their differences are not yet overcome. The decision in *GE/Honeywell*[174] may serve as an illustrative example for the procedural and cultural, or rather philosophical, divergence still existing[175]. In addition, technical differences may entail different outcomes of US or EU proceedings.

For example, there is a great distrust of large market players prevailing in the EU, a greater willingness to interfere with industrial structure due to the historically high degree of state intervention as a more activist approach, a less thorough acceptance of the consumer welfare model and finally a tendency to consider individual competitors' interests rather than the preservation of effective competition in general[176]. Also, EU authorities focus heavily on due proc-

---

[165] J. Wilson, *Globalization and the Limits of National Merger Control Laws*, 2003, 196.

[166] EEC Regulation 4064/89 [OJ 1990, No. L257/13], as amended by Council Regulation (EC) No 1310/97 [OJ 1997, No L180/1].

[167] J. Wilson, *ibid.*, 197.

[168] Case IV/M53 [1991] OJ L334/42, [1992] 4 CMLR M2.

[169] *Airtours v. Commission* (Case T-342/99) [2002] OJ C191/24.

[170] *Schneider Electric SA v. Commission* (Case T-310/01) [2003] OJ C55/24.

[171] *Tetra Laval BV. v. Commission* (Case T-5/02) [2003] OJ C19/34.

[172] Compare G. Stirati, *The Appraisal of Collective Dominance and Efficiency Gains under the Substantive Test of the New EU Merger Regulation*, in: 1(3) Erasmus Law and Economics Review 2004, 261.

[173] Compare G. Stirati, *The Appraisal of Collective Dominance and Efficiency Gains under the Substantive Test of the New EU Merger Regulation*, in: 1(3) Erasmus Law and Economics Review 2004, 276 et sqq, referring to paras. 76 et sqq. of the Guidelines.

[174] Case No. COMP/M.2220 - *GE Honeywell*, 3 July 2001.

[175] Compare Y. Akbar, *Grabbing Victory from the Jaws of Defeat: Can the GE/Honeywell Merger Facilitate International Antitrust Policy Co-operation?* 25(4) Journal of World Competition 2002, 404, 412 et sqq.

[176] *J.* Wilson, *ibid.*

ess and legal fairness, whereas US authorities apply a results-oriented approach[177].

Second, the US approach is generally more consumer-oriented in general, placing much of an emphasis on the merger's effect on prices. US authorities are tolerant of single firm growth and even dominance, assuming that economic strength due to efficient use of resources and innovation must not be punished *per se*. The EU approach, on the other hand, stresses a merger's effects on competitors and a possible effect of leverage. In doing so, an expansive definition of what dominant firm behaviour is considered to be unlawful is applied. The appraisal of the transaction's effects on consumers will only be realized as a secondary analysis.

Third, from a historic point of view, merger regulation has come into play in the United States long after the respective market had been guaranteed by the Commerce Clause of the constitution. Therefore, US antitrust authorities have as their main responsibility the maintenance of fair competition. In comparison, given the market integration goals of the European Union, the European competition authorities have been responsible for the creation as well as the maintenance of the Common Market[178].

Finally, from a procedural and institutional point of view, differences may be detected in the degree to which *ex-post* control is possible. Arguably, the degree to which *ex-post* control is admitted to US authorities is much greater than the European Merger Regulation has foreseen for their European counterparts. Thus, in order to compensate for this lack of control, European authorities will apply stricter rules from the outset in order to prevent any anti-competitive behaviour in the future. Moreover, the EU authorities have fewer personnel and are jury and judge at the same time[179]. This may imply a certain individualization of the decision-making process of European authorities.

To sum up the above, there are considerable inherent differences within the individual national transformations of merger regulation, despite some substantive convergence.

6. Application and borders of domestic competition law

6.1. Definition of the relevant market

Market definition is a core aspect and fundamental prerequisite to all areas of competition law. Basically, it is only by defining the relevant market that restrictive business practices can be identified and, consequently, be assessed in

[177] Y. Akbar, *ibid.*, 413 et sqq.
[178] Compare J. Wilson, *Globalization and the Limits of National Merger Control Laws*, 2003, 192 et sqq.
[179] Y. Akbar, *ibid.*, 412 et sqq.

light of the applicable domestic regulation with regard to their effect on effective competition on a given market *within the jurisdiction at issue*. The purpose of market definition is to determine the substitutability of products or services for one another in the eyes of their potential consumers, so as to determine which products or services operate as competitive restraints on producers of the substitutable goods[180]. In this determination, the specific product features[181] are considered together with geographical aspects as well as temporal aspects[182] from both a supply and demand point of view[183].

Competition enforcement authorities tend to apply a rather narrow definition of the relevant market to facilitate proof of restrictive practices. Nevertheless, market definitions occur on a case to case basis and will depend on the assessing authorities' individual analysis of *inter alia* international integration, specific regional preferences or transport costs. Consequently, the individual perceptions of the relevant markets may differ. Under EC competition law, the markets are traditionally defined particularly narrow[184].

As a general rule, domestic competition law is directed toward a particular product market within that jurisdiction's territory. In case of international relevant markets across multiple jurisdictions' territories, the assessing authorities may adopt different market definitions. This may give rise to conflict, and also raise questions relating to the territorial application of domestic law.

6.2. Geographical scope: Principle of Territoriality v. Effects Doctrine

The geographical scope of domestic competition law may be limited by either national borders, or the effects of a given practice on domestic markets. Thus, the principle of territoriality and the effects doctrine are the two regulatory alternatives available to domestic competition law rule makers[185].

---

180 A. Jones/B. Sufrin, *ibid.*, 38 et sqq.

181 E.g. Product characteristics, price and intended use, compare EC Commission, *Notice on the definition of the relevant market for the purposes of Community competition law*, OJ 1997, No. C372/5, para. 7. in line with Anglo-Saxon antitrust tradition, the EC Commission has adopted the "Small but Significant Non-transitory Increase in Price" – test ("SSNIP - test") verifying the cross-elasticity of demand, which has been criticized for practical difficulties to measure the consumers' reactions to a hypothetical price rise, compare H. Wins, *Eine internationale Wettbewerbsordnung als Ergänzung zum GATT*, 2000, 36; A. Jones/B. Sufrin, *ibid.*, 45.

182 The temporal aspect is of minor practical importance. For an EC case where the temporal aspect was considered compare Case 27/76, *United Brands Co and United Brands Continental BV* v. *Commission* [1978] ECR 207, [1978] 1 CMLR 429.

183 E.g. EC Commission, *Notice on the definition of the relevant market for the purposes of Community competition law*, OJ 1997, No. C372/5, para. 15 et sqq; US Department of Justice, *Horizontal Merger Guidelines*, revised April 8,1997, s. 1, available at: http://www.usdoj.gov/atr/public/guidelines/hmg.htm (29.05.2005).

184 Compare the criticized approach adopted by the ECJ for the geographic market of replacement tires in Case 322/81, *Nederlandsche Banden-Industrie Michelin* v. *Commission* [1983] ECR 3461 [1985] 1 CMLR 282, para. 23 et sqq.

185 H. Wins, *Eine internationale Wettbewerbsordnung als Ergänzung zum GATT*, 2000, 39 et sqq.

Albeit being a generally recognized principle of delimitation of both domestic subject-matter and enforcement jurisdiction by public international law, the territoriality principle has only a minor role in competition policy matters. In fact, it has been adopted by a only limited number of countries[186] which have thereby limited their jurisdiction in competition law matters to their particular territory. The majority of states have taken into consideration the effects doctrine, modelled on the predominant example provided by the United States. These states have thereby empowered themselves to extraterritorially apply their domestic law to foreign businesses located abroad.

In the United States, although the concept of "comity"[187] has partly expanded into legal practice[188], the effects doctrine has been the dominating approach from an early point in time. The 1982 Foreign Trade Antitrust Improvement Act sets out that export transactions are excluded from the Sherman Act unless they directly, substantially and reasonably foreseeable affect US Commerce, and has come to be regarded as a statutory formulation of the effects doctrine. It does not, however, address any balancing criteria, as foreseen by the Third Restatement of the Foreign Relations Law of the United States[189] or the Set of Antitrust Enforcement Guidelines for International Operations[190] in line with the mentioned legal practice. In *Hartford Fire Insurance*[191], the Supreme Court recognized the claims of comity, but nevertheless applied the effects doctrine to a boycott agreed on by re-insurers based in London with parties in the US. Later, the Department of Justice has even commenced criminal procedures against a Japanese company for price fixing[192]. Recently, however, the US Supreme Court appears to have placed limits on the reach of US antitrust laws in its decision in *F. Hoffman-La Roche Ltd. et. al.* v. *Empagram S.A.* It held that where price fixing harmed both American and Non-Americans, foreign plaintiffs could not use American Courts to sue unless the harm they suffered was directly dependent on the harm to US plaintiffs[193]. Nevertheless, with regard to criminal enforcement, the DOJ generally seeks more jail time for individual US and foreign defendants found guilty of cartel crimes. Also, the DOJ supports

186 E.g. Korea, Sri Lanka, compare H. Wins, *ibid.*

187 "Comity" generally refers to the notion of "living peacefully with other nations in mutual respect and accommodating the other nations' interests", compare A. Jones/B. Sufrin, *ibid.*, 1041.

188 In *Timberland Lumber Co.* v. *Bank of America*, 549 F.2d597 at 613 (9th Cir.1976), it has been recognized that the effects test itself is incomplete as it would "fail to consider the other nation' interest", and the three criteria of *(i)* tripartite analysis, *(ii)* cognizable injury and *(iii)* sufficiently strong effect so as to justify an assertion of extra-territorial authority have been developed. Those criteria were subsequently expanded in *Mannington Mills Inc.* v. *Congoleum Corp.*, 595 F, 2d 1287 (3rd Cir.1979). Compare A. Jones/B. Sufrin, *ibid.*

189 American Law Institute, 1995, at sec. 403.

190 Department of Justice and Federal Trade Commission, *Antitrust and Trade Reg. Rep. (BNA)*, Special Supplement (6 Apr. 1995).

191 *Hartford Fire Insurance Co.* v. *California*, 509 US 764,113 S Ct. 2891 (1993).

192 *United States* v. *Nippon Paper Industries Co.*, 109 F, 3d (1st Cir. 1997).

193 US Supreme Court, *F. Hoffman-La Roche Ltd. et. al.* v. *Empagram S.A.*, June 14, 2004, compare Sandra Rubin, *US Antitrust Reach Shortened*, Financial Post 30.6.2004, FP11, at: http://www.mcmillanbinch.com/Upload/News/JWRowley_USantitrust_reach_063004.pdf (29.05.2005).

legislation before Congress that would significantly increase penalties for antitrust violations[194]. In light of these contradictory trends among US antitrust institutions, private parties will have to face increased legal uncertainty and a threat of considerable fines.

The European authorities have dealt with the question of extraterritorial application as early as in *Dyestuffs*[195]. In that case, however, one of the parties was based in the EC. Subsequently, in *Woodpulp*[196], although formally adhering to the principle of territoriality[197], the ECJ held that entities established outside the Common Market were nevertheless subject to EC Competition Law where they "implemented" price concertation through their branches within the EC. In *Gencor*[198], the CFI, arguing with an "immediate and substantial effect in the Community", prohibited a merger in the South African platinum and rhodium industry on the grounds that it would create a position of oligopolistic dominance in the Common Market. Arguably, this legal practice has not yet clarified the meaning of "implemented", and also left undefined the precise links required for an alleged jurisdiction over a foreign nation[199].

In addition to these two major proponents of the effects doctrine, various other states have endorsed it[200]. Being a unilateral method to address cross-border restrictive business practices, the effects doctrine clearly touches on the national sovereignty of states where the foreign addressees of domestic law are being located. Moreover, the application of domestic competition law to situations occurring on foreign markets without mutual consideration of the effects domestic restrictive practices might have on markets located abroad is potentially discriminatory[201].

Notably, some countries have recently endorsed a system of implicit exclusion, by abolishing their explicit exemptions for practices only affecting markets abroad. *Bhattacharjea* argued that this would imply further hindrances for effective enforcement in the countries actually affected by such practices. Different than in case of a published infringement with subsequent exemption, the affected countries would hardly be able to obtain information about the prac-

---

[194] J. S. Magney/R. C. Anderson, *Recent Developments in Criminal Enforcement of US Antitrust Laws*, in 27(1) Journal of World Competition 2004, 101 et sqq.

[195] Case 48/69, *ICI* v. *Commission (Dyestuffs)* [1972] ECR 619, [1972] CMLR 557.

[196] Cases 89, 104, 114, 116, 117 and 125-1129/85, *A. Ahlström Oy* v. *Commission* [1988] ECR 5193, paras. 12 et sqq.

[197] H. Wins, *ibid.*, 40.

[198] European Court of First Instance, Case IV/M 619 [1997] OJ L11/30, [1999] 4 CMLR 1076.

[199] E. Fox, *The Merger Regulation and its Territorial Reach* [1999] ECLR 335-336.

[200] Compare s. 130 para 2 of the German "Gesetz gegen Wettbewerbsbeschränkungen" (GWB): (2) "Dieses Gesetz findet Anwendung auf alle Wettbewerbsbeschränkungen, die sich im Geltungsbereich dieses Gesetzes auswirken, auch wenn sie außerhalb des Geltungsbereichs dieses Gesetzes veranlaßt werden"; compare also the Austrian equivalent in s. 24 para 2 of the Austrian "Kartellgesetz" (KartG): "(2) Dieses Bundesgesetz ist nur anzuwenden, soweit sich ein Sachverhalt auf den inländischen Markt auswirkt, unabhängig davon, ob er im Inland oder im Ausland verwirklicht worden ist.

[201] *H. Wins*, ibid., 40 et sqq.

tices' existence at all under a system of implicit exclusion, as the practices would not be documented or published by the authorities of the country where the practices occurred[202].

Thus, the effects doctrine must clearly be considered an imperfect method to address restrictions of competition with a cross-border dimension. From a competition policy perspective, however, a system of explicit exemption must be preferred over a system of implicit exclusion.

E. Conclusion

In light of the above, the author argues that the existing individual domestic approaches to competition law differ to a considerable extent. Despite being based on common economic rationales, the concrete underlying policy goals may vary largely. In particular, the underlying policy goals of competition laws depend on individual political or institutional aspects of the jurisdiction at issue, and extend to certain competition-extrinsic factors such as industrial policy or public policy goals.

Domestic competition laws are *ex lege* bound to the national territory of the enacting states. In light of the emergence of global markets, the number of competition law investigations with international aspects is growing. Consequently, the question must be raised as to whether traditional competition law instruments and the current institutional setup of domestic competition enforcement authorities are still adequate in light of the amended market circumstances. In the following, therefore, the author shall examine in more detail *(i)* the changes in the market circumstances, and *(ii)* the adequacy of the existing normative systems of domestic competition laws in the light of the amended market circumstances.

---

[202] A. Bhattacharjea, *The Case for a Multilateral Agreement on Competition Policy: A Developing Country Perspective,* in: 9(2) Journal of International Economic Law 2006, 299.

III. The Case for International Competition Rules from a Competition Policy Perspective

A. Liberalisation & Integration of World Markets

1. The International Trading System after Bretton Woods

For an examination of the world market's structures prevailing today, we must first consider the changes in the international trading regime that have occurred since World War II, and the system of international institutions that has been established. Arguably, a growing linkage in international economic relations has taken place. This linkage has occurred in three phases[203]. The first happened through increased trade in line with the dismantling of tariffs and other governmental barriers to trade during the 1950s and 60s. The second phase was commenced by three commodity and oil shocks which occurred in the 1970s. The third one has been referred to as "globalization", being characterized by sharply increased foreign direct investment, mainly built on the transfer of capital and technology.

To begin with, the developments initiated by the negotiations at Bretton Woods, which resulted in the creation of the IMF, the World Bank and the GATT have markedly influenced today's international economic relations. So did the United Nations and the OECD. Today, trade laws and policies are operating in an international context and focus on the liberalisation of *governmental* measures restricting or distorting international trade. Such governmental measures may consist in border regulations (e.g. tariffs and quantitative restrictions), internal regulations (e.g. discriminatory internal taxation), or in government participation in trade (e.g. state trading enterprises, government procurement procedures). Thus, a variety of multilateral treaty instruments and organizations have been designed for commodity regulation, transport regulation, taxation, and many other subjects[204]. In addition, various regional arrangements have emerged. As a European example, the European Union, formerly the European Economic Community (EEC), the European Free Trade Area (EFTA) and the European Economic Area (EEA) can be mentioned. For the Americas, the NAFTA between the United States, Canada and Mexico can be cited[205].

An excellent example for the history of economic integration is the GATT/WTO System. The GATT, which replaced the failed ITO Charter in

[203] M. J. Trebilcock, *Competition Policy and Trade Policy. Mediating the Interface,* in: 30(4) Journal of World Trade 1996, 72 et sqq.

[204] J. H. Jackson, *Alternative Approaches for Implementing Competition Rules in International Economic Relations,* in: 49(II/III) Aussenwirtschaft 1994, 178.

[205] Jackson/Davey/Sykes, *ibid.*, 447 et sqq.

1948[206], has prompted the reduction of barriers to trade in goods among democratic and market oriented industrial economies. It is not a single agreement, but rather a series of over two hundred agreements, protocols, procès-verbaux, and "Schedules of Concessions" expressing an individual country's tariff limits. Based on the principle of reciprocity[207], the main objective of GATT is to advance trade liberalisation[208] in order to promote global welfare[209]. Thus, governments are constrained from imposing or continuing a variety of measures that restrain or distort international trade. Such measures include tariffs, quotas, internal taxes and internal regulation discriminating against imports, subsidy and dumping practices, state trading as well as customs procedures and other "non-tariff" events. In addition, the "Most Favoured Nation Clause"[210] prohibits discrimination between other countries' products by means of government import or export regulation. Likewise, the obligation of "National Treatment" in Article III GATT stipulates that imports shall be treated no worse than domestically produced goods under internal taxation or regulatory measures.

During eight rounds of trade negotiations between 1948 and 1994, tariffs have been continuously reduced. Already during the first round in 1947, 45,000 tariff concessions were achieved, which affected US $ 10 billion of trade. By 1979, the average custom duty on industrial products had been brought down to 4.7%[211]. Subsequently, anti-dumping measures[212] and non-tariff measures[213] were brought to the agenda, followed by services, intellectual property, dispute settlement, textiles and agriculture[214]. By 1999, tariffs for industrial commodities had sunk below 4% from 40% in 1947[215]. These achievements are considerable in light of the GATT's problematic legal structure prior to 1994. First, GATT was applied by means of the "Protocol of Provisional Application",

---

[206] J. H. Jackson, *Alternative Approaches for Implementing Competition Rules in International Economic Relations*, in: 49(II/III) Aussenwirtschaft 1994, 178.

[207] Jackson/Davey/Sykes, *ibid.*, 215.

[208] Compare the recitals to the GATT 1947, paras. 2 & 3.

[209] Based on David Ricardo's book *The Principles of Political Economy* published in 1917 and the "Theory of Comparative Advantage" established therein, International Trade Theory seeks to demonstrate that free international trade substantially broadens the contract opportunity set available to private economic actors and hence the mutual gains realizable from exchange as parties with different endowments of certain special resources or skills are able to reap the gains from their differential advantages and disadvantages through trade, compare M. J. Trebilcock/R. Howse, *The Regulation of International Trade*, 2002, 3 et sqq.

[210] Article I GATT.

[211] See WTO, *The GATT Years: From Havana to Marrakesh*, available at: http://www.wto.org/english/thewto_e/whatis_e/tif_e/fact4_e.htm (15.7.2004)

[212] Kennedy Round (1964-1967), details available at: http://www.wto.org/english/thewto_e/whatis_e/tif_e/fact4_e.htm (15.7.2004).

[213] Non-tariff barriers were first examined during the Tokyo Round from 1973 to 1979, available at: http://www.wto.org/english/thewto_e/whatis_e/tif_e/fact4_e.htm (15.7.2004).

[214] The latter issues were first raised during the Uruguay Round between 1986 and 1994, compare: http://www.wto.org/english/thewto_e/whatis_e/tif_e/fact4_e.htm (15.7.2004).

[215] G. Koopmann, *Internationalisierung der Wettbewerbspolitik: Korrelat zur internationalen Handelspolitik?* In: 56(II) Aussenwirtschaft 2001, 162.

which provided for an "existing legislation clause" in its paragraph 1(b)[216]. Second, GATT never had the formal status of an organization, although operating as one in practice[217]. Third, the Agreement was nearly impossible to amend due to the cumbersome amending provisions. As a result thereof, an elaborate system of "side agreements or codes" was established, with an unclear relationship to the General Agreement. Moreover, such side agreements only bound those governments accepting them, and have, therefore, contributed to what was referred to as "GATT à la carte"[218]. Fourth, the efficacy of the dispute settlement process was questionable due to *(i)* a consensus requirement in that the adoption of panel reports could be blocked, *(ii)* the absence of time frames, *(iii)* its nature as a "power-ruled" system[219], and *(iv)*, certain incidents of non-compliance[220].

Arguably, these shortcomings have been mostly overcome by the creation of the World Trade Organization through the 1994 Marrakesh Agreement Establishing the World Trade Organisation (hereafter "WTO Agreement"). The WTO Agreement now *inter alia* comprises all Multilateral Agreements like the revised GATT 1994, the previous Side Agreements[221], the General Agreement on Trade in Services (GATS), the General Agreement on Trade-Related Intellectual Property Rights (TRIPS), the Dispute Settlement Understanding and four optional Plurilateral Agreements[222]. The WTO Agreement established an international organization with legal personality[223], and promotes legal and practice continuity with GATT[224]. The "single package" idea has been reinforced in that countries accepting the Uruguay Round must accept the entire package. Another important aspect is the facilitation of the extension of the institutional structure to the new subjects that have been negotiated during the Uruguay Round, in particular services and intellectual property. Also, recognizing the necessity for providing security and predictability to the multilateral trading system, the dispute settlement system has been reformulated by Dispute Settlement Understanding[225] and thereby been transformed into a rule-based system.

---

216 This provision put the so-called "Grandfather Rights" in place, by which the GATT did not have to be applied in inconsistency with mandatory national legislation in existence in a state before becoming a contracting party to GATT, Jackson/Davey/Sykes, *ibid.*, 217.

217 Jackson/Davey/Sykes, *ibid.*, 208.

218 Jackson/Davey/Sykes, *ibid.*, 215.

219 Different from an adjudicative, rule-based system, a negotiation, power-based system will imply settlement by negotiation and agreement with reference to the relative bargaining power of the parties, see J. H. Jackson, *The World Trading System*, 1997, 109.

220 *European Communities – Regime for the Importation, Sale and Distribution of Bananas*, DS32/R (3 June 1993) [Bananas I Panel Report], DS38/R (1995) [Bananas II Panel Report].

221 For example, Agreement on the Application of Sanitary and Phytosanitary Measures, Textiles and Clothing, Safeguards, Subsidies and Countervailing Measures, Technical Barriers to Trade, or Agreement on Agriculture.

222 Such agreements exist for government procurement, trade in civil aircraft, bovine meat and dairy.

223 Jackson/Davey/Sykes, *ibid.*, 221.

224 Article XVI:1 of the Marrakesh Agreement establishing the World Trade Organization.

225 Annex 2 to the WTO Agreement.

Thus, the GATT/WTO experience may serve as an illustrative example of how economic interdependence[226] and mutual trans-national economic awareness among individual states have been substantially fostered by the international trading regime since World War II. The degree of economic integration has been continuously augmented so that governments are increasingly restricted in the domestic regulation of their economies. Given the high density of regulation and the agreed enforceability, a member state's national sovereignty concerning domestic regulation has been significantly affected by the predominant obligation to grant market access to other states. Arguably, the interdependence among states has deepened to an extent that almost any domestic policy or regulation may affect the economic activities in other countries[227].

2. *International Production & Foreign Direct Investment*

Apart from the increase in cross border sales that has occurred trough the trade liberalisation under the GATT, international production under the common governance of trans-national companies (TNCs) is fostering the integration process of today's world economy. Thereby, TNCs have been creating a cohesive global production system, in which "deep integration" is occurring alongside with traditional market integration strategies[228]. In particular, TNCs are systematically locating certain specialized activities across numerous states on a long-term basis. This is due to the ongoing fall of barriers to investment, trade and information, which entails increased competitive pressure for TNCs to variably locate their activities in order to enhance economic efficiency. The most important cross-border flows relate to finance, trade, personnel, know-how and technology, i.e. to both business-related and internal administrative activities[229]. This trend of deep integration can be expected to rise with growing competition as well as increased familiarity with and efficiency of a given location[230].

The relative importance of international production to global economy can, albeit only imprecisely, be measured by Foreign Direct Investment (FDI) and other TNC activities, in particular sales, assets, gross-product, employment and

---

[226] Jackson/Davey/Sykes, *ibid.*, 1.

[227] A. S. Grewlich, *Globalisation and Conflict in Competition Law. Elements of Possible Solutions*, in: 24(3) Journal of World Competition 2001, 367.

[228] In light of technical developments, intensified competition and liberalisation and the resulting decrease in transportation and communication costs, TNCs have increasingly been put in the position to distinctively integrate production as well as other corporate functions across various countries (so-called "deep integration"), UNCTAD, *World Investment Report 2000. Cross-border Mergers and Acquisitions and Development*, 30, available at:
http://www.unctad.org/en/docs/wir2000_en.pdf (29.05.2005). Deep integration can take various forms, such as locating certain corporate functions abroad (e.g. accounting, marketing, R& D), or splitting certain production steps across multiple countries in order to benefit from lower relative costs and logistic advantages, UNCTAD, *World Investment Report (WIR) 2000*, Chapter I, 9.

[229] UNCTAD, *WIR 2000*, Chapter I, 15.

[230] UNCTAD, *WIR 2000*, Chapter I, 9 et sqq.

export of foreign affiliates, all of which have constantly increased since the 1980s[231]. For instance, before they distinctly declined between 2001 and 2003, global sales of foreign affiliates alone were about twice as high as global exports in 1999, compared to almost parity at the beginning of the 1980s[232]. In 2003, international production was carried out by more than 900.000 foreign affiliates for over 61.000 TNCs worldwide. This accounts for about one third of world exports, and for approximately 10% of the worldwide gross domestic product[233], which is about double compared to two decades ago[234].

Foreign direct investment occurs in two ways. Mainly it occurs through foreign market participants acquiring an existing local firm or merging with it. Alternatively, it can also occur through "greenfield investment" of foreign market participants into new local facilities, mostly in developing countries[235]. During the 1990s, most of the growth in international production has occurred through cross-border M&A transactions. The value of completed cross-border transactions has risen from less than US $100 billion in 1987 to US $720 billion in 1999, which equals about 10% of world exports[236]. The vast majority of these transactions are acquisitions[237]. Many host countries and in particular developing host countries have issued concerns that FDI entry by means of takeovers of domestic firms was more harmful to local economic development than entry by establishing new facilities. Allegedly, foreign acquisitions would not add productive capacity, but only constitute a simple transfer of ownership, resulting in foreign control, layoff of employees or even closings, and most probably servicing the new owner in foreign exchange. From a competitive point of view, concerns have been raised that if an acquirer was a global oligopolist, a dominant position might be created through the acquisition. Also, cross-border M&As could be calculatingly deployed to reduce competition in the domestic market at issue, thereby threatening local undertakings and endangering local capacity building. It has also been pointed out that the commercial expectations of the underlying transactions could often not be realized, which would additionally endanger the local and often fragile economies[238].

Given the potential importance of FDI to national economies, it is not surprising that many countries have sought to attract foreign investors by liberalizing the regulatory conditions for investment and, subsequently, supplementing this

---

231 UNCTAD, *World Investment Report 2004. The Shift toward Services,* Table I.3, Chapter 1, 9, available at: http://www.unctad.org/en/docs/wir2004_en.pdf (29.05.2005).

232 UNCTAD, *WIR 2000,* Chapter I, 4 et sqq.

233 UNCTAD, *WIR 2004,* Chapter I, 8 et sqq.

234 In 1982, the global gross product attributed to foreign affiliates amounted to approximately 5%, compare UNCTAD, *WIR 2000,* Chapter I, 4.

235 UNCTAD, *WIR 2000,* Chapter II, 99.

236 G. Koopmann, *Internationalisierung der Wettbewerbspolitik: Korrelat zur internationalen Handelspolitik?* In: 56(II) Aussenwirtschaft 2001, 165.

237 Compare UNCTAD, *WIR 2000,* Overview, xix. According to UNCTAD's survey, 97% of cross-border M&A transactions are acquisitions, compared to only 3% mergers.

238 UNCTAD, *WIR 2000,* Overview, xxiii.

regulatory basis through other instruments, e.g. bilateral investment or double taxation treaties[239]. For instance, of the 140 statutory amendments to FDI laws in 1999, 131 resulted in their liberalisation[240]. For developing countries, these liberalisation measures most prominently include the removal or limitation of sectoral restrictions for foreign entry, as well as the liberalisation of operations for formerly closed industries[241]. For developed countries with largely liberalized FDI regimes, the measures introduced could be described as complementary "second level liberalisation measures", mainly aimed to ensure *(i)* a competitive environment in the markets liberalized for FDI and *(ii)* certain public policy goals. With regard to the first goal, many developed countries strengthened their domestic competition law regimes, whereas for the second, developed countries amended their regulatory environment for corporate governance, consumer and environmental protection[242].

3. *The effects of trade liberalization and international production on competition and domestic competition policy*[243]

The pre-eminent effect of market liberalisation on competition policy is that the relevant geographical market is enlarged due to decreasing costs for cross-border activities. From an efficiency point of view, this enlargement may have positive effects on competition. Due to increased export possibilities, the degree of concentration on domestic markets will decrease. In the light of the diverse institutional backgrounds of the competitors, their production costs may vary. Consequently, markets are less transparent and collusion is less likely to occur. Thus, prices will decrease, which prompts innovation and, thereby, stimulates competition. Yet, the increased competition renders the individual competitors' position and market power more vulnerable. As a result, liberalisation also provides an incentive for individual competitors to engage in restrictive business practices so as to limit competitive pressure[244], for example through market foreclosing or market sharing at the international level[245].

---

239 For a brief overview of the contentious discussion on the Multilateral Agreement on Investments compare P. Hilpold, *The Multilateral Agreement on Investments. Are the Fears justified?* In: 16 Academia 1999, available at:
http://www.eurac.edu/Press/Academia/16/Artikel2.asp (29.05.2005).

240 UNCTAD, *WIR 2000,* Chapter 1, 6.

241 UNCTAD, *WIR 2000,* Chapter 1, 7.

242 UNCTAD, *WIR 2000,* Chapter 1, 7.

243 This chapter is to provide a basic summary of the implications of trade liberalisation and international production on competition. For a more detailed analysis of both possible private and public practices see Chapter IV. C. below.

244 G. Koopmann, *Internationalisierung der Wettbewerbspolitik: Korrelat zur internationalen Handelspolitik?* In: 56(II) Aussenwirtschaft 2001, 165 et sqq

245 M.-C. Malaguti, *Restrictive Business Practices in International Trade and the Role of the World Trade Organization,* in: 32(3) Journal of World Trade 1998, 119.

With regard to international production, similarly ambiguous effects on competition can be discerned. M&A activities increase[246]. Clearly, barriers to entry are reduced for potential foreign competitors located abroad. Consequently, competition on domestic markets is intensified and efficiency increases. Foreign investors can often make use of economies of scale resulting from the regional splitting of intra-company services. Therefore, foreign investors are more easily in the position to compensate for domestic economies of scale of established domestic competitors, or for sunk costs required for investments to enter a particular market, than a domestic potential competitor would be[247]. Apart from possible efficiency gains due to increased competition, however, the technological supremacy of foreign competitors may give raise to strategic or structural barriers to entry and, thereby, also increase concentration in a given market. Thus, the creation or possibly even the abuse of dominant positions may be fostered[248].

Therefore, for an examination of the effects of the ongoing reduction of barriers to international trade and production on competition, two aspects must be considered[249]. First, enforcement of existing restrictive business practices among private market actors is hampered due to increased transparency and the reduction of barriers to entry. Practice partners might consider the increased number of foreign competitors with competitive advantages from cost benefits or strategic or structural conveniences a sufficient incentive to cheat on existing arrangements in order to raise their profits. Therefore, undertakings will find it more difficult to sustain tacit or explicit collusion[250]. Second, given the increased competitive pressure on price policy due to possible cost advantages of foreign competitors, competing undertakings on extended markets are subject to an increased incentive to engage in restrictive practices, and in particular to agree to fix higher prices.

For domestic enforcement of competition laws, the implications are similarly multi-faceted. First, increased competitive activity may imply efficiency gains and, thus, a positive development for the purposes of domestic competition law enforcement. All the same, the workload for domestic enforcement authorities will not be reduced in light of the described incentives to engage in collusion. Moreover, M&A activities have increased, and so have cases where the relevant geographical market extends beyond national borders. Extraterritorial application or other ways of dealing with international competition law situations might not be consistent with existing inter-governmental obligations.

---

246 Compare UNCTAD, *WIR 2000*, Overview, xix.

247 G. Koopmann, *ibid.*, 170.

248 This is supported by the fact that according to UNCTAD, the majority of foreign direct investment occurs through horizontal mergers between former competitors of a given market, compare UNCTAD, *WIR 2000*, Overview, 10. See also G. Koopmann, *ibid.*, 170.

249 G. Koopmann, *ibid.*, 170.

250 "Nash equilibrium" or "Prisoner's Dilemma", compare Chapter II.A. above.

4. Conclusion

In light of the foregoing, International Trade and Foreign Direct Investment can be held to mutually reinforce each other. In turn, trade liberalisation and international production clearly affect competition on domestic markets, which is increasingly foreign controlled. At the same time, the revenue created by the competitors at issue is allocated across various states. National legislators attempt to optimize these effects of liberalisation on competition for their economies through supplementary regulation and competition law instruments in particular. Therefore, a clear correlation between international trade liberalisation, private market behaviour and domestic regulatory and enforcement activities can be established for competition law matters. This reciprocity implies a distinct need for governance in domestic competition law matters, so as to ensure that the contractual obligations vis-à-vis other states as agreed under multilateral trade agreements are not infringed.

For a more detailed analysis of the question as to whether an internationalization of competition policy is required from a competition policy point of view, the author will in the following undertake an in-depth study of the effects of market integration due to trade liberalisation and international production on competition from both an individual competitor's as well as an individual state's point of view.

B. Competition on Global Markets: Implications for Individual Competitors

1. Business Perspectives

As outlined above, parallel to the developments at the state level, private business activity shows an increased degree of international economic interdependence. Businesses are taking advantage of the openness created at the state level, which caused considerable growth both in international production and cross-border trade. In many industries, businesses are competing on world wide markets. If companies are not present in all the countries where they are engaging in business activities, they often form strategic alliances to penetrate new, foreign markets in international partnerships. This is especially true for all high-technology sectors like telecommunications, information technology or entertainment[251]. In addition, the activities of TNCs have increased in number and reach[252].

[251] Karel Van Miert, *Foreword to the 1998 Competition Report*, in: EC Commission, *Commission's XXVIIIth Report on Competition Policy*, 1998, 3-4.

[252] J. Jackson/W. Davey/A. Sykes, *ibid.*

The underlying business case is more or less established: In a market economy, competitors on a given market will likely seek to extend their market power in order to be in the position to restrict output, increase prices above competitive level and earn monopoly profits. However, market power can only arise in relation to a specific market[253]. Where markets are international and extend beyond national borders, firms are thus likely to seek to extend their business activities accordingly. In order to prevent any efficiency and welfare losses, competition policy must target practices within a given international market[254].

While domestic competition law is targeted at the protection of competition within the borders of a specific country, international market power is based on domestic market power. Thus, in order to briefly outline possible restrictive business practices for international markets from a competitor's point of view, the author shall differentiate between practices building on domestic market power "only" as opposed to practices building on international market power[255]. Given that these practices may basically comprise *any* restrictive conduct, agreement, transaction or practice that could be deployed on domestic markets, this outline can by no means be exhaustive.

1.1. International restrictive business practices building on domestic market power

1.1.1. Foreclosure against imports

(i) Strategic unilateral deployment of barriers to entry

In light of increased competition from abroad, the incentive for domestic competitors to unilaterally deny or impede market access for foreign competitors through anti-competitive conduct has increased. When adopting an effects-based definition[256], barriers to entry may take the two basic forms of *(a)* absolute incumbent advantages, and *(b)* strategic incumbent advantages[257].

(a) Absolute (cost) advantages

Absolute cost advantages imply that the production costs for potential competitors are higher than the incumbents' productions cost, independent of the quantity of sales. They may result from natural monopolies or certain state-imposed factors, such as certain public grants for the purposes of innovation policy,

[253] A. Jones/B. Sufrin, *ibid.*, 38.
[254] This is why a correct definition of the relevant market is indispensable.
[255] In doing so, the author is following H. Wins in his analysis at *ibid.*, 44 et sqq.
[256] This approach has heavily influenced today's industrial economy, and was first introduced by J.S. Bain of the Harvard School, as opposed to the narrower definition building on production costs as the main aspect constituting significant barriers to entry adopted by G.J. Stigler of the Chicago School, compare D. Harbord and T. Hoehn, *Barriers to Entry and Exit in European Competition Policy,* 14 International Review of Law and Economics 1994, 413 et sqq.
[257] A. Jones/B. Sufrin, *ibid.*, 57 et sqq.

which might not be available for later potential competitors. Alternatively, they may arise due to the incumbents' conduct[258]. First, incumbents may deny access to superior production techniques or charge royalties to potential new entrants. Second, strategic factor supplies may be owned or controlled by established domestic firms, which are, therefore, in the position to deny access to "essential facilities"[259] or materials. Incumbents may, for example, aggravate access to resources such as input factors or distribution channels, so that market access becomes considerably more expensive if not uneconomic for potential entrants, or could require the development of new resources[260].

(b) Strategic advantages

Strategic entry barriers typically arise from "first-mover advantages" in relation to sunk costs[261] and associated behaviour. The most relevant examples for strategic entry barriers[262] for potential competitors from abroad are economies of scale, vertical foreclosure and exclusion (e.g. through vertical integration by means of conglomerate mergers, exclusive dealing, tying, refusal to supply), strategic deployment of intellectual property rights or product differentiation, advertising, goodwill and capital.

Economies of scale occur where efficiency in production is achieved through increased output. Where average cost of producing a commodity is high, established domestic firms may make use of economies of scale more easily than potential new entrants. Once efficiency in production is achieved[263], incumbents may attract and, subsequently, bind consumers through aggregated rebates or volume discounts and, thereby, restrict market access for potential competitors who cannot yet afford the same end user prices[264].

Established domestic firms may likewise erect barriers to or within a domestic market through vertical restraints or control. For instance, incumbents may deploy exclusive dealing contracts, engage in geographical market partitioning, resale price maintenance, franchise agreements or create "total" vertical control

---

258 J. S. Bain, *Barriers to New Competition*, 1956, at 144 et sqq.

259 "Essential facilities" can be defined as assets that are a prerequisite to production, e.g. a railway bridge, a nation-wide telephone network or an electricity network. In the USA, there is an established tradition in competition policy to apply the "essential facilities doctrine" so as to require individual competitors to provide access to essential facilities to other competitors in order to keep markets open, compare H. Wins, *ibid.*, 51. After a rather liberal decision of the ECJ in *RTE&ITP v. Commission (Magill), Cases C-241 to 241/91P [1995] ECR I-743*, the EC Commission applied a rather strict definition under a 3-factor test in order to establish whether access must be granted in *Case C-7/97 Oscar Bronner GmbH & Co. KG* v. *Mediaprint* [1998] ECR I-7791.

260 H. Wins, *Eine internationale Wettbewerbsordnung als Ergänzung zum GATT*, 2001, at 45.

261 "Sunk costs" have a crucial role in entry or exit decisions, as they cannot be recouped upon exiting a market, but are a prerequisite for a potential competitor's ability to enter a market. Consequently, sunk costs oblige a firm to stay in a market. Examples may relate to capacity building, R&D, patents, brand proliferation, advertising, vertical control; compare D. Harbord and T. Hoehn, *ibid.*, at para. 2.3.

262 Compare Office of Fair Trading, *Barriers to Entry and Exit in UK Competition Policy*, Research Paper 2, para 5.1.2.

263 "Minimum efficient scale", see A. Jones/B. Sufrin, *ibid.*, 8.

264 H. Wins, *ibid.*, 45.

through vertical integration[265]. A commonly cited example for market access restrictions through vertical agreements or conglomerate mergers is the Japanese *"Keiretsu"* - system[266]. *"Keiretsu"* refers to a group of vertically integrated undertakings, in which producers, suppliers and sales agents are conducting substantially all relevant transactions among each other. Albeit this system generally does not discriminate among domestic and foreign potential competitors, it allegedly limits market access for potential competitors through a complex system of exclusive purchase or selling agreements in their distribution channels[267].

Moreover, intellectual property rights may be deployed so as to restrict market access for potential foreign competitors. The various IP rights such as patents, trade marks or copy right provide an incentive to innovation through a monopoly annuity. Incumbents may strategically use their monopoly so as to refuse to supply intellectual property rights at all or to grant the license only under additional conditions. Incumbents can tie the supply and licensing of their products to the supply of related products or after-markets to restrict their potential competitors' market access[268]. In addition to these non-territorial restraints, incumbents can deploy territorial limitations. As intellectual property is generally bound to national territory, potential foreign competitors may be hindered trough geographical market segmentation, e.g. through exclusivity or import and export restrictions. Incumbents who are erecting barriers to entry to a given market by means of intellectual property rights may implement both an abuse of a dominant position as well as restrictive business practices.

With regard to product differentiation, "buy-national" initiatives may be cited as an example of strategic advantages. Such initiatives build on domestic cost advantages through established demand preferences for certain products and distribution arrangements[269].

(ii) Abuse of a dominant position through unilateral predatory behaviour

Where domestic firms enjoy a dominant position, they may deploy unilateral conduct so as to drive foreign competitors from the market or prevent their

[265] Compare A. D. Mitchell, *Broadening the Vision of Trade Liberalisation. International Competition Law and the WTO*, in: 24(3) Journal of World Competition 2001, at 349.

[266] By arguing that there is fierce competition among the various Keiretsu-systems and that this system also has efficiency enhancing effects, the Japanese government has repeatedly insisted on the innocuousness of this system. This approach was harshly criticized, compare H. Wins, *ibid.*, 47 et sqq.

[267] Compare in this regard WTO Case *Japan – Measures affecting Consumer Photographic Film and Paper*, WTO/DS44/R, with comments in Jackson/Davey/Sykes, *ibid.*, 277 et sqq. In this case, market access was allegedly in particular impeded for foreign potential competitors.

[268] H. Wins, *ibid.*, 49.

[269] From a competition policy point of view, these practices are not necessarily problematic if they are purely privately initiated, as they build on legitimate consumer preferences. Nevertheless, they do impede market access for foreign competitors. In the special case of the EU as a Common Market, such initiatives have been condemned under Article 28 EC as a "measure having equivalent effect" to a quantitative restriction of trade between Member States fostered by one Member State's government, compare the ECJ's judgment in Case 249/81 *Commission v. Ireland* [1982] ECR 4005.

market access from the outset. For example, they could engage in predatory pricing in that they price so low that competitors are driven from the market[270]. Moreover, "non-price predation" is possible. For instance, dominant firms may engage in "predatory product or process innovation", which occurs when a product or process is introduced without technical or other improvement, but rather so as to exclude competitors, e.g. through technical incompatibility. Allegedly, the range of possible non-price predatory practices is wide. For instance, dominant firms may refuse to supply in order to exclude competitors from ancillary or downstream markets, in tying or exclusive dealing. Common to all practices is the rise in costs for rivals.

Such conduct is likely to constitute an abuse of that dominant position. However, in particular for non-price predation, the line between normal competition and abusive practices may be difficult to draw in practice[271].

(iii) Multilateral conduct: Import cartels

Given the potential cost advantages or economies of scale of foreign entrants, domestic competitors will have a certain incentive to engage in bilateral or even multilateral agreements or other concerted conduct targeted against foreign competitors once these foreign competitors have entered the domestic market. Import cartels are used by established domestic competitors as a means against potential new entrants to secure their monopoly profits through agreements on quantity or price. This is due to the fact that any cartel can only be sustained if its members can deter potential entries which their uncompetitive profits or reduced output attract[272]. To that end, incumbents may *inter alia* block distribution channels through collective refusal to supply against distributors purchasing from foreign producers[273]. Another example could be the engaging in collective price discrimination.

1.1.2. Restrictions affecting export markets

(i) Export cartels

Domestic export cartels are agreements between firms established in one country and operating in the same product market, by which these firms agree to

---

[270] In practice, economists have argued that predatory pricing is hardly ever a rational business strategy and therefore very rare. Also, identifying predatory pricing is difficult in practice. Under the *Areeda-Turner Test*, a price lower than reasonably anticipated short-run marginal cost is considered predatory. However, for reasons of computing, average variable costs are being used instead of short-run marginal cost. For an overview of the practical problems inherent in the *Areeda-Turner Test* compare A. Jones/B. Sufrin, *ibid.*, at 335 et sqq. For a demarcation of predatory pricing against "dumping" as sanctioned under Article VI GATT see below.

[271] R. Rapp, *Predatory Pricing and Entry Deterring Strategies: the Economics of AKZO*, in: [1986] ECLR 233 et sqq.

[272] P. B. Marsden, *Dealing with International Exclusion. The Right Focus for the WTO Working Group on Trade and Competition Policy*, in: 21(2) Journal of World Competition 1997, 97.

[273] H. Wins, *ibid.*, 46 et sqq.

refrain from competing against each other when exporting their substitutable products[274]. Likewise, export cartels may be international where its members are located in multiple countries. Depending on whether only foreign markets or both foreign and domestic markets are affected, export cartels can be "pure" or "mixed" ones.

Export cartels may, in particular, fix prices for exports to a certain country or divide market territories among their members. From an individual market participant's perspective, the strategic goals of export cartels range from aggressive considerations, such as the capturing of new markets abroad, to rather defensive considerations, such as responding to foreign monopolies or foreign governmental restrictions to trade. Arguably, sustaining export cartels presupposes domestic market power of its members, as efficient control of exports would hardly be feasible without domestic power[275].

(ii) Dumping

"Dumping" as defined under the GATT occurs where products are being exported from one country to another at less than the normal value, meaning *(i)* less than the comparable price for a like product destined for consumption in the exporting country, *(ii)* less than the highest comparable price for a like product for export, or *(iii)* less than the cost of production in the country of origin plus a reasonable addition for selling cost and profit, i.e. transport costs or customs duties[276]. From an individual market participant's point of view, dumping may have two basic economic rationales, *(i)* predatory pricing or *(ii)* international price discrimination.[277].

Arguably, dumping by means of predatory pricing constitutes the most questionable restrictive business practice from a competition policy point of view[278], as exporters thereby harm the export market on a permanent basis while at the same time recouping any resulting monopoly profits themselves. With regard to international price discrimination, it has been argued that the traditional arguments for a prohibition of discriminatory pricing, namely output reduction and welfare losses through market segregation and inducing monopolies are not convincing[279]. Rather, consumers in the export markets would benefit from

---

[274] F. Amato, *International Antitrust: What Future?* In: 24(4) Journal of World Competition 2001, 455.

[275] H. Wins, *ibid.*, 52 et sqq.

[276] Article VI.1. of the GATT 1994.

[277] M. J. Trebilcock, *The Regulation of International Trade*, at 177. Trebilcock also identifies intermittent dumping over a long period of time as a third economic rationale behind dumping, but argues that the structural conditions required for this third instance are hardly ever given in practice.

[278] H. Wins, *ibid.*, 55.

[279] M. J. Trebilcock, *The Regulation of International Trade*, at 179 argues that there is decisive empirical answer to the question whether output will de- or increase under discriminatory pricing, and that certain balancing factors and possible efficiency enhancements have been neglected.

lower prices while the dumper's home country would bear the dumper's costs of market segregation and social costs[280].

1.2. International restrictive business practices building on international market power

1.2.1. International cartels

Empirical evidence shows a numerical increase of international cartels[281]. International cartels can be agreements to fix prices or to allocate geographic markets between multinational corporations operating in the same product market[282]. A cartel will have to be rated "international" where the agreement is affecting more than one national market, where collusion concerns actors from more than one jurisdiction or where the product or service to be supplied or provided is situated in more than one country[283].

The most common object of international cartels is the segmentation of international markets through isolation of the participants' domestic markets[284]. This partitioning along national borders through private practices replaces the governmental restrictions to cross-border trade which the international trading regime has sought to diminish. Arguably, from a practical and enforcement point of view, market segmentation along national borders through international cartels is relatively easy to maintain, as no detailed regulation of quotas, prices or allocation of monopoly annuities to individual members is required. Rather, domestic markets including export markets where no member is located are simply attributed to the individual member located therein[285].

In light of reduced transport costs in integrated markets and the increased incentive for arbitrage, the market segmentation achieved through an international cartel must be upheld through the combination of horizontal with vertical agreements, such as strategic deployment of intellectual property rights. In particular, international patent pools have been cited as one efficient means to support territorial segmentation through cross-licensing among the members. However, apart from territorial market segmentation, patent pooling is equally suited for qualitative and quantitative segmentations concerning production or distribution. Moreover, the strategic accumulation of patents may create barriers to entry for potential competitors[286].

---

280 M. J. Trebilcock, *ibid.*, 177.

281 WTO, *Annual Report 1997*, at 40.

282 F. Amato, *International Antitrust: What Future?* In: 24(4) Journal of World Competition 2001, 454.

283 F. R. Schoneveld, *Cartel Sanctions and International Competition Policy: Cross-Border Cooperation and Appropriate Forums for Cooperation*, in: 26(3) Journal of World Competition 2003, 436.

284 H. Wins, *ibid.*, 58.

285 H. Wins, *ibid.*, 58.

286 H. Wins, *ibid.*, 58.

1.2.2. Strategic alliances and joint ventures

Strategic alliances of independent undertakings are playing an important role in the internationalisation of global economy[287]. Typically, strategic alliances consist of international participants and are aimed at international markets. High technology sectors are primarily concerned, as the main incentives of such alliances are the exploitation of technological complementarities, mutual learning and acceleration of the period between invention and marketing, e.g. by engaging in common R&D activities[288] or other forms of cooperation. At the same time, strategic alliances seek to extend market power or to isolate markets from potential competition by creating barriers to entry[289], and must therefore be held to share certain common features with international cartels[290]. This conclusion is reinforced by the fact that strategic alliances mainly occur in highly competitive market sectors[291].

Joint ventures are commercial arrangements among two or more firms, by which the independent undertakings involved integrate part of their operations and put them under joint control, so as to realize one particular commercial goal[292]. While co-operation must not be rated uncompetitive in general[293], there are certain competitive concerns with regard to *(i)* the risk of collusion as "spill-over-effects" of the underlying joint venture, *(ii)* the reduction of actual or potential competition between the undertakings at issue, and *(iii)* the risk of market foreclosure for potential competitors[294]. Also, joint ventures incorporate a certain risk of market segmentation with a subsequent limitation of competition among the individual segments[295].

1.2.3. Restrictive business practices of TNCs

Generally, international market power builds on domestic market power. Thus, TNCs will typically explore the potential of domestic selling markets before expanding to foreign export markets once the potential for growth on the domestic market has been exhausted. As illustrated above, the efficiency gains of TNCs due to efficient international production can enhance competition in a given market. Also, compared to domestic competitors, TNCs have certain competitive advantages relating to technical and organizational know-how, resources, economies of scale or easier access to various capital markets. How-

---

287 G. Koopmann, *Internationalisierung der Wettbewerbspolitik: Korrelat zur internationalen Handelspolitik?* In: 56(II) Aussenwirtschaft 2001, 165 et sqq.

288 G. Koopmann, *ibid*

289 G: Koopmann, *ibid.*

290 H. Wins, *ibid.*, 60.

291 H. Wins, *ibid.*, 60.

292 A. Jones/B. Sufrin, *ibid.*, 813.

293 Compare European Commission, *Guidelines on the applicability of Article 81 of the EC Treaty to horizontal cooperation agreements*, [OJ 2001, No. C3/02], at para. 1.1.3.

294 A. Jones/B. Sufrin, *ibid.*, 813.

295 H. Wins, *ibid.*, 61.

ever, in particular with regard to TNCs' activities in developing countries, there are commonly expressed concerns with regard to the possible leverage of TNCs' market power to other markets. Although most TNCs do remain subject to a domestic competition law regime as a predominant proportion of them have their registered business seats located in industrialized countries with sophisticated competition laws, these concerns appear legitimate under certain circumstances[296].

(i) Abuse of international market power

Just like any "normal" competitor, TNCs can abuse their market power through pricing strategies, e.g. through raising prices to an uncompetitive level or through engaging in predatory dumping. In light of the *Effects Doctrine*, TNCs might be very easily in the position to leverage market power to countries in transition or developing countries.

(ii) International oligopolies

As far as international markets are concerned, the risk of oligopolistic market structures is particularly distinct on high technology markets[297], as there are few large players with homogenous goods as opposed to a stable and inelastic demand and high barriers to entry[298]. Under these prerequisites, tacit or even express concertation is likely to occur. Nevertheless, there is no empirical evidence as to whether TNCs are more or less inclined to collude than Non-TNCs[299].

(iii) Trans-national mergers

A merger transaction will be "trans-national" where the uniting entities will be situated in different jurisdictions[300]. In light of foreign direct investment and international production, the number of trans-national mergers has experienced considerable growth since the 1980s[301].

From an economic perspective, a trans-national merger with an established competitor may serve to overcome barriers to entry for a new entrant, and, therefore, promote competition and bring about a welfare enhancement. Also, a merger may be one way to overcome barriers to exit[302]. At the same time, trans-national mergers may have adverse effects in that they may reduce competition where two former competitors merge. Another fundamental objective of a trans-national merger with adverse effects to competition is the amplification of

---

296 H. Wins, *ibid.*, 62 et sqq.
297 H. Wins, *ibid.*, 64.
298 A. Jones/B. Sufrin, *ibid.*, 639.
299 UNCTAD, *World Investment Report 1997*, available at: http://www.unctad.org/en/docs/WIR97_en.pdf (20.05.2005), at 156 et sqq.
300 See J. Wilson, *Globalization and the Limits of National Merger Control Laws*, 2003, 199 et sqq.
301 Compare Chapter III.A.
302 A. Jones/B. Sufrin, *ibid.*, 701.

market power, in that a merger might facilitate monopolisation by thinning out the competitive structure of a given market and by increasing concentration.

However, even where a merger and the resulting business activity are competition enhancing, any efficiencies created from a business point of view may result in consequences generally perceived as negative, such as unemployment. By definition, TNCs are "big business". Therefore, both positive as well as adverse effects of their business activities are perceived to be particularly striking due to their numerical effects on a domestic economy. Consequently, additional non-economic factors have grown in significance for those opposed to trans-national mergers. In addition to unemployment, their concerns also relate to possible adverse socio-political consequences of concentration of private power in that democracy could be harmed and individual freedom restricted[303]. Moreover, in light of trans-national activity in politically sensitive areas such as press or industries related to national security[304], fears of overseas control have been expressed.

2. *Compliance*

As illustrated above by outlining the EU and the US approaches toward certain individual legal instruments[305], individual domestic competition policy and also its implementation into domestic law may feature considerable variations. The variations among national competition law approaches and instruments may consist in material and/or procedural aspects. Moreover, institutional considerations[306] may bear a substantial influence on the outcome of competition law proceedings.

Thus, private market participants wishing to spread their business activity across multiple jurisdictions will need the flexibility to act in accordance with the diverse national legal systems at issue. In the following, the author shall discuss possible problems areas relating to compliance created through the traditionally domestic orientation of competition law instruments for private market actors engaging in trans-national business activity, relating to:

1. *The necessity of multiple filings;*
2. *The problem of less legal certainty;*
3. *The extraterritorial application of national laws.*

303 Compare A. Jones/B. Sufrin, *ibid.*, 706 et sqq.

304 E.g. Oil, defense equipment or other vital industries, compare A. Jones/B. Sufrin, *ibid.*, 707.

305 For a summary of the EU and US approaches compare A. S. Grewlich, *Globalisation and Conflict in Competition Law. Elements of Possible Solutions*, in: 24(3) Journal of World Competition (2001), 376 et sqq.

306 Compare International Competition Policy Advisory Committee to The Attorney General and Assistant Attorney General for Antitrust, *Final Report 2000* ("ICPAC-Report"), available at: http://www.usdoj.gov/atr/icpac/forward.htm and http://www.usdoj.gov/atr/icpac/chapter1.htm, (29.05.2005).

2.1. Multiple filings

A single transaction might require multiple filings in the various jurisdictions involved. From a procedural point of view, this implies increased costs, efforts, research and analysis being required as well as a longer duration of individual proceedings.

Competition law procedures are usually very elaborate, costly and complex, as profound economic analysis will be indispensable for a determination of the relevant circumstances of the case. Therefore, a multiplication of these costs and efforts through multiple filings has noticeable economic consequences for the undertaking at issue. These consequences may be further reinforced where a particular jurisdiction places the burden of analysis predominantly on the parties themselves. In this regard, the European Union's recent amendments in Article 81 EC proceedings must be kept in mind. Undertakings will be expected to self-assess the compatibility of their agreements with Article 81 EC as a consequence of the Commission's monopoly of exemption being lifted and a new system of direct application of Article 81 EC being introduced[307]. In addition, given the links with multiple jurisdictions, international business transactions, and mergers in particular, will also impose other strategic challenges to business management. *Prima facie,* one might expect that this would reduce the costs for filing transactions in the EU. Nevertheless, in light of increased legal uncertainty and the necessity to involve counsel, the potential for cost reductions seems very limited.

The potential impact of the requirement of multiple filings on the business can be illustrated by the *GE Honeywell* merger case[308]. In October 2000, GE and Honeywell announced the world's largest proposed industrial merger at that time, worth US $ 42 billion. As part of the process of completing that merger, GE and Honeywell had to notify the relevant competition authorities around the world. Of these, the most important ones were the US Department of Justice, the Canadian authorities and DG Competition for the European Union. After having received rapid regulatory approval from both the United States and Canadian authorities, an equally rapid decision was being expected from the EU Competition Authorities. However, after several months of investigation, the EU authorities rejected the proposed merger as it was considered to be anti-competitive. This decision was based on the considerations that *(i)* GE's 62% market share of the large commercial jet engine market compared to 15 and 22 % of the nearest competitors would be further secured by the merger, which would undermine the rivals' positions, and that *(ii)* GE's financial and leasing entity GECAS was going to be used to leverage market power to avionics and

[307] These amendments have been introduced by Regulation 1/2003, see analysis under B. IV. 2. above.

[308] Compare Y. Akbar, *Grabbing Victory from the Jaws of Defeat: Can the GE/Honeywell Merger Facilitate International Antitrust Policy Co-operation?,* in 25(4) Journal of World Competition 2002, 403 et sqq; D. Giotakos/L. Petit/G. Garnier/P. de Luyck, *General Electric/Honeywell – An insight into the Commission's investigation and decision,* EC Competition Policy Newsletter Number 3, October 2001, 5 et sqq.

other equipment, and, thereby, to bundle avionics and other equipment at a lower price then separate purchases of engine and avionics, which could force competitors out of business. The remedy suggested by DG Competition, namely the divestiture of most of GE's ownership in GECAS, would have, arguably, undermined a major rationale for the proposed merger in the first place. After several months of negotiations, the merger was blocked by DG Competition in July 2001.

In light of the risks concerning the outcome of multiple proceedings, strategic considerations inherent in international business transactions will have to be adapted to the individual competition policy considerations prevailing in a particular jurisdiction. For instance, it will be harder for businesses to estimate the duration of the procedures, as multiple authorities will have to be approached for their respective decisions. Also, differences in competition law may influence the bargaining power of the parties in a certain transaction. Another aspect is the possible inconsistency of remedies for parallel investigations, which may put an additional burden on the parties and create conflict[309]. Consequently, business strategy must consider individual differences relating to competition law from one jurisdiction to another.

The strategic problems inherent to management decisions relating to international mergers feature at least three aspects[310]. First, any international business activity will require, besides operational aspects, complex prior research on the regulatory environment for the envisaged operation so as to understand the differences among the models of competition law used by different authorities in different countries. Second, for a successful completion of the envisaged transaction, management decisions will also have to consider cultural differences in the policymakers' decision making process. In this regard, it has been pointed out that the traditional view of Anglo-Saxon management is that regulation is a "non-market issue". Conversely, public policymakers will usually consider the role of regulation as a means to ensure the market's functioning. This conflict is further reinforced by the fact that certain European economies are traditionally regulated to a greater extent than their US counterparts. Thirdly, the strategic incentive for mergers will predominantly consist in the desire to increase market share so as to reduce competition. This, however, may be problematic in jurisdictions where it is the pronounced interest of the policymaker at issue to maintain plurality of supply. Thus, managers will have to consider a broader, more market- based view of their strategy rather than emphasizing operational, synergy-based objectives[311]. Given the fact that the GE/Honeywell proposal was drafted in three days, it can easily be reckoned that these complexities have

---

309 L. Fullerton/C. C. Mazard, *International Antitrust Co-operation Agreements,* 24(3) Journal of World Competition 2001, 411.

310 Y. Akbar, *ibid.*, 417.

311 Y. Akbar, *ibid.*, 418.

not been sufficiently appreciated for the various jurisdictions concerned in that concrete case[312].

Another issue is confidentiality, which is essential for a successful international business operation. Where multiple filings of merger transactions are required, confidential information will have to be submitted to each authority, and public filings of notifications might be required. Thus, it has been argued that this would multiply the risk of disclosure, and would thus put the individual transactions at risk[313].

2.2. Less legal certainty

As far as substantive law is concerned, being subject to various domestic jurisdictions and various different competition laws will mean that private parties engaging in international business activity must face the risk of less legal certainty with regard to *(i)* the feasibility of their transaction from the outset, and *(ii)* the ultimate compliance upon effective implementation. Again, this lack of legal certainty is particular cumbersome for a business if there is only limited official guidance available for certain transactions, e.g. through the abolishment of individual exemptions under Article 81 EC through Regulation 1/2003[314].

In particular, one jurisdiction might consider a certain transaction to be lawful, while another one might not. To begin with, similar situations might be rated differently. For example, recommended resale prices may be considered unlawful price fixing in formerly centralized economies, while such recommendations are considered lawful in the United States or the European Union. Furthermore, different presumptions attributed to a certain market share may contribute to divergent outcomes in the assessment of like behaviour in different jurisdiction. For example, it is worth noting that some jurisdictions, such as the Czech Republic and Lithuania, have adopted a legal presumption of dominance at thirty and forty percent, respectively, and the European Union has adopted a corresponding legal practice. Compared to the treatment of single firm conduct in the United States, these presumptions contribute to the generally perceived wide disparity among jurisdictions[315]. Worse, a transaction might be considered unlawful in multiple jurisdictions, resulting in an accumulation of fines. For example, the ECJ in 2006 explicitly rejected the application of the *ne bis in idem* principle to an international cartel in *SGL Carbon v. Commission.*

---

[312] Y. Akbar, *ibid.*
[313] Compare comments under III.B.2.1.
[314] Compare FN 47.
[315] M. G. Egge, *ibid.*

2.3. Risk of extraterritorial application

A third challenging aspect for trans-national business activity with both procedural as well as substantive implications is the extraterritorial application of domestic competition law rules to situations which are taking place abroad but allegedly affect the home market[316].

Given the differences in legal practices as illustrated by the example of the change in US legal practice and official statements as described above, and given also the remaining ambiguities as illustrated by EC legal practice, the concept of extraterritorial application implies considerable legal uncertainty for businesses engaging in cross-border business activity. For example, where an international agreement has no link to a given jurisdiction by contracting party, subject matter or fulfilment, that jurisdiction might nevertheless consider its market affected and apply its competition law to the transaction at issue.

This is particular bothering for individual market participants where there are possible sanctions of nullity[317]. International agreements between two trans-national companies regularly consist of one international master agreement between the parent companies and several local agreements among the various subsidiaries locally implementing the obligations under the framework agreement. Where nullity is the sanction foreseen for that particular agreement under a given domestic competition law and where that jurisdiction at issue provides for the extraterritorial application of its competition law, both the local agreement *and* the master agreement[318] could be threatened with at least partial nullity[319]. Therefore, a single jurisdiction's competition law could endanger the feasibility of the overall master agreement concluded among the parent companies. Consequently, significant resources are required for a detailed *ex ante* analysis of the risks inherent to a particular transaction. These burdens are further reinforced by the differences in enforcement mechanisms among the vari-

---

316 Compare II.D.6.2.

317 Compare Article 81 para. 2 EC: "Any agreements or decisions prohibited pursuant to this Article shall be automatically void"; or similarly the wording of s. 22 of the Austrian Cartel Act: "Kartellverträge sind unwirksam, soweit ihre Durchführung verboten ist".

318 For the EC approach compare the CFI's decision in *Gencor,* Case IV/M 619 [1997] OJ.L11/30, [1999] 4 CMLR 1076. For an example of an EC Member State compare s. 6 of the Austrian Cartel Act, which provides for the extraterritorial application of the Act to situations taking place abroad but affecting the Austrian market, see the text of the cited provision above. S. 6 of the Austrian Cartel Act has been interpreted by Austrian legal practice to derogate the general rule of s. 35 of the Austrian International Private Law Act (implementing the "Convention on the law applicable to contractual obligations" – "Rome Convention"), according to which contracts are to be assessed under the law expressly or conclusively agreed by the parties to that contract.

319 According to Austrian legal practice, only the specific clauses of an agreement bringing about the prohibition are threatened with nullity under the specific competition law at issue, whereas the remaining clauses of the agreement – and in particular the question of severability - must be assessed in light of the applicable law as originally agreed by the parties in the agreement; compare H.-G. Koppensteiner, *Österreichisches und europäisches Wettbewerbsrecht*[3], at 73, quoting the corresponding Austrian Supreme Court's practice *(unpublished decision).*

ous jurisdictions, and also by the unpredictability of an assertion of jurisdiction, as the borders of extra-territorial application have become increasingly unclear.

Thus, extra-territorial application of domestic competition laws brings about considerable risks for individual competitors engaging in cross-border business activity. The legal uncertainty thereby created is particularly burdensome for businesses where private suits are admitted to Courts and where damages are awarded to successful private parties[320].

3. Conclusion

It has been demonstrated that integrated markets provide extended possibilities for individual competitors to engage in competition with competitors abroad so as to gain market shares of international markets. Individual competitors can, thereby, promote overall efficiency gains on the one hand, but also engage in restrictive business practices to extend or abuse national or international market power on the other.

At the same time, the new business opportunities that have been created since *Bretton Woods* may also imply considerable challenges for individual competitors inasmuch as their business transactions may be subject to a variety of domestic competition laws. Compliance with all competition laws potentially applied to a given transaction implies the need for additional personal and financial resources, strategic analysis *ex ante*, flexibility as well as consideration of inherent financial risks in the balance sheets. Individual competitors have to face reduced legal certainty with regard to the viability of their transactions.

Despite the possible additional burdens, the differences among individual competition laws can also be regarded as advantageous productions factors. Regulatory competition is an important aspect for international production, as the efficiency of possible locations for production will also depend on the applicable regulation of competition. This may partly also explain one reason why TNCs have placed a considerable proportion of their production to developing countries, which traditionally do not have a sophisticated competition law in place.

Nevertheless, some within Academia seem to support (at least partial) convergence of domestic competition law instruments and international co-operation in order to overcome the mentioned shortcomings. In the following, the author shall examine the implications of global economy for domestic competition policy from a state's point of view so as to assess the case for multilateral competition rules from a national perspective. This analysis will consider both the domestic competition policy perspective as well as the relationship of competi-

---

[320] In this regard, see S. 4 of 15 USC Sec.15 (Clayton Act) for the United States. For the EC, the Case C-453/99 *Courage* v. *Crehan* [2001] 5 CMLR 28 should be noted, where it was held that even a business which itself is party to an anti-competitive agreement can claim damages.

tion policy with existing governmental obligations resulting from the multilateral trading rules agreed to under the GATT.

C. Competition Policy and Global Markets: Implications at State Level

1. *Regulatory Perspectives: "Booming Competition Laws"*

International organizations promoting the liberalisation of international trade have commonly argued that restrictive business practices can have significant effects on the competitive functioning of international markets and, therefore, are of concern to international trade policy[321]. Thus, as early as in 1948, the proposed International Trade Organization's Charter contained nine articles dealing with restrictive business practices, obligating Member States to "take appropriate measures" and to "co-operate with the Organization in order to prevent, on the part of private or commercial public enterprises, business practices affecting international trade which constrain competition, limit access to markets, or foster monopolistic control, whenever such practices have harmful effects on the expansion of production or trade and interfere with the achievement of any of the other objectives set forth in Article 1 [of the charter]"[322].

However, none of these articles in the Havana Charter was ever incorporated in the General Agreement. Nevertheless, competition issues where also approached by other organizations, such as the Organization for Economic Co-Operation and Development (OECD) or certain organizations under the auspices of the United Nations. This mainly happened via recommendations rather than substantive obligations.

The OECD, for instance, focussing its work on the interaction of trade and competition and on co-operation of enforcement authorities, has issued the OECD Recommendation of the Council concerning Co-operation between Member Countries on Anticompetitive Practices affecting International Trade[323], and, subsequently, the OECD Recommendations concerning effective action against hard core cartels[324]. Also, the OECD Guidelines for Multinational Enterprises of 1976, which were revised in 2000, contain several provisions relating to competition.

---

321 Compare OECD, *Competition and Trade Policies: Their Interaction* (1984), 112-113.

322 Havana Charter for an International Trade Organization (ITO-Charter), Article 46 para 1, available at: http://www.wto.org/english/docs_e/legal_e/havana_e.pdf (29.05.2005).

323 27 July 1995 - C(95)130/FINAL, available at: http://webdomino1.oecd.org/horizontal/oecdacts.nsf/Display/D3E757937B1812EAC1256FC2007101BF?OpenDocument (29.05.2005). The Recommendation *inter alia* provides for mutual information on violations and cases of interest for another Member State, positive comity, information sharing insofar as permitted by national confidentiality laws, co-ordination of investigation and remedies.

324 25 March 1998 - C(98)35/FINAL.

The United Nations Commission for Trade and Development (UNCTAD) has adopted the Set of Multilaterally Agreed Equitable Principles and Rules for the Control of Restrictive Business Practices[325] in 1980 as one of the most detailed internationally agreed statement on restrictive business practices[326]. It stipulates that independent enterprises should refrain from certain practices where those practices would impede market access or otherwise unduly restrain competition, and also touches on situations where dominant positions could be abused by limiting market access or other competitive restraints[327].

More recently, competition issues have been closely investigated under the patronage of the WTO Working Group on the Interaction between Trade and Competition Policy (WGTCP) which was established at the Singapore Ministerial Conference in 1996[328]. Subsequent to a more detailed proposal on a Multilateral Framework Agreement on Competition Policy submitted by the European Community in 2000[329], the WTO Members agreed at the Fourth WTO Ministerial Conference in Doha in 2001 that negotiations on WTO competition law would start at the following Ministerial Conference[330]. Despite the subse-

---

325 U.N.Doc. TD(RBP/10 (1980).

326 Jackson/Davey/Sykes, *ibid.*, 1120.

327 Set of Multilaterally Agreed Equitable Principles and Rules, U.N.Doc. TD/RBP/10 (1980), paras. D.3. & D.4.

328 Singapore Ministerial Declaration, WT/MIN(96)/DEC18 December 1996, decision item 20, which reads: "Having regard to the existing WTO provisions on matters related to investment and competition policy and the built-in agenda in these areas, including under the TRIMs Agreement, and on the understanding that the work undertaken shall not prejudge whether negotiations will be initiated in the future, we also agree to:

- establish a working group to examine the relationship between trade and investment; and
- establish a working group to study issues raised by Members relating to the interaction between trade and competition policy, including anti-competitive practices, in order to identify any areas that may merit further consideration in the WTO framework.

These groups shall draw upon each other's work if necessary and also draw upon and be without prejudice to the work in UNCTAD and other appropriate intergovernmental fora. As regards UNCTAD, we welcome the work under way as provided for in the Midrand Declaration and the contribution it can make to the understanding of issues. In the conduct of the work of the working groups, we encourage cooperation with the above organizations to make the best use of available resources and to ensure that the development dimension is taken fully into account. The General Council will keep the work of each body under review, and will determine after two years how the work of each body should proceed. It is clearly understood that future negotiations, if any, regarding multilateral disciplines in these areas, will take place only after an explicit consensus decision is taken among WTO Members regarding such negotiations."

329 Compare *Communication of 21 September 2000 from the European Community and its Member States to the WTO Working Group*, WT/WGTCP/W/152, available at: http://docsonline.wto.org/gen_search.asp?language=1 (18.09.2004).

330 Ministerial Declaration of 20 November 2001 ("Doha Declaration"), WT/MIN(01)/DEC/1, 20 November 2001, No. 23-25, available at: http://www.wto.org/english/thewto_e/minist/min01_emindecl_e.htm (18.09.2004). The declaration reads: "[...] 23. Recognizing the case for a multilateral framework to enhance the contribution of competition policy to international trade and development, and the need for enhanced technical assistance and capacity-building in this area as referred to in paragraph 24, we agree that negotiations will take place after the Fifth Session of the Ministerial Conference on the basis of a decision to be taken, by explicit consensus, at that Session on modalities of negotiations.

24. We recognize the needs of developing and least-developed countries for enhanced support for technical assistance and capacity-building in this area, including policy analysis and development so that they may better evaluate the implications of closer multilateral cooperation for their development policies and objectives, and human and institutional development. To this end, we shall work in cooperation with other rele-

quent failure of the Cancún Ministerial Conference of September 2003, the Doha Declaration arguably remains the basis for future developments from a legal point of view, as the question of competition in the ambit of WTO law still has not dropped from the Agenda[331].

Common to all initiatives cited is *(i)* the examination of existing domestic competition law instruments, and *(ii)* the promotion of certain basic principles of competition law generally recognized as being detrimental to efficiency and consumer welfare, such as, *inter alia,* price fixing, the limitation of production or the sharing or division of markets by allocating customers. This increased scrutiny at the international level has, arguably, contributed to what has been identified as "nothing short of an explosion in competition law enactment and enforcement" during the last years[332].

A century ago, only the United States had a comprehensive competition law in place. In the course of the reconstruction period following World War II, a number of jurisdictions in Western Europe, Japan and also some Latin American regimes developed competition or antitrust laws in some form[333]. By 1948, at the beginning of the multilateral liberalisation process, five countries had adopted a domestic competition law regime. By 1980, this number had risen to less than 40[334]. Today, approximately 80 to 100 jurisdictions of the 148 WTO Member States have competition regimes in place[335]. Nevertheless, there are only few states with an established history of competition laws[336]. Approximately 60% of the codes existing today took effect during the last decade[337], so that the majority of those laws have to be regarded as newly established or renewed.

---

vant intergovernmental organizations, including UNCTAD, and through appropriate regional and bilateral channels, to provide strengthened and adequately resourced assistance to respond to these needs. 25. In the period until the Fifth Session, further work in the Working Group on the Interaction between Trade and Competition Policy will focus on the clarification of: core principles, including transparency, non-discrimination and procedural fairness, and provisions on hard-core cartels; modalities for voluntary cooperation; and support for progressive reinforcement of competition institutions in developing countries through capacity-building. Full account shall be taken of the needs of developing and least-developed country participants and appropriate flexibility provided to address them. [...]"

331 J. Drexl, *International Competition Policy after Cancún: Placing a Singapore Issue on the WTO Development Agenda,* in: 27(3) Journal of World Competition 2004, at 421.

332 M. G. Egge, *The Harmonization of Competition Laws Worldwide. Remarks,* in: 2(1) Richmond Journal of Global Law & Business 2001, 93 et sqq.

333 International Competition Policy Advisory Committee to the Attorney General and Assistant Attorney General for Antitrust, *Final Report 2000 ["ICPAC-Report"],* available at: http://www.usdoj.gov/atr/icpac/chapter1.htm (16.7.2004).

334 G. Koopmann, *Internationalisierung der Wettbewerbspolitik: Korrelat zur internationalen Handelspolitik?* In: 56(II) Aussenwirtschaft 2001, 160.

335 J. Drexel, *International Competition Policy after Cancun: Placing a Singapore Issue on the WTO Development Agenda,* in; 27(3) Journal on World Competition 200, 422. These countries usually pursue a free market-economy approach, compare. F. Amato, *International Antitrust: What Future?* In: 24(4) Journal of World Competition 2001, 451.

336 For example the United States or Germany.

337 R. Pitofsky, *Competition Policy in a Global Economy – Today and Tomorrow,* in: 2(3) Journal of International Economic Law 1999, 403-411.

Given the continued liberalisation of international trade and the opened frontiers to foreign competitors, market participants are more and more engaging in trans-border business transactions. International mergers have become daily business[338]. Therefore, even in jurisdictions which already have developed a tradition of competition law enforcement such as the European Community or the United States, this new international perspective of business life and the fact that each business transaction might be re-examined under the competition laws of other countries have added a new dimension to competition law and enforcement. Clearly, this new dimension has made the influence of competition laws in everyday commercial decision-making processes a predominant one.

As illustrated above, the implications of the global market place for private parties have affected competition enforcement authorities in their day-to-day acting. Given that cartels or mergers or other potentially restrictive business practices increasingly have an international dimension[339], cross-border antitrust enforcement has increased. This trend has in particular been ascribed to *(i)* the increasing globalization of business activity, *(ii)* the growing proliferation of new antitrust laws in various countries, *(iii)* the increasing resort to extraterritorial application of domestic competition law to situations abroad, and *(iv)*, the liberalisation of state-sponsored trade barriers so that market access by foreign-based competitors is more likely[340].

For merger transactions in particular, an increased share of international transactions can be identified. Given the increased international merger activity, the number of notifiable merger transactions has considerably augmented over the last several years[341]. This can be exemplified by the enforcement activities in both the United States and the European Union. For example, the US Department of Justice has reported a growth of reviews of international matters from 2 to 3% annually in the early 1990s to approximately 40% in 1998, whereas the US Federal Trade Commission reported that in 1999, almost every second merger it investigated had impact on consumers in more than one country. For the EC, the number of mergers notified with one party being a US company has risen from approximately 10 such mergers in each of 1992 and 1993, to 125 in 1999[342]. In light of the increased complexity of mergers in particular, challenges may arise from the limited resources available to enforcement authorities. This will be particularly true for countries where merger control regimes have been newly created.

---

338 Hawk, B. E., *Convergence in International Antitrust Law*, WuW 9/2001, available at: http://www.canada-europe.org/en/CD-Rom/pdf/BDI.pdf (16.7.2004)

339 Compare III.A.

340 L. Fullerton/C. C. Mazard, *International Antitrust Co-operation Agreements*, 24(3) Journal of World Competition 2001, 405 et sqq.

341 M. G. Egge, *ibid.*, 94.

342 ICPAC Report, *ibid.*, 47.

With regard to cartel activity, a certain degree of escalation can be observed as well. For instance, fines for cartel activity have increased dramatically[343]. In the United States, US $ 29 million were obtained annually in criminal fines during the 10 years prior to 1997. In 1997, US $ 205 million were collected, a sum thus 500% higher than during any previous year. For the period from 1997 until spring 2001, the Antitrust Division of the U.S. Department of Justice has obtained over US $ 1.7 billion dollars in criminal fines. This sum is many multiples higher than the sum total of all criminal fines imposed for violations of the Sherman Antitrust Act dating back to 1890. Well over 90 percent of these fines were imposed in connection with the prosecution of international cartel activity, which has been said to affect a large volume of U.S. commerce. Of that amount, more than US $ 500 million came from a single enforcement matter[344].

Thus, given the increased adoption of domestic competition laws and the enlarged trans-national economic business activity of private actors after liberalisation of international trade, it can easily be asserted that competition laws and enforcement efforts have amplified in prominence[345], and that the operations of competition enforcement authorities have been strongly affected by the changing market structures and the increasing trans-national business activity. More concretely, these effects can constitute considerable challenges for enforcement authorities. In particular, it has been argued that national or regional competition authorities are, besides jurisdictional restraints, ill-equipped to tackle problems posed by (anti-) competitive behaviour outside their territories. In the following, therefore, the author shall evaluate the case for international competition rules by discussing the limits of the application of domestic competition law instruments in more detail.

2. *Limits to Domestic Enforcement*

With regard to the potential inadequacy of domestic competition law for international situations, it must be borne in mind that domestic law is in general clearly confined to domestic territory. The territoriality principle stems from the sovereignty of states as a basic principle of public international law[346]. Consequently, domestic competition law can generally not be applied to situations taking place abroad. Nevertheless, in light of the important underlying policy

343 Compare for example the speech of James M. Griffin, Deputy Assistant Attorney General, Antitrust Division, U.S. Department of Justice, at the 49th Annual Spring Meeting of the American Bar Association, Section of Antitrust Law, presented on March 28, 2001, available at: http://www.usdoj.gov/atr/public/speeches/8063.htm (16.7.2004).

344 On appeal *Empagram SA v. Hoffman-LaRoche,* US Court of Appeal D.C. Circuit, Decision of 17 January 2003, No. 01-7115.

345 M. G. Egge, *ibid.*

346 Compare S. Hobe/O. Kimminich, *Einführung in das Völkerrecht*[8] (2004), at 96 et sqq. For a reproduction of this principle in an international treaty compare Article 2 of the Charter of the United Nations, available at: http://www.un.org/aboutun/charter/ (06.05.2005).

goals of competition laws, many states have chosen to extra-territorially apply their domestic laws to situations abroad where they consider these situations to affect their domestic markets[347].

The practice of extra-territorial application of competition law to situations which are taking place abroad and allegedly affect the home market has gained in prominence during the last years. In particular, the effects test as applied by the United States has gained increasing acceptance in recent years. Besides the European Union[348], other foreign jurisdictions have started to adopt their own versions of the test[349]. The issue of extraterritoriality has become increasingly important with the advancement of trans-border economic activity, as it becomes more and more impossible to isolate the effects of an individual transaction to a given national market[350]. Thus, in order to protect their national markets, enforcement authorities have increasingly claimed jurisdiction over foreign territory by applying their domestic competition law to situations abroad[351]. Consequently, a variety of not necessarily congruent approaches to allegedly anti-competitive behaviour taking place outside the initiating authorities' jurisdictions may be observed.

Therefore, leaving aside for a moment the discussion of the legitimacy of applying domestic law to actors or situations located outside a state's territory, a need for international competition rules might first arise with regard to the deliberate *application* of domestic competition law to transactions having an international dimension. In particular, national enforcement agencies might be incapable of efficiently addressing restrictive business practices with an international dimension. This may be true even where the state is applying the effects doctrine to extend the range of its domestic competition law. Thus, the need for international competition rules must first be considered from a purely domestic point of view, in that *(i)* one state might not be able to target all restrictive practices potentially affecting its domestic market, and *(ii)* another state might consider its national sovereignty infringed through the first state's subsequent recourse to the effects doctrine so as to apply its domestic competition law extra-territorially into the second state's jurisdiction.

---

347 For a general overview refer to Chapter II.D.6.2. above.

348 Compare *Gencor/Lenrho*, under C. III. above.

349 Compare L. Fullerton/C. C. Mazard, *International Antitrust Co-operation Agreements*, 24(3) Journal of World Competition 2001, 408 et sqq. In the *Woodpulp* Case, the CFI has confirmed that Article 81 EC could be applied extraterritorially. The Community concept of extraterritorial jurisdiction was based on "implementation" rather than the strict endorsement of the effects doctrine as postulated by the US, compare Cases 89, 104, 114, 116, 117, 125-129/85, A. Ahlström Oy v Commission [1988] ECR 5193, [1988] 4 CMLR 901, para 16. Subsequently, this EC approach was very much adapted to the "classical" US notion of the effects doctrine in the CFI's judgment in *Gencor*, where the application of EC Merger Regulation 4064/89 was "justified under public international law when it is foreseeable that a proposed concentration will have an immediate and substantial effect in the Community", Case T-102/96, *Gencor Ltd v. Commission* [1999] ECR II-753, [1999] 4 CMLR 971. Compare A. Jones/B. Sufrin, *ibid.*, 1053 et sqq.

350 Compare A. Jones/B. Sufrin, *ibid.*, 1039.

351 Compare L. Fullerton/C. C. Mazard, *International Antitrust Co-operation Agreements*, 24(3) Journal of World Competition 2001, 407 et sqq.

Generally, therefore, the problems identified for competition authorities wishing to enforce can be attributed to two main groups[352]. On the one hand, national competition authorities may not be in the position to fully protect their citizens from trans-national anti-competitive conduct, in particular when arising in the form of international cartels[353] or global oligopolies or monopolies. On the other hand, competition authorities' enforcement policies may conflict with each other, which may give rise to practical problems and even diplomatic conflicts between the nations at issue. The various inherent problem areas[354] are largely overlapping.

2.1. Procedural and substantive frictions

2.1.1. Pre-decision phase

An enforcement authority might have to face considerable obstacles in obtaining evidence where a restrictive business practice has an international dimension. It might be difficult to obtain evidence if a party has its registered business seat abroad.

Apart from the collection of evidence or issues relating to information sharing in general, the protection of confidential information will also be of immediate concern. Given the necessity of having detailed economic information for a comprehensive assessment in competition law matters, this information will most likely comprise information that is of economic or strategic value to the undertakings at issue. Enforcement agencies will have to define procedural guarantees so as not to infringe any statutory obligation not to disclose such confidential information or business secrets by sharing them with other enforcement agencies.

Given the differences in the individual policy goals and their respective implementation in substantive law, a certain kind of behaviour might not be considered unlawful in a certain country, and the authorities there will therefore be unwilling to condemn such behaviour, whereas the same behaviour might be sanctioned by others. Therefore, there is a certain risk of incoherent or contradictory decisions being reached by different enforcement authorities[355], which

---

[352] Compare D. K. Tarullo, *Norms and Institutions in Global Competition Policy,* [Vol. 94:478] The American Journal of International Law 2000, 479 et sqq.

[353] Resulting in price fixing or territorial allocation across national borders, see D. K. Tarullo, *Norms and Institutions in Global Competition Policy,* [Vol. 94:478] The American Journal of International Law 2000, 479 et sqq.

[354] Compare Karel Van Miert, *Foreword to the 1998 Competition Report,* in: EC Commission, *Commission's XXVIIIth Report on Competition Policy* (1998), 3-4.

[355] Besides preventing a coherent enforcement strategy from the individual enforcement authorities' point of view, the inconsistencies thereby created will be of immediate concern to the parties involved. The outcome of an envisaged transaction will largely depend on a uniform appraisal by the authorities involved, as one negative decision will most certainly frustrate the whole transaction.

may imply jurisdictional frictions and disadvantages from a regulatory competition point of view.

2.1.2. Post-decision phase

Once a decision is taken by the investigating agency, it might be difficult to enforce against individuals or entities situated abroad[356]. In particular, efficient enforcement of administrative or judicial decisions abroad will depend on whether the foreign competitors at issue do have assets in the jurisdiction of the state applying its competition law, or whether the countries at issue have agreed on bilateral co-operation agreements[357]. The efficacy, and hence, credibility of an antitrust enforcement agency will be seriously impaired, however, where it cannot provide for a coherent enforcement of its decisions.

Moreover, the efficacy of cartel sanctions imposed by competition authorities has been questioned in light of the prevailing international market structures. Generally, sanctions for cartels are for purposes of deterrence, punishment and compensation or restitution of harm caused by the cartel. For these purposes, four types of sanctions can be distinguished, namely pecuniary fines, prison sentences for individuals, court actions for damages and restitution, and disqualification to act as a company director[358]. The approaches among the various jurisdictions as to the availability of the individual sanctions and the determination of the level of sanction to apply to an international cartel will, however, feature significant differences. For instance, the level of fines to be imposed can be problematic. In the European Union, fines can amount to 10% of a cartel member's worldwide turnover[359], whereas in the United States, the fine will be calculated on the basis of the loss suffered or a percentage of "affected commerce", which is not limited to a percentage of the turnover[360]. Also, the individual approaches with regard to the possibility of court actions for those suffering loss through the conduct of cartels may be very different[361].

---

[356] Compare Karel Van Miert, *Foreword to the 1998 Competition Report,* in: EC Commission, *Commission's XXVIIIth Report on Competition Policy* (1998), 3-4.

[357] E. U. Petersmann, *Proposals for Negotiating International Competition Rules in the GATT-WTO World Trade and Legal System,* in: 49 (II/III) Aussenwirtschaft 1994, at 244.

[358] Compare F. R. Schoneveld, *Cartel Sanctions and International Competition Policy: Cross-Border Cooperation and Appropriate Forums for Cooperation,* in 26(3) Journal of World Competition 2003, 437 et sqq.

[359] See Article 25 of Regulation (EC) No 1/2003, OJ 2003 L1/1.

[360] F. R. Schoneveld, *Cartel Sanctions and International Competition Policy: Cross-Border Cooperation and Appropriate Forums for Cooperation,* in 26(3) Journal of World Competition 2003, 438, citing the *US Sentencing Guidelines.*

[361] In this regard, the United States have been identified as the friendliest jurisdiction for such claims for damages or restitution by individuals, see F. R. Schoneveld, *Cartel Sanctions and International Competition Policy: Cross-Border Cooperation and Appropriate Forums for Cooperation,* in 26(3) Journal of World Competition 2003, 439. For the European Union, the ECJ has also recognized that private actions for damages can contribute to the maintenance of effective competition in the Common Market, see Case C-453/99 *Courage Ltd. V. B. Crehan,* [2001] ECR I-06297. Still, the tradition of private court action for damages is less pronounced in the European Union than it is in the United States.

Consequently, a number of concerns have been raised with regard to sanctions in international cartel cases[362]. In particular, given the competition enforcement authorities' practice to leave sanctioning of international cartels to other jurisdictions, such sanctions might be insufficient for effective deterrence. Also, those imprisoned should not be punished twice by different authorities in different jurisdictions for the same conduct. Moreover, case specific evidence[363] has been presented which suggests that heavy sanctions can trigger certain business transactions such as mergers and acquisitions, joint ventures or strategic alliances which reduce competition and which thereby lead to excessive concentration on a given market. The reasoning behind this concern is based on the strategic disadvantages of a company whose directors were disqualified, whose management was imprisoned or on which severe fines were imposed due to its membership in a cartel. Arguably, such companies are prime candidates for take-overs. Take-overs, however, will reduce the number of competitors and result in a more concentrated market. The author does not support this line of argument, as in her view, a legitimate sanction due to an infringement of competition law cannot reasonably be put into question in light of potential economic disadvantages caused. Rather, the very purpose of a sanction is to punish by imposing economic disadvantages.

In addition, different application of leniency programs[364] may bring about a disincentive for participation in such programs, where an application for leniency in one jurisdiction will expose the applicant to severe sanctions in another. Thereby, the individual domestic policy rationale behind such leniency programs might be frustrated without further coordination of their application.

2.2. Competency and diplomacy

First, the increasing practice of competition enforcement agencies targeting foreign individuals or entities abroad implies an enlarged need to access evidence located in foreign jurisdictions. Accessing such evidence, however, may

---

362 F. R. Schoneveld, *Cartel Sanctions and International Competition Policy: Cross-Border Cooperation and Appropriate Forums for Cooperation*, in 26(3) Journal of World Competition 2003, 448 et sqq.

363 Compare F. R. Schoneveld, *Cartel Sanctions and International Competition Policy: Cross-Border Cooperation and Appropriate Forums for Cooperation*, in 26(3) Journal of World Competition 2003, 453, citing the EC Commission's Decision of 18 January 2002, Case No. COMP/M.2502, *Cargill/Cerestar*, where *Cargill's* acquisition of *Cerestar* followed the EC and US imposition of fines in this citric acid cartel case. Also, the *Oil Country Tubular Goods* market has been held as another example. In that case, the EC fined several European and Japanese OCTG steel manufacturers for price fixing in 1999. Arguably, since the break-up of the cartel, every former member has joined one of three large international alliances, the largest one of which holds a 25% share of the world market in OCTG. Arguably, thus, the level of competition was reduced to a large extent as a result of the fines imposed, compare S. Evenett et al., *International Cartel Enforcement: Lessons from the 1999's*, available at: http://www.econ.worldbank.org/files/2454_wps2680.pdf (29.05.2005).

364 Leniency programs provide incentives for "whistle blowing" by offering certain reductions of complete immunity from the sanctions normally imposed for a certain anti-competitive behaviour, compare for example *EC Commission Notice on immunity from fines and reduction of fines in cartel cases*, [OJ 2002, No. C45/03].

be difficult to achieve. Without active support on part of the relevant national enforcement authorities at issue and without co-operation agreements, the information might not be obtainable at all.

Second, the international activity of competition authorities may provoke negative reactions by foreign governments, as they might consider such actions to be in violation of their sovereignty. Possible reactions by foreign governments may take various forms. For example, governments might insist on being notified of proceedings initiated against their nationals. Alternatively, they may approach the initiating authorities with requests for co-operation. Also, the initiating authorities might be asked to take traditional "negative" comity into account[365].

Third, given that the same conduct may be investigated by multiple competition authorities, each of them applying their own procedural as well as substantive law, additional problems may be created. From a procedural point of view, several competition authorities might claim jurisdiction over the same subject matter, to begin with. In addition, the coordination among the investigating authorities during the procedures of taking evidence or with regard to the sharing of information might entail problems relating to the question of authority, and thus the need for regulation.

2.3. Interim Summary

The increasing international reach of private business transactions entails considerable challenges for competition enforcement agencies. Specifically, competition enforcement agencies have encountered serious problems in securing an effective scrutiny of cross-border transactions under their respective antitrust law provisions. The individual shortcomings identified may relate to jurisdictional, organizational, procedural and also substantive factors, and may result in diplomatic frictions between the sovereign states involved. Therefore, national provisions with a domestic scope are inadequate to deal with cross-border transactions[366], and anticompetitive conduct may elude national regulation, as national competition authorities cannot fully protect their citizens from transnational anticompetitive conduct by international cartels or global oligopolies and monopolies[367]. Consequently, a need for international rules can be established, with the minimum requirement of an obligation to co-operate.

International institutional co-operation in competition policy has been called for at both bilateral and multilateral level. A number of understandings and

[365] L. Fullerton/C. C. Mazard, *International Antitrust Co-operation Agreements,* 24(3) Journal of World Competition 2001, 410.

[366] For many, see M. Todino, *International Competition Network. The State of Play after Naples,* in: 26(2) Journal of World Competition 2003, 285.

[367] D. K. Tarullo, *Norms and Institutions in Global Competition Policy,* [Vol. 94:478] The American Journal of International Law 2000, 479 et sqq.

agreements for co-operation have been signed at the bilateral level[368]. At the multilateral level, various international organizations have discussed possible coordination of competition law issues, such as the International Competition Network (ICN) [369], the Organization for Economic Cooperation and Development (OECD)[370], the United Nations Conference on Trade and Development (UNCTAD)[371] or the World Trade Organization (WTO)[372]. These various initiatives and their respective approaches will be examined in more detail below.

3. *Incomplete Coverage of Domestic Competition Policies*

In addition to the arguments raised above, the need for international competition rules from a state's perspective might equally result from *(i)* the non-existence of competition law instruments, or *(ii)* the deliberate non-application of existing domestic competition law to certain situations. The author has demonstrated that international market power builds on national market power first. In certain cases, national market power may be disregarded by domestic competition policy due to a lack of restrictions of competition or other negative effects on the home market as an immediate effect of this market power. This may, however, result in the leverage of domestic market power against international market power and, consequently, to the creation of international restrictions of competition[373]. In turn, this leverage may lead to welfare losses. A common example is that many states do not sanction export cartels, as they do not have any immediate negative affect on competition on the exporting country's markets. Nevertheless, the tolerance of export cartels may restrict competi-

---

[368] For example, the European Union has concluded bilateral cooperation agreements with Canada (*Council and Commission Decision of 29 April 1999 concerning the conclusion of the Agreement between the European Communities and the Government of Canada regarding the application of their competition laws*, Official Journal L 175, 10.07.1999), the United States (E.g. *Agreement between the European Communities and the Government of the United States of America on the application of positive comity principles in the enforcement of their competition laws*, Official Journal L 173, 18.06.1998), and many Eastern European countries. In comparison, the United States have concluded bilateral cooperation agreements with Australia, Brazil, Canada, Japan and Mexico, for example, compare F. R. Schoneveld, *Cartel Sanctions and International Competition Policy: Cross-Border Cooperation and Appropriate Forums for Cooperation,* in 26(3) Journal of World Competition 2003, 433.

[369] Arguably, the ICN, being focused entirely on competition topics, is currently the most promising, albeit informal, forum for international dialogue among national competition authorities, compare M. Todino, *International Competition Network. The State of Play after Naples*, in 26(2) Journal of World Competition 2003, 283 et sqq.

[370] Compare for example OECD, *Recommendation of the Council concerning Co-operation between Member Countries on Anticompetitive Practices affecting International Trade*, 27 July 1995 – C(95)130/FINAL, available at:
http://webdomino1.oecd.org/horizontal/oecdacts.nsf/Display/17A98914E131EFF5C1256EE3006CB9CE?OpenDocument (29.05.2005).

[371] For a comprehensive analysis of the work within the UNCTAD, see P. Brusick, *UNCTAD's role in promoting Multilateral Co-operation on Competition Law and Policy,* in 24(1) Journal of World Competition 2001, 23 et sqq.

[372] See for example WTO, Working Group on the Interaction between Trade and Competition Policy, *Report on the Meeting of 22-23 March 2001, Note by the Secretariat,* WTO Document WT/WGTCP/M/14.

[373] Compare H. Wins, *ibid.*, 44.

tion in the particular export market or have negative implications for global welfare. The potentially fragmentary application of domestic competition policies may therefore result in negative economic after-effects for individual states.

In the following, the author shall undertake an assessment of possible defaults in the application of domestic competition policies, which may support the case for international competition rules. To that end, the prevailing domestic competition law practices toward international restrictive business practices shall be examined.

3.1. International restrictive business practices building on domestic market power

3.1.1. Foreclosure against imports

Generally, state-initiated or state-tolerated restrictions against imports are dealt with under the GATT[374], which shall be analysed in Chapter IV. of this book. At this point, the analysis will be limited to potential shortcomings from a competition policy perspective.

(i) Strategic unilateral deployment of barriers to entry

As illustrated above, barriers to entry may take the two basic forms of *(a)* absolute advantages, and *(b)* strategic advantages[375].

With regard to absolute advantages, the author has demonstrated that they may in particular arise through preventing access to distribution channels or other resources, or through protectionist use of intellectual property rights. The first group of barriers to entry can in particular be implemented through vertical agreements or mergers. Generally, such measures do not only prevent market access for foreign potential competitors, but also for domestic ones. Nevertheless, the immediate threat of potential foreign competition results primarily in the formation of such barriers to entry, because its inherent risks are harder to compute and estimate for the incumbents than for a familiar domestic competition[376]. In any case, these restrictions are usually caught by the competition laws of the importing country. However, where the importing country does not regulate such agreements or mergers, there is an increased risk of (defensive) concentrations.

In comparison to developing countries, developed countries have adopted competition laws very early. By 1980, 40 mostly developed nations had adopted

---

[374] For an overview of the applicable GATT rules, see H. Hauser/R. E. Schoene, *Is there a Need for International Competition Rules?* In: 49 (II/III) Aussenwirtschaft 1994, at 207 et sqq.

[375] Compare Chapter III.B.1.1.1.(i) above.

[376] H. Wins, *ibid.*, 44.

competition laws. By 2003, this number had risen to 93, with an increasing proportion of developing and transition countries among them[377]. In light of the total number of UN Member States, this number equals around 48% of total membership[378]. Although many of these newly enacted laws follow well-proven models[379], the individual laws adopted may feature considerable differences. In addition, it is far from clear that all of the 48% of UN Member States having a competition law in place are in a position to efficiently enforce it. For instance, many developing countries lack the resources and expertise, in particular with regard to large cross-border mergers, abuse of dominant position, or vertical restraints[380]. These practices typically require a vast amount of evidence[381] as well as a profound economic analysis in order to establish a restriction of competition.

As far as vertical restrictions are concerned, there are considerable differences in the individual national perception of their detrimental effects on competition and, consequently, in the individual national approaches to enforcement[382]. Nevertheless, even the adoption of a very strict approach cannot guarantee market access to foreign competitors wishing to enter a particular market. The most prominent example in this regard is the Japanese "Keiretsu" system. Arguably, the Japanese Monopoly Law can be considered as formally one of the strictest of its kind[383]. Yet, arguably, Japan has failed to adopt an enforcement policy efficient enough to ensure market access for potential new entrants from abroad[384].

Equally, domestic competition policy may allow for strategic deployment of intellectual property rights against potential new entrants through clauses taking advantage of the monopoly-like position of intellectual property right hold-

---

377 UNCTAD, *World Investment Report 2003. FDI Policies for Development: National and International Perspectives*, available at:
http://www.unctad.org/en/docs/wir2003_en.pdf (08.05.2005), at 135.

378 Currently, the UN has 191 Member States, compare the information provided by the United Nations at: *http://www.un.org/Overview/unmember.html* (08.05.2005).

379 E.g. the EC Competition Law regime's model has been copied by many of the new EU Member States prior to their accession after the conclusion of association agreements. Others have followed the UN Model Law on Competition, albeit taking account of their particular economic situation, judicial systems or degree of development; compare UNCTAD, *World Investment Report 2003. FDI Policies for Development: National and International Perspectives*, available at:
http://www.unctad.org/en/docs/wir2003_en.pdf (08.05.2005), ibid.

380 UNCTAD, *World Investment Report 2003*, ibid.

381 E.g. details relating to market shares, market structure, potential efficiencies created.

382 As explained above, different from the approach adopted in the US, the EC authorities have long hesitated to embrace any efficiency considerations inherent in vertical restrictions. This has only changed with the rather recent adoption of the EC Commission's *Guidelines on Vertical Restraints*, [2000] OJ C291/1.

383 H. Wins, *ibid.*, 48.

384 Generally, the "Keiretsu" system is preventing market access for both domestic and foreign potential competitors. Still, a possible worse treatment of foreign potential competitors is supported by the fact that Japan has produced a considerable surplus in its balance of trade, although no appreciable state-initiated or state-supported protectionist measures can be observed; compare H. Wins, *ibid.*

ers, e.g. through grant-back clauses[385], clauses prohibiting imports or exports, exclusivity clauses or through clauses tying supply from the licensor's after-markets[386]. This allowance may result from the non-rigorous application of domestic competition rules. Likewise, such practices may be subject to control of abuse. Such control may for example assess if a franchisor legitimately ties the licenses to use his trademarks to additional obligations to obtain certain good or services from the franchisor[387]. The suitability of intellectual property rights to be used as an uncompetitive barrier to entry will very much depend on the individual domestic interpretation of the incentives for innovations granted through monopoly rents. For instance, the US applies a doctrine under which intellectual property right owners are denied monopoly protection when they "overstep their intellectual property rights in a manner that violated the antitrust laws, and threatened to reduce innovation"[388]. Also, the EC authorities have endorsed a very strict approach regarding territorial protection and market segregation resulting from the use of intellectual property rights[389]. However, given the lack of underlying market integrationist motives as applied by the EC authorities or even the lack of competition laws at all, other countries might be hesitant to prosecute similar practices in their jurisdiction. For example, developing countries being mostly importers of technology, they try to improve the bargaining position of their local firms by a rather lax application of intellectual property rights[390]. In this regard, it is also worth noting that since the TRIPS Agreement, intellectual property regimes have undergone a certain degree of standardization in that all WTO Member States are required to provide for certain minimum standards, which might facilitate the strategic deployment of intellectual property rights as a barrier to entry[391].

Moreover, access to essential facilities may be prevented by incumbents. Essential facilities are commonly regarded as natural monopolies and, therefore, subject to the individual regulatory regime at issue, and the individual degree of

---

385 Under grant-back clauses, the licensee is required to assign his inventions based on the licensed technology back to the licensor; E.-U. Petersmann, *International Competition Rules for Governments and for Private Business,* 30(3) Journal of World Trade 1996, 10.

386 H. Wins, *ibid.*, 50.

387 H. Wins, *ibid.*, 50.

388 Anne K. Bingeman, *Competition and Innovation: Bedrock of the American Economy,* Speech before the University of Kansas Lawschool, Sept. 19, 1996, available at: http://www.usdoj.gov/atr/public/speeches/960919ks.htm (09.08.2005). *A. Bingeman* is citing *inter alia* the cases *United States v. Microsoft Corp., United States v. S.C. Johnson & Son, Inc. & Bayer A.G., and United States v. General Electric Co.*

389 Compare the ECJ's approach in Cases 56&58/64 *Consten & Grundig v Commission* [1966] ECR 299. Despite the ECJ has adopted a *rule of reason* approach in its later decision Case 258/78 *Nungesser* v. *EC Commission* [1982] ECR 2015, [1983] 1CMLR 278 and has found in Case 27/87 *Erau-Jacquéry* v. *La Hesbignonne* [1988] ECR 1919, [1988] 4 CMLR 576 that even an export ban could be outside Article 81(1) EC, the EC Commission has taken a rather restrictive view of *Nungesser* and has interpreted the concept of "new technology" very narrowly until *Sicasov* [1999] OJ L4/27, [1999] ECMLR 192.

390 UNCTAD, *World Investment Report 2003,* at 130, available at: http://www.unctad.org/en/docs/wir2003_en.pdf (08.05.2005).

391 H. Wins, *ibid.*, 50.

liberalisation prevailing[392]. From a competition policy point of view, the United States is the only country with a tradition of enforcing access to essential facilities for potential entrants through rigid application of the essential facilities doctrine[393]. The EU, in contrast, has not explicitly endorsed that doctrine, and has, after a short departure in *Magill*[394], presented a rather rigid test for an obligation to supply under Article 82 EC in *Bronner*[395]. Thus, a potential entrant's chances to penetrate a new market will very much depend on the individual regulation and enforcement approach prevailing in the country at issue.

(ii) Abuse of dominant position through unilateral predatory behaviour against importers

Generally, governmental control of abuses of dominant positions through an undertaking is part of most existing competition laws as this practice is considered a hard-core restriction very detrimental to domestic markets and, consequently, domestic welfare. In countries with existing competition laws, therefore, predatory behaviour against importers is generally caught by domestic competition law just like predatory behaviour against domestic competitors. However, if there is no domestic competition law in place to sanction this kind of behaviour, importers will likely be subject to particularly hostile behaviour, as potential competition from abroad is generally perceived as especially harmful by domestic incumbents[396]. Likewise, where existing competition laws cannot be enforced due to a lack of resources or know-how, these practices against importers will escape governmental control. In addition, domestic enforcement might be less concerned with predatory behaviour against importers than they are for domestic producers, as the number of domestic competitors is not reduced by predatory behaviour against importers[397]. In all three cases, a non-avenged abuse of a domestic dominant position will increase domestic market power and may therefore give rise to international market power. However, international market power cannot yet be effectively controlled under the current system of largely uncoordinated coexistence of existing domestic competition laws.

---

[392] E.g. Telecommunications facilities are largely liberalized in the EC since EC Commission Directive 96/19/EC, March 13, 1996.

[393] Until now, only the lower courts have explicitly acknowledged an "essential facilities" doctrine, although the US Supreme Court in *Kodak* has decided that a firm can only refuse to deal with its competitors if there are "legitimate competitive reasons for the refusal", Case *Eastman Kodak Co.* v. *Image Technical Services Inc.*, 504 US 451, 119 L. Ed. 2d 265, 112 S.Ct. 2072 (1992); compare B. Doherty, *Just What Are Essential Facilities?* In: 38 Common Market Law Review 2001, 402 et sqq.

[394] In Cases 241/91P etc *RTE and ITP* v. *Commission* [1995] ECR I-743, [1995] 4 CMLR 718, the Court found "exceptional circumstances" on which it based an obligation to supply.

[395] ECJ, Case C-7/97, *Bronner*, [1998] ECR I-7791.

[396] H. Wins, *ibid.*, 44.

[397] This will depend on the extent to which the domestic competition law at issue is concerned with the protection of individual competitors or groups of competitors in addition to the protection of overall efficiency.

(iii) Multilateral conduct: Import cartels

Import cartels can rarely be considered as efficiency enhancing. This could only be the case when coordination of import logistics led to output increases or cost reductions for transport, insurance or storage that were subsequently passed on to the consumer[398]. Therefore, most states with competition laws prohibit import cartels in light of their detrimental effects on domestic markets. Mostly, the general prohibition of cartels is extended to import cartels by legal practice. Some states even have provided for an explicit prohibition of import cartels[399]. Generally, therefore, this kind of restriction against imports will only escape domestic competition law where the jurisdiction at issue does not have a competition law in place. Thus, compared to other restrictive practices, the need for international competition rules is less pronounced with regard to import cartels[400].

3.1.2. Restrictions affecting export markets

From a competition policy perspective, this area of restrictive business practices with an international dimension is the one deserving most attention. Generally, as restrictions on export markets do not directly affect competition in the exporting countries, an appreciable lack of action against these practices can be perceived in the exporting countries. As opposed to net importers who tend to over-regulate anticompetitive behaviour in case they can apply their laws to foreign activities, net exporters tend to under-regulate such behaviour[401]. Given that these practices necessarily build on domestic market power, the lack of domestic regulation and/or sanctions may give rise to international market power. Again, under the prevailing system of an incongruent patchwork of domestic competition laws, international market power cannot sufficiently be addressed and can consequently lead to losses in efficiency and welfare.

(i) Export cartels

Since export cartels primarily affect competition in the country of delivery, the country of origin usually does not have any interest in sanctioning export cartels. In practice, the assessment of export cartels from a competition policy point of view will require a detailed analysis as to which geographical market is affected and from which countries the cartel's members originate[402]. In fact,

---

398 H. Wins, *ibid.*, 46 et sqq.

399 The United States have adopted an explicit prohibition of import cartels which reduce external trade or lead to price increases in the Wilson Tariff Act, 15 U.S.C. s. 8, *Trusts in restraint of import trade illegal; penalty*, available at: http://www.usdoj.gov/atr/foia/divisionmanual/ch2.htm#a2 (12.05.2005). Likewise, the German "Gesetz gegen Wettbewerbsbeschränkungen" has switched from the notification system to a general ban of import cartels in its 6th amendment of August 26, 1998, BGBl. 1998 I, 2546.

400 H. Wins, *ibid.*, 46 et sqq.

401 A. T. Guzman, *Is International Antitrust Possible?* In: 73 New York University Law Review 1998, at 1504.

402 H. Wins, *ibid.*, 53.

many countries either explicitly tolerate or exempt "pure" export cartels from the application of their domestic competition law instruments in light of the effects doctrine[403]. Supporters argued that this exemption was justified because it would "sensibly allocate enforcement responsibility" to the government whose consumers' interests are at risk[404]. Moreover, export cartels would benefit both exporters and their customers, and therefore result in a win-win situation for all parties. In addition, export cartels would have an "undeniable positive impact on export trade"[405].

From an economic policy point of view, however, this approach has been criticized as a "beggar-thy-neighbour" policy, since export cartels help to reap higher prices on foreign export markets and, consequently, artificially amend the terms of trade[406]. From a competition policy perspective, this practice must equally be disapproved of for several reasons.

To begin with, export cartels are predominantly anticompetitive[407]. This is certainly true for aggressive export cartels, which are used for active capturing of foreign markets and to replace local incumbents. Where aggressive export cartelists succeed in the creation of a dominant position on the export market from abroad, prices can be raised above competitive to monopolistic levels. The effects of the subsequent exploitation of the export market's demand are tantamount to import restrictions on competitors from other foreign markets concerned and, consequently, bring about similarly detrimental effects[408]. As far as defensive export cartels are concerned, they are maintained to counteract foreign monopolistic market structures or governmental trade barriers, and may enhance international competition where they help to overcome barriers to entry on export markets. Arguably, however, the negative effects of defensive export cartels on competition generally outweigh the positive ones. First, export cartels provoke anti-competitive countermeasures on part of the incumbents in

---

403 For a comprehensive overview of individual states' approaches compare A. Bhattacharjea, *Export Cartels – A Developing Country Perspective,* in: 38(2) Journal of World Trade 2004, at 336 et sqq. For instance, EC Competition Law is operating by an implicit exemption, in that Article 81 EC only targets "cartels which may affect trade between Member States and which have as their object or effect the prevention, restriction or distortion of competition within the Common Market." Similarly, many EU Member States are operating a similar implicit exemption, e.g. the UK has switched from an explicit exemption in the 1976 Restrictive Trade Practices Act to an implicit one in Chapter I of the 1998 Competition Act; and Germany has recently abolished its registration requirement of export cartels in the 6th amendment of the *Gesetz gegen Wettbewerbsbeschränkungen.* Australia and New Zealand do require authorization of export cartels, whereas Japan and Spain provide for an prior authorization of export cartels. The same is true for the United States of America, where export cartels are regulated in the *1918 Webb-Pomerene Act* and the *1982 Export trading Companies Act* together with the *Foreign Trade Antitrust Improvements Act.* On the other hand, Canada, Greece and Mexico have adopted explicit exclusions of export cartels from their domestic competition laws.

404 J. R. Magnus, *Joint Export Trade Provisions in Antitrust Laws: A Supporter's Perspective,* in: 39(1) Journal of World Trade 2005, 181 et sqq.

405 J. R. Magnus, *ibid.,* 182.

406 H. Wins, *ibid.,* 54. This aspect shall be considered in more detail below.

407 A. D. Mitchell, *Broadening the Vision of Trade Liberalisation. International Competition Law and the WTO,* in: 24(3) Journal of World Competition 2001, at 348.

408 H. Wins, *ibid.,* 52 et sqq.

the export markets, or lead to anti-competitive agreements between the exporters and the incumbents. Second, defensive export cartels easily convert to aggressive ones. Consequently, economic theory implies that both aggressive and defensive export cartels may create international market power and, thus, have detrimental effects on the efficiency of international markets[409].

Some have rated the exclusion or toleration of export cartels from domestic competition laws as unproblematic, since anti-competitive behaviour by exporters on export markets should economically be dealt with best by applying the national antitrust law of the importing country to the foreign cartelists[410]. Given the yet incomplete coverage of competition laws worldwide[411], this argument cannot be accepted, as a certain amount of anti-competitive export practices would remain untouched. Possible efficiency considerations of export cartels should best be evaluated by the importing countries where possible detrimental effects on consumers would be realized[412]. Nevertheless, the realization of such assessment might not be possible for many competition enforcement agencies due to their lack in expertise or resources.

Likewise, efficiency and welfare enhancement being the underlying policy objectives of competition laws, the overall credibility of these policy goals and their implementation through the strict prohibition of hard-core restrictions in domestic competition law is damaged where efficiency losses through the behaviour of exporting firms subject to that very domestic competition law are - explicitly or implicitly - tolerated[413]. Any governmental enforcement policy which is letting escape export cartels despite their established anticompetitive effects would appear to be arbitrary and untrustworthy. This finding is reinforced by the argument that the harm done by export cartels to consumers in the importing countries is usually outweighing the benefits for the colluding firms in the exporting country[414]. Consequently, the exclusion of export cartels from the scope of domestic competition law does not only result in a random and fragmentary domestic enforcement policy, but also in global welfare and efficiency losses. Thus, from a competition policy point of view, the allowance for export cartels must not be tolerated, as it enables one state to either accept welfare and efficiency losses to the detriment of another state, or even to deliberately assign such losses to another state once sufficient evidence of an export cartel has been collected by domestic enforcement authorities.

---

409 H. Wins, *ibid.*, 53.

410 H. Hauser/R. E. Schoene, *Is There a Need for International Competition Rules?*, in: 49(II/III) Aussenwirtschaft 1994, at 211 et sqq.

411 According to the materials provided by UNCTAD, only 48% of UN Member States had encated a competition law by 2003; compare UNCTAD, *World Investment Report 2003. FDI Policies for Development: National and International Perspectives*, available at: http://www.unctad.org/en/docs/wir2003_en.pdf (08.05.2005), at 135.

412 A. Bhattacharjea, *Export Cartels – A Developing Country Perspective*, in: 38(2) Journal of World Trade 2004, at 332.

413 H. Wins, *ibid.*, 55.

414 F. Amato, *International Antitrust: What Future?* In 24(4) Journal of World Competition 2001, at 455.

(ii) Dumping

As previously stated[415], "dumping" basically refers to exporting at prices below the products' normal value. In particular, pricing at dumping level may either imply predation or discrimination. For the purposes of our analysis from a competition policy point of view, two aspects must be considered. First, an examination must occur to establish whether predatory or discriminatory pricing across national borders is anti-competitive and should therefore be addressed by the domestic competition law of the exporting country. If answered in the affirmative, an examination must occur if this practice is sufficiently addressed. In addition, possible reactions and potential anti-competitive retorts on part of the importing country must be considered to assess the necessity of international competition rules.

With regard to the first aspect, dumping by means of predatory pricing deserves particular attention. Exporters thereby harm the export market on a permanent basis while recouping the resulting monopoly profits themselves. Dumping as international price discrimination can, however, potentially be efficient on balance[416]. Moreover, the typical counterarguments of output reduction and welfare losses through market segregation and inducing monopolies have been considered as not convincing from an economic theory point of view[417], as it is the consumers in the export markets who benefit from lower prices, while the related costs of market segregation and social costs would have to be borne by the exporting country[418].

Economic theory shows that predatory pricing in practice can (if at all[419]) only occur under very limited circumstances. In particular, the elements of *(i)* a dominant position in terms of very high market share; *(ii)* the possibility of recoupment of the costs for dumping; and *(iii)*, sufficient evidence of investment in the elimination of a certain competitor have been required to accept predatory pricing as a rational business strategy deliberately deployed to reduce the number of competitors in the exporting markets[420]. In addition to these restrictions, it may be difficult in practice to identify the cost level of predatory pricing. Under the *Areeda-Turner Test,* a price lower than reasonably anticipated short-run marginal costs is considered predatory[421]. Due to differences in com-

---

[415] Compare Chapter III.B.1.1.2.(ii) above.

[416] W. Bishop, *Price Discrimination under Article 86: Political Economy in the European Court,* 44 MLR 1981, 288.

[417] M. J. Trebilcock, *The Regulation of International Trade,* at 179 argues that there is decisive empirical answer to the question whether output will de- or increase under discriminatory pricing, and that certain balancing factors and possible efficiency enhancements have been neglected.

[418] M. J. Trebilcock, *ibid.,* 177.

[419] For instance, R. Bork has totally denied the existence of predatory pricing, see *The Antitrust Paradoxon: A Policy at War with Itself,* at 154. The majority of economists do not share this extreme position.

[420] R. T. Rapp, *Predatory Pricing and Entry Deterring Strategies: the Economics of AKZO,* in [1986] ECLR 233 et sqq.

[421] P. Areeda/D. Turner, *Predatory Pricing and Related Practices Under Section 2 of the Sherman Act,* in 88 Harv. L. Rev. 1975, at 697.

puting the marginal costs, however, the average variable costs are used as a surrogate[422].

Consequently, in case the criteria specified apply and where a computation of the cost level proves predatory pricing, the business strategy at issue must be considered restrictive of competition. While predatory cross-border pricing will be of minor quantitative importance, it should be clearly addressed by the domestic competition law in the exporting country in light of the existing market power, or dominance, at national level and the risk of leverage to international market power. This argument is reinforced by the fact that besides its effect of eliminating individual competitors, predatory pricing itself may also constitute a barrier to entry for potential competitors[423], and must therefore be rated particularly detrimental to efficiency.

However, in light of the effects doctrine and the resulting reference to practices affecting the domestic market only, domestic competition laws commonly do not sanction predatory pricing with regard to exports. Again, concerns relating to *(i)* credibility and scope of domestic competition policy and *(ii)* leverage of welfare losses to abroad as established for export cartels also apply to predatory dumping. This is in particular supported by the fact that the existing degree of market power required to engage in predatory pricing is already (at least close to) that of dominance. Given this degree of domestic market power, the exporter can subsequently very easily establish international market power. The exporting jurisdiction should therefore be prevented from shifting this responsibility to abroad. This argument is underlined by the level of detail required for establishing predatory cost levels. Arguably, the economic evidence necessary for this assessment is disproportionately harder to obtain for enforcement agencies located abroad than local agencies.

With regard to the second aspect of the discussion, the author shall now consider possible countermeasures initiated by the importing country's attitude toward dumped imports. Many countries have enacted antidumping laws as a trade remedy against material injury caused to domestic producers of "like products" through dumped imports[424]. In addition to their possible immediate implications for trade policy, the enforcement of these laws may also interact with competition policy. For instance, antidumping laws may allow for practices such as price undertakings or quantitative restrictions which are commonly prohibited by competition law, or punish other types of price differentia-

---

[422] The *Areeda-Turner Test* has been endorsed by both US and EC Legal Practice; compare the ECJ's statement in Case C-62/86, *AKZO Chemie BV* v. *Commission* [19991] ECR I-3359,m [1993] 5 CMLR 215, which was further developed in Case C-333/94 p, *Tetra Pak International SA* v. *Commission (Tetra Pak II)* [1996] ECR I-5951, [1997] 4 CMLR 662.

[423] A. Jones/B. Sufrin, *ibid.*, 334.

[424] M. J. Trebilcock, *The Regulation of International Trade*[2], at 166. For WTO Member States, the legal basis for the adoption of antidumping laws is to be found in Article VI of the GATT 1994 and the *Agreement on Implementation of Article VI of the General Agreement on Tariffs and Trade 1994*.

tions that might be justified under competition law. These differences can be attributed to the different policy objectives of antidumping and competition laws. The first are a trade remedy for domestic industries injured by import competition at dumped prices, the latter aims at the promotion of consumer welfare and productive efficiency, for which import competition is a fundamental prerequisite in order to obtain market access[425].

The EC and the United States being major users of antidumping actions[426], it is interesting to note that for both jurisdictions, the primacy of competition law over antidumping law is a recognized principle[427]. The European legislation ensures this primacy of competition policy *(i)* in Article 3 (g) EC in conjunction with Article 81 EC and *(ii) inter alia* in Article 21 of Council Regulation No. 384/96 by reference to a wider "Community interest"[428]. As far as the United States is concerned, the *Noerr-Pennington Doctrine* was established by the US Supreme Court by the 1960s[429], which provides immunity for private actors from antitrust liability for lobbying and other attempts to influence government action, even where the object of such lobbying is to restrict competition or trade. However, the limits of these privileges have been clearly based on considerations of effective competition[430].

For both the EU and the US, this principle of supremacy of competition laws over antidumping laws has in principle been endorsed by legal practice[431].

---

425 Compare J. Tavares de Araujo Jr., *Legal and Economic Interfaces Between Antidumping and Competition Policy*, in: 25(2) Journal of World Competition 2002, at 159. The cited policy objectives must of course be considered in proportion to the individual perceptions of the goals of competition policy, as described in above. Consequently, the protection of individual competitors may equally be a goal of certain competition laws, compare for example the interpretation of the EC through the EC Commission or the ECJ.

426 Between July 1980 and June 1988, the actions brought by the United States (30%), Australia (27%), Canada (22%) and the European Union (19%) accounted for 97,5% of all antidumping actions filed during that period; M. J. Trebilcock, *The Regulation of International Trade², at 166.*

427 Compare J. Tavares de Araujo Jr., *Legal and Economic Interfaces Between Antidumping and Competition Policy*, in: 25(2) Journal of World Competition 2002, at 163.

428 Article 21 para. of Council Regulation 384/96 (EC) No 384/96 of 22 December 1995 on protection against dumped imports from countries not members of the European Community, Official Journal L 056 , 06/03/1996 p. 1, reads: "A determination as to whether the Community interest calls for intervention shall be based on an appreciation of all the various interests taken as a whole, including the interests of the domestic industry and users and consumers; [...] In such an examination, the need to eliminate the trade distorting effects of injurious dumping and to restore effective competition shall be given special consideration. [...]". In addition, Recital 15 of the mentioned regulation explicitly lays down that "in accepting undertakings, care should be taken that the proposed undertakings, and their enforcement, do not lead to anti-competitive behaviour".

429 Compare the US Supreme Court's judgments in *Eastern Railways Presidents Conference v. Noerr Motor Freight, Inc.*, 365 U.S. 127 (1961); *United Mine Workers of America v. Pennington*, 381 U.S. 657 (1965).

430 Compare US DOJ Antitrust Division and Federal Trade Commission, *Antitrust Enforcement Guidelines for International Operations 1995*, available at: http://www.usdoj.gov/atr/public/guidelines/internat.htm (15.05.2005).

431 Compare in particular ECJ Case C-358/89 *Extramet Industrie SA.* v. *Council* European Court Reports 1992, I-3813, where Advocat General Jacobs has argued for the importance of the consideration of competition policy in antidumping measures. In the *Soda-Ash-Solvay Case [1991] OJ L152/21,* the EC Commission suspended an antidumping review during the antitrust investigation; Similarly, in the *Ferrosilicon Case, Investigation No. 751-TA-21-27, US International Trade Commission Publication 3218, Washington, D.C.,*

Nevertheless, antidumping and competition enforcement may result in controversial and unclear decisions[432]. Besides, despite the prevailing legal supremacy of competition policy, competition policy considerations appear to be only insufficiently considered in antidumping procedures[433]. This may be attributed to the fact that the economic interaction between antidumping and competition policy is rather intransparent. Nevertheless, this interaction must be held to be established. This is supported by the finding that a certain proportion of parties in cartel cases have also been involved in antidumping procedures for the same products[434].

At any rate, there is at least certain evidence that the competition policy goals of promoting efficiency and consumer welfare are hindered by market distortions through antidumping measures[435]. In particular, the regular use of antidumping measures may result in an additional rise in the costs of conventional trade barriers. These costs may *inter alia* be ascribed to price increases, barriers to entry through higher concentration, incentives for collusion or retaliation among oligopolists or trade diversion, and may, arguably, exceed conventional trade barriers' standard welfare costs[436]. Thus, despite the fact that the exact consequences are difficult to compute, it can be assumed that antidumping laws may preclude the realization of competition policy.

Moreover, it has been argued that antidumping laws are not suited to meet the competition patterns currently prevailing in today's high-technology markets, and have, therefore, lost their immediate importance. Rather, antidumping laws primarily remain a protectionist remedy in traditional industry such as steel, chemical, textiles or other commodities whose competition mechanisms are technologically limited[437].

Without going into the details of the corresponding controversy about antidumping laws or the academic criticism relating to their possible economic or legal justification from a trade policy perspective, it can be argued that antidumping laws should be integrated in, if not totally replaced by competition laws. Consequently, as dumping by definition affects cross-border transactions, a case for international competition rules for dumping can be established from a competition policy perspective from both the exporting as well as the importing

---

1999, the ITC revoked antidumping benefits when the antitrust proceedings showed that the ferrosilicon market was neither competitive nor price sensitive; compare J. Tavares de Araujo Jr., *ibid.*, at 165.

432 D. Baetge, *Das Verhältnis zwischen Antidumpingrecht und Wettbewerbsrecht im Recht der Europäischen Gemeinschaft*, in: 62 RabelsZ (1998), at 673, who argues that as an example, the concept of the "Community Interest" has been applied rather inconsistently by the EC antidumping authorities.

433 D. Baetge, *ibid.*, at 676.

434 P. A. Messerlin, *Antidumping Regulations or Pro-Cartel Laws? The EC Chemical Cases*, 13 World Economy 1990, at 491.

435 J. Tavares de Araujo Jr., *ibid.*, at 166.

436 J. Tavares de Araujo Jr., *ibid.*

437 J. Tavares de Araujo Jr., *ibid.*, at 172.

country's perspective[438]. This case shall equally be sustained from a trade policy perspective below.

3.2. International restrictive business practices building on international market power

3.2.1. International Cartels

International cartels will only be effective if *(i)* all of its members adhere to the agreement, and *(ii)* their members enjoy market power in their home jurisdictions. Thus, the control of market power on domestic markets is crucial. Given the achievements of domestic competition policy and the severe sanctions adopted for cartels in light of their classification as hard-core restrictions in many jurisdictions[439], the successful fighting of domestic cartels has diminished the incentives for organizing international ones[440]. Nevertheless, the annual costs of international cartels to the world economy are still in the multi-billions of dollars[441].

Despite the aggressive investigation and prosecution of international cartels on the part of competition enforcement authorities of certain developed jurisdictions, it is important to note that these enforcement efforts primarily focus on the anticompetitive effects of international cartels and the harm thereby caused in their own respective home markets. However, in light of the amount of evidence required to deal with practices building on international market power and its potentially extended geographic scope, domestic enforcement may be difficult due to the jurisdictional limitations of domestic competition law[442]. Vigorous prosecution of an international cartel in one country is not enough to prevent harm occurring in other countries targeted by that international cartel[443].

Consequently, in order to provide for full-scope protection against international cartels, a complete and consistent network of domestic competition laws is required. It must also be considered, however, that even where competition laws exist, their enforcement may be insufficient due to a lack of resources[444] or the

---

438 In contrast, it has been argued that antidumping laws should be dropped without any substitute, as existing antitrust laws of all countries referring to antidumping measures would provide sufficient remedies against predatory pricing; compare H. Hauser/R. E. Schoene, *Is There a Need for International Competition Rules?* In 49(II/III) Aussenwirtschaft 1994, at 214. This argument cannot be shared due to the incomplete coverage of domestic competition laws, compare Chapter III.C.3. above.

439 The United States and the European Union may serve as an example.

440 H. Wins, *ibid.*, 59.

441 R. D. Anderson/P. Holmes, *Competition Policy and the Future of the Multilateral Trading System*, in: Journal of International Economic Law 2002, at 543.

442 F. Amato, *International Antitrust: What Future?* In: 24(4) Journal of World Competition 2001, 455.

443 R. D. Anderson/P. Holmes, *ibid.*, at 543 et sqq.

444 Arguably, many countries in Latin America, Africa and the Far or Middle East have not yet enacted domestic competition laws , compare H. Wins, *ibid.*

exemption of export cartels[445]. Therefore, the adoption of international competition rules providing for minimum standards or for capacity building for countries with no or weak competition laws would be required in order to ensure congruent and efficient action against international cartels. At minimum, comprehensive international co-operation and notification requirements should be laid down for cases where one enforcement authority comes across evidence of an international cartel in order to prevent overall efficiency or welfare losses.

3.2.2. Strategic alliances and joint ventures

From an enforcement point of view, strategic alliances and joint ventures have to be rated as either co-operation by agreement or concerted practice on the one hand, or as a concentration on the other. The final characterization will depend on the degree of financial or corporate integration. However, an unambiguous classification is not always possible in practice, which may give rise to frictions as the individual legal consequences differ[446].

The first group shares certain similarities with international cartels, and the issues raised for international cartels are therefore largely valid. With regard to the second group, an efficient control of concentrations is vital. However, not all jurisdictions have yet adopted a merger control regime[447]. Thus, relevant situations of concentrations might escape domestic merger control.

In addition, strategic alliances and joint ventures may give rise to international conflicts due to the possible trade-offs between efficiency gains and restrictions of competition among the countries involved. A set of international competition rules should, therefore, include consultation mechanisms to overcome possible conflicts[448].

3.2.3. Restrictive business practices of TNCs

The phenomenon of TNCs is closely linked to foreign direct investment and international production[449]. At the same time, there is a direct and growing interrelation between the liberalisation of foreign direct investment policies and competition policy[450].

Provided that the regional or global markets where TNCs are operating remain contestable through the interaction of trade liberalisation and a liberal foreign

---

[445] H. Wins, *ibid.*, 59.
[446] H. Wins, *ibid.*, 61.
[447] Compare UNCTAD, *World Investment Report 1997*, Annex Table A.22, at 291, available at: http://www.unctad.org/en/docs/WIR97_en.pdf (16.05.2005). For a more detailed overview of domestic merger control regimes in light of international concentrations compare below.
[448] H. Wins, *ibid.*, 61 et sqq.
[449] Compare Chapter III.A. above.
[450] UNCTAD, *World Investment Report 1997*, available at: http://www.unctad.org/en/docs/WIR97_en.pdf (19.05.2005), 183 et sqq.

direct investment scheme, TNCs' business activities are likely to increase competition and achieve welfare gains through cost effects, quality or innovation. However, foreign direct investment affects both market structure and competitors' conduct.

With regard to market structure, foreign direct investment by TNCs can under certain circumstances reduce the number of competitors, thereby increasing the degree of concentration prevailing on a market. Yet, the precise relationship between foreign direct investment and the degree of concentration is still unclear. The particular motivation of a given transaction will be decisive[451]. At the same time, although foreign direct investment in developing countries occurs primarily through green-field investment as opposed to FDI by means of M&A activities in developed countries[452], empirical evidence shows that increased TNC activity results in increased concentration on developing countries' markets. This increased concentration has *inter alia* been attributed to the distinct degree of TNCs' specialization and competition through product differentiation[453].

Consequently, in order to ensure the maximum benefit from inward foreign direct investment and the associated liberalisation measures, countries need to adopt competition laws so as to ensure that the abandoned statutory obstacles to market contestability are not replaced by private anticompetitive conduct of either domestic or foreign firms. Albeit (in particular developing[454]) countries are increasingly adopting competition laws, the overall coverage is not yet satisfying.

This need for domestic competition rules is reinforced by the fact that in addition to their effects on market structure, TNCs can by means of their very inherent features[455] also bear an anti-competitive influence on conduct, and thus, also performance[456] of the market at issue, thereby outweighing any initially competition enhancing effects by raising the number of competitors, the introduction of new products or lower prices[457]. For instance, where market contestability is low, the efficiency improvements in light of integrated interna-

---

451 UNCTAD, *ibid.*, at 142, is citing a merger with a view to down-scaling the size of operations or eventually the shut-down of the acquired firm as being intended to increase the level of concentration prevailing, as opposed to a merger with a view to the increase of efficiency through a decrease in production costs.

452 Arguably, the creation of a new entity as opposed to merging with or acquiring an existing one would result in an increase of the number of sellers and, thus, in a decrease of concentration in that market, compare UNCTAD, *ibid,* at 142.

453 UNCTAD, *ibid,* at 148. 169.

454 UNCTAD, *ibid.*, 189.

455 E.g. their competitive advantages through technical innovation, size, cost allocation through international production, their tendency to operate on concentrated markets, to be market leaders or to have larger than average market shares.

456 The *Structure->Conduct->Performance* paradigm was influenced by the *Harvard School* and has led to an extremely interventionist enforcement approach in the 1960s. Albeit toned down to some extent by the *Chicago School*, this paradigm remains a major tool of antitrust analysis; compare A. Jones/B. Sufrin, *ibid.*, 20. Compare Analysis in Chapter II.C.1. above.

457 UNCTAD, *ibid.*, 150 et sqq.

tional production can lead to additional barriers to entry for potential competitors as well as to predatory behaviour or exclusionary co-operation agreements or alliances relating to innovation which might give rise to dominance in the future[458].

However, anti-competitive practices by TNCs may entail circumstances for which domestic competition laws and domestic competition enforcement authorities are ill-equipped, and which therefore support the case for international competition rules.

(i) Abuse of international market power

Given the generally rather high market shares of TNCs, they are perhaps more likely to abuse a dominant position than "normal" competitors. In particular, trans-nationality could facilitate predatory behaviour, and especially discriminatory pricing, e.g. through the manipulation of transfer prices by intra-group sales at excessive low prices[459]. Generally, however, the same considerations relevant in the assessment of a potential abuse of domestic market power will also apply to the potential abuse of international market power.

Most TNCs have their registered business seats in developed countries with competition laws in place. Consequently, abuse of international market power with an effect on the home market will most likely be addressed by the home country's competition law. Nevertheless, the home country's enforcement authorities will only be active where the potentially abusive measure results in detrimental effects on the home country's market. Where TNCs behaviour is directed abroad and does not affect the home country's market, it will usually remain unsanctioned where the country of destination does not itself have a competition law in place. Again, developing countries in particular may lack competition laws. Yet, because the degree of concentration is prone to be high in developing countries, the consequences for the home industry may be particularly severe.

In addition, proceedings to which TNCs are a party might be especially cumbersome. Given the fact that their operations are typically located across various jurisdictions, TNCs may have certain advantages for procedures affecting multiple jurisdictions. For instance, information concerning transfer pricing will be difficult to obtain due to information transfers within the group[460]. Likewise, intra-group trade and accounting will aggravate the calculation and representations of discriminator prices for the investigating authorities[461].

---

458 UNCTAD, *ibid.*, 170 et sqq.

459 The anti-competitiveness of discriminatory pricing has been questioned, compare Chapter III.C.3.1.2.(ii) above.

460 Compare UNCTAC, *ibid.*, 158.

461 H. Wins, *ibid.*, 63.

In total, the differences with regard to the issues raised for potential abuse of international market power through TNCs as opposed to the ones raised for domestic abuse are mainly a matter of degree. Thus, besides overcoming the shortcomings identified in the foregoing chapters, no special regime for TNCs is required.

(ii) International oligopolies

For TNCs, tacit concertation might be relatively easy to sustain where co-operation among enforcement authorities is not yet established. The lack of comprehensive co-operation among domestic enforcement authorities is thus a major shortcoming of the current situation. In light of the general approval[462] of export cartels through either explicit legal exceptions or the application of the effects doctrine, a certain incentive might be created for concertation among international oligopolists[463].

(iii) Trans-national mergers

Depending on the territorial scope of merger control laws, four basic types of laws can be distinguished[464]. First, merger control laws can apply to only domestically registered entities[465]. Second, merger control laws can apply to transactions whereby foreign firms acquire domestic firms (inward foreign direct investment). Third, merger control regulations can cover acquisitions of foreign firms by domestic firm (outward foreign direct investment). Fourth, regulations can also apply to transaction purely effectuated abroad, such as mergers or acquisitions between foreign firms[466].

Merger control is an area of competition policy where states, under certain circumstances, investigate outward or even purely foreign transactions. As a basic principle, however, countries will only review such transactions where these transactions would have an effect on their domestic market[467]. The EC, for instance, has interpreted the concept of the "Community dimension" accordingly[468]. The major concern of domestic enforcement authorities in this regard

---

[462] Compare Chapter II.D.6.2. above.

[463] H. Wins, *ibid.*, 64.

[464] UNCTAD, *World Investment Report 1997*, available at: http://www.unctad.org/en/docs/WIR97_en.pdf (21.05.05), at 193.

[465] E.g. Hungary until 1997.

[466] Compare the EC Commission's interventions in *Aerospatiale-DeHavilland* [1991] OJ L334/42; [1992] CMLR M2, in Case No IV/M.877 *Boeing/McDonnell Douglas* [1997] OJ L336/16; and the decision of the CFI in Case T-102/96 *Gencor v. Commission* [1999] ECR II-753; [1999] 4 CMLR 971.

[467] Compare Federal German Cartel Office, *Guidelines on Domestic Effects of Mergers Completed Abroad*, available at: http://www.bundeskartellamt.de/wDeutsch/download/pdf/Merkblaetter/Merkblaetter_englisch/99_Inlandsauswirkung_e.pdf (21.05.05).

[468] Article 1 para. 1 of Council Regulation (EC) No 139/2004 [2004] OJ L24/1 – just like its predecessor – only refers to turnover thresholds. In addition, Recital 10 of Council Reg 139/2004 stipulates that the Community dimension is irrespective of a company's incorporation or assets within the Community.

is whether the outward investing firm acquires control of a foreign entity that would otherwise have competed in the country of the acquiring entity[469].

Thus, subject to the enactment of a merger control regime, no general lack of *application* of domestic merger regulations to situations with foreign links can be detected. Nevertheless, countries that engage in outward-directed control are likely to face situations where multiple countries are reviewing the same case. The procedural challenges have already been discussed above[470]. In addition, jurisdictional issues may arise. With regard to the individual states concerned, the results of individual merger control in one country might lead to unacceptable results for another country investigating the same transaction[471]. In particular, as merger control is directed at market structure as opposed to competitors' conduct, the implications of enforcement measures may not be easily limited to a given market. Rather, a state's individual domestic industrial policy may be seriously impaired by merger control enforcement measures set by another state. Moreover, different underlying merger control policy goals might lead to different efficiency defences and, consequently, conflicting outcomes of individual cases.

In *Gencor*[472], for instance, the EC Commission found the merger between Gencor Ltd and Lenrho Plc to be incompatible with the common market, as the sales within the platinum group metal sector in the Community would have the effect of creating a duopoly position there. In contrast, the South-African authorities would rate the merger's effect to bring about equally matched competitors as preferable to the situation of one dominant firm prevailing[473].

Consequently, merger control is arguably one of the most controversial areas of competition policy, with the highest potential for inter-jurisdictional conflict and the most distinct need for a coordinated approach. At the same time, international convergence of substantive rules is particularly unlikely in light of the differing underlying policy objectives of competition policy[474].

In addition to jurisdictional and policy conflicts, the as-is situation of domestic merger control laws may also entail welfare losses, where world wide dominant positions are being facilitated through *non-application* of domestic competition laws. For instance, a merger transaction might facilitate global oligopolistic coordination or concertation among a limited number of competitors, thereby reducing the contestability of a worldwide market[475]. There are only few cases

---

469 UNCTAD, *ibid.*, at 199.
470 Compare Chapter III.C.2.1. above.
471 UNCTAD, *ibid.*, at 200.
472 European Court of First Instance, Case T-102/96 *Gencor v. Commission* [1999] ECR II-753; [1999] 4 CMLR 971.
473 A. Jones/B. Sufrin, *ibid.*, 1060.
474 H. Hauser/R. E. Schoene, *Is There a Need for International Competition Rules?* In: 49(II/III) Aussenwirtschaft 1994, at 215.
475 UNCTAD, *ibid.*, at 201.

where competition authorities have investigated transactions that were likely to lead to a worldwide dominant position[476]. Moreover, where an enforcement authority started investigations, it would only focus on the transaction's anticompetitive effects in its own jurisdiction. Consequently, the cost and benefit analysis will not take into account possible efficiency or welfare implications at the international level[477].

In light of the above, merger control regimes should be aligned at the international level. Increased co-operation between jurisdictions so as to overcome the procedural issues is required. In addition, minimum substantive standards could improve the area coverage of domestic merger control laws. However, harmonized substantive rules appear to be politically infeasible in this sensitive area of industrial policy[478].

4. Conclusion

As illustrated above, the current situation of co-existing and un-coordinated domestic competition laws is ill-equipped to deal with international business activity. On the one hand, domestic competition authorities cannot fully protect domestic competition and competitors from offences with an international dimension. There is no complete coverage of domestic competition laws yet, and the capacities of existing competition laws may be insufficient under certain circumstances. Where a state does have a domestic competition law, its application and enforcement is *ex lege* bound to the legal territory of that state. On the other hand, states try to overcome potentially negative effects on their territory by applying the effects doctrine to situations having an international dimension, thus potentially causing inter-jurisdictional conflicts. Structural or industrial policy related considerations might bring about different conflicting outcomes if more than one state investigates the same situation. At the same time, states may decide not to apply their domestic competition rules to situations with no anti-competitive effect in their home-market and, thus, cause detrimental welfare implications for other states due to immediate negative effects of the same situation in their respective markets. Therefore, the case for international consolidation can be supported from a competition policy point of view.

[476] E.g. EC Commission, *Aerospatiale-DeHavilland* [1991] OJ L334/42; [1992] CMLR M2; European Court of First Instance, Case T-102/96 *Gencor* v. *Commission* [1999] ECR II-753; [1999] 4 CMLR 971.
[477] UNCTAD, *ibid.*, 202.
[478] H. Hauser/R. E. Schoene, *ibid.*, at 218.

D. Existing Approaches to Overcome the Identified Shortcomings

In the following, existing approaches to overcome the shortcomings identified will be discussed. From an individual competitor's perspective, the ideal approach would be total harmonization of competition laws. However, binding international convergence is clearly not the approach generally favoured by sovereign states, as they fear a loss of national sovereignty and discretionary power. Consequently, at the international level, the existing initiatives are predominantly focussing on unilateral measures on the one hand, and on co-operation among competition enforcement authorities on the other. It is only at the regional level that binding harmonized international competition rules currently exist.

1. Extraterritorial application of domestic competition law: The unilateral approach

It has already been shown that the extraterritorial application of domestic competition law or the effects doctrine has gained in prominence as a means to overcome jurisdictional limits. On the one hand, the unilateral approach can be regarded as a "robust concept"[479] allowing for national self-protection against inbound restraints launched abroad, which works quite efficiently for nations with a long-standing tradition of competition law and requires only minimal institutional regulation. On the other hand, however, the unilateral approach features serious deficiencies relating to both the efficiency and legitimacy of the application of domestic competition law abroad.

With regard to efficient protection against inbound restraints, two principal shortcomings exist[480]. First, developing countries are easy targets of anticompetitive conduct from abroad, as they either do not have a competition law in place or do not have adequate resources to enforce it. Second, extraterritorial enforcement may be inefficient due to the difficulties of obtaining evidence from abroad. With regard to efficient enforcement against outbound restraints, the most prominent issue is that national law commonly does not prohibit conduct which does not bring about detrimental effects within that nation's territory[481]. This exemption brings about a gap in a world wide competition system, which hampers global efficient competition. Moreover, it has been argued that the effects doctrine results in allocative inefficiency, as the inefficiencies result-

479 E. M. Fox, *International Antitrust and the Doha Dome,* in: 43 VA. J. INT'L. L. 911 (2003), at 916.

480 E. M. Fox, *ibid.*

481 At the same time, the regulation of conduct which primarily affects a foreign country and its consumers so as to open up these foreign markets would have to be considered illegitimate due to its disregard for the foreign nation's export or investment policy and, thus, due to its disregard of foreign sovereignty, compare E. M. Fox, *ibid.*

ing from the anticompetitive practices themselves are supplemented by the costs resulting from potential trade sanctions or other retaliation measures[482].

Extraterritorial application of domestic competition law also brings about concerns of legitimacy. To begin with, the basic concern is the illegitimate infringement of foreign sovereignty. Although it results from a wide application[483] of the principle of territoriality that a state harmed by anticompetitive conduct launched abroad is entitled to enforce its domestic law against that conduct, diplomatic conflicts may arise when the enforcing state infringes the other's sovereignty through excessive action in the course of the proceedings. Apart from intrusive enforcement action against anticompetitive conduct from the target country taking effect within the enforcing nation's territory, such infringement may in particular result from the attempt to enforce market access in the target country[484]. The individual perception of infringement may, however, differ from case to case. In addition, a lack of consensus may be perceived among nations to recognize the effects doctrine[485]. Moreover, states acknowledging this doctrine have adopted varying definitions. Certain countries such as Japan have been reluctant to apply it, whereas other states such as the United Kingdom have adopted special laws so as to defend foreign authority on their nationals[486]. Furthermore, the application of the effects doctrine may bring about jurisdictional conflicts due to different appraisal of similar situations, which may lead to political frictions[487]. The *U.S. v. IBM*[488] case or the *GE/Honeywell*[489] case may serve as illustrative examples. Moreover, the extraterritorial application of domestic competition law may be regarded as illegitimate due to the potential discrimination from a global community perspective, when a given state excludes its own nationals engaging in conduct harmful to foreign sovereigns, while attacking the same foreign sovereigns so as to ensure market access in that latter country[490]. Concerns for legitimacy may furthermore arise where the application of domestic competition law abroad conflicts with industrial policy in the target country. Consider the U.S. enforcement against the members of the *Uranium Cartel* as an example[491]. Given the lack of

[482] D. Fritz-Aßmus, *Zum Ordnungsrahmen einer internationalen Wettbewerbspolitik.* In: Fritz-Aßmus, Dieter/ Tuchtfeldt, Egon (Hrsg.): *Die Ordnung des Welthandels* (1997), at 209.

[483] S. Hobe/O. Kimminich, *Einführung in das Völkerrecht*, 97.

[484] E. M. Fox, *ibid.*, at 920.

[485] U. Immenga, *Comment: The Failure of Present Institutions and Rules to Respond to the Globalization of Competition*, in: 49 (II/III) Aussenwirtschaft 1994, 201.

[486] U. Immenga, *ibid.*, at 202, referring to the British "Blocking Statutes".

[487] U. Immenga, *ibid.*, at 202.

[488] Compare E. M. Fox, *ibid.*, citing the Assistant Attorney General's statement in the Hearing Before the Senate Comm. On the Judiciary, 97th Cong., 56-130 (1982) that after having withdrawn the U.S. monopoly case against IBM, the EC Commission's plan to order IBM to disclose certain interface changes was illegitimate.

[489] For a comprehensive case analysis compare Y. Akbar, *Grabbing Victory from the Jaws of Defeat: Can the GE/Honeywell Merger Facilitate International Antitrust Policy Co-operation?* In: 25(4) Journal of World Competition 2002, 403 et sqq.

[490] E. M. Fox, *ibid.*, 920.

[491] After underproduction of Uranium caused by a U.S. embargo, certain British, Canadian, South African, Australian and French producers were supporting mining and marketing of uranium on their territory. U.S.

international authority for extraterritorial application of competition law, such conflicts are currently solved on a national basis. However, national-only decision making can distort the resolution of such problems at the interface of competition and industrial policy[492]. These frictions are further reinforced by the threat of comparably high claims for compensation in certain states[493]. Furthermore, the extraterritorial application of domestic competition law may bring about legal uncertainties in light of public international law. For instance, applying the effects doctrine may conflict with the "principle of non-intervention"[494] on the one hand and the "acts of state doctrine"[495] on the other.

In light of the above, the author argues that the exterritorial application of domestic competition law is an imperfect approach to address anticompetitive practices with an international dimension. Domestic competition law should therefore be supplemented by inter-governmental co-operation or multilateral rules.

2. Intergovernmental co-operation

2.1. Bilateral co-operation

Bilateral co-operation understandings and agreements are the most common type of co-operation. Many of them take the bilateral agreements concluded between the European Union and the United States of America as a model[496]. Typically, therefore, the scope of these agreements is extended beyond informal communication or technical assistance[497] to additional formal obligations such as "positive comity". According to that concept, an antitrust enforcement authority of one country may refer a matter to another country's authority if a given conduct appears to have an adverse effect on the latter country[498]. Apart from the agreement between the U.S. and the EU, the agreement between the

---

nationals being confronted with price rises sued the members of this latter cartel in the United States. Albeit these nationals' governments resisted the U.S. suits, considerable political frictions did arise, as the U.S. judgments against the cartel members were perceived illegitimate abroad. Compare E. M. Fox, *ibid.*, at 918.

492 E. M. Fox, *ibid.*, at 917 et sqq.

493 For example the U.S. system of private actions with awards for considerable damages, compare H. Wins, *ibid.*, 78.

494 U. Immenga, *ibid.*

495 H. Wins, *ibid.*, 79 et sqq. Wins refers to the importance attributed to the Act-of-State Doctrine in the United States and cites the example of the dismissal of claim filed against OPEC's pricing policy in 1974, which was dismissed on the grounds that OPEC itself was based on an Act of State, and therefore not subject to review under Antitrust Law.

496 E.g. *Agreement between the European Communities and the Government of the United States of America on the application of positive comity principles in the enforcement of their competition laws*, Official Journal L 173, 18.06.1998. Another agreement was concluded in 1991.

497 A. D. Melamed, *International Cooperation in Competition Law and Policy: What Can Be Achieved at the Bilateral, Regional, and Multilateral Levels*, in: Journal of International Economic Law 1999, at 425 et sqq.

498 A. D. Melamed, *ibid.*, at 428.

U.S. and Canada may be cited as an example[499]. Alternatively, antitrust-specific mutual assistance agreement may regulate the obtaining and sharing of confidential information, based on stringent conditions of confidentiality and reciprocity[500]. Another tool for co-operation in competition matters is the conclusion of bilateral mutual legal assistant treaties (MLATs). Although not being specific to competition matters, such MLATs obligate the parties to mutual assistance in certain criminal matters by obtaining evidence in one country for the benefits of enforcement investigations initiated in another country. The United States for instance were party to approximately twenty of such agreements by 1999[501].

Although this approach is certainly helpful for some problems of international competition, and although the number of bilateral enforcement agreements has risen, there are still shortcomings.

First, the scope of bilateral agreements tends to be fragmentary and incomprehensive. For example, co-operation between the United States and the European Union is largely focussed on merger enforcement. The co-operation between the United States and the European Union is regarded as a major role model for intergovernmental co-operation by some, and has also brought about a certain degree of convergence of substantive merger laws. Nevertheless, co-operation between the U.S. and the EU in the area of cartel enforcement is considerably less developed. Consequently, the United States and the EC Commission cannot yet co-ordinate enforcement in cartel matters to the same degree as would be possible for the United States in relation to Canada[502]. Also, limitations must be discerned in the fact that by 2002, the positive comity provisions applicable between the EU and the U.S. have only been activated on a single instance. Furthermore, the sharing of confidential information such as commercially sensitive material largely depends on the consent of the companies at issue, and may anticipate effective co-operation[503].

Second, bilateral co-operation agreements are not suitable means to overcome divergent policy goals[504]. This can be illustrated by the *GE Honeywell* case, where the US DOJ has been putting much of an emphasis on consumers' interests by permitting GE/Honeywell to offer bundled services at lower prices. DG

[499] C. S. Goldman/J. F. Rill, *The Internationalization of Competition Law and the Need for Global Convergence*, available at: http://www.europe-canada.org/en/CD-Rom/pdf/BIAC.pdf (04.08.2005), p. 11.

[500] Compare the authorization under the U.S. International Antitrust Enforcement Assistance Act of 1994, available at: http://www.ftc.gov/ogc/stat2.htm (21.05.2005).

[501] A. D. Melamed, *ibid.*, at 427.

[502] L. Fullerton/C. C. Mazard, *International Antitrust Co-operation Agreements*, in: 24(3) Journal of World Competition 2001, at 417.

[503] S. Woolcock, *International Competition Policy and the World Trade Organisation, Paper for the LSE Global Dimensions/Federal Trust Forum on the 'Singapore Issues' in the WTO, March 25-27th 2003, London School of Economics*, available at: http://www.lse.ac.uk/collections/globalDimensions/tradepolicy/papers/woolcock.htm (24.02.2005).

[504] S. Woolcock, *ibid.*

Competition was arguably more apprehensive of the potential displacement of individual competitors and the potential reduction of plurality of players within the Single Market[505]. In light of the different underlying policy approaches, co-operation efforts could not prevent the resulting conflicting decisions.

Third, certain problems relating to competition enforcement may neither be solved at the national nor at the bilateral level[506]. This may be due to the geographical reach or the material grasp of a given practice. For instance, where competition policy intersects with industrial policy, the consequences of a given governmental measure relating to competition policy may result in broader industrial policy implications for Third Party states. According the measure at the bilateral measure would not change such industrial policy implications.

Fourth, bilateral co-operation agreements may be considered imperfect as their closing and individual design may not only consider mutual efficiency gains, but also to a considerable extent the individual "bargaining chips" of a given state negotiating the agreement. Thus, countries with little bargaining power may not be in the position to enter such agreements at all[507]. This applies to developing countries in particular.

Moreover, with regard to the often cited potential of capacity building through co-operation, bilateral co-operation *per definitionem* offers less potential for mutual learning and transfer of know-how than a broader forum would. In light of global markets and global competition and the resulting case for international capacity building, bilateral co-operation is not a suitable means to the integration of a wider community.

Thus, although providing a valuable forum for the coordination of enforcement efforts and for communication purposes, bilateral co-operation by itself cannot be rated a universal remedy for global competition problems.

2.2. Multilateral co-operation

Besides bilateral co-operation, various regional or other multilateral co-operation initiatives have emerged. The main differences in characteristics are *(i)* the membership being dominated by developed or developing countries, and *(ii)* the individual emphasis on either the creation of binding rules and the actual process of enforcement on the one hand or mere discussion and capacity building on the other one. The latter criterion will very much depend on the individual degree of legal integration. The more legally integrated the participating countries are, the more likely the transition from pure co-operation among

505 Y. Akbar, *Grabbing Victory from the Jaws of Defeat: Can the GE/Honeywell Merger Facilitat International Antitrust Policy Co-operation?* In: 25(4) Journal of World Competition 2002, at 415.

506 E. M. Fox, *International Antitrust and the Doha Dome,* in: 43 VA. J. INT'L. L. 911 (2003), at 917.

507 E. M. Fox, *ibid.*

the participating jurisdictions to convergence of these jurisdictions' domestic competition laws.

2.2.1. Regional initiatives

With regard to regional co-operation initiatives, the Asia Pacific Economic Co-operation (APEC) serves as an example for an informal forum of co-operation at the "lower end" of the integration scale, focussing on discussion and mutual learning[508]. More formally, there are initiatives which place a focus on the actual process of enforcement and legal or administrative assistance. This focus's emphasis rises in proportion with the existing degree of political and legal integration among the member states. Consider the European Competition Authorities (ECA) as an example, which is comprised of EEA Member States' competition enforcement authorities. Although it is an informal association, the ECA is aimed at the contribution to efficient enforcement of EC Competition law. For instance, it has set up procedures for information exchange during multi-jurisdictional merger investigations, and has agreed on revised principles on the application of Articles 4(5) and 22 of the revised EC Merger Regulation within the EEA[509].

Since the effective date of Regulation 1/2003 and the resulting parallel enforcement of Article 81 EC by both the EC Commission and national authorities, the degree of integration in competition law matters has been further reinforced. In particular, in addition to the competition regime under the EC, the European Competition Network (ECN) has lately been urged by the Commission to cooperate in a close and complementary manner[510]. Besides providing general procedural rules relating to mutual information and case allocation, an Advisory Committee consisting of national enforcement authorities has been created to discuss individual cases as well as general issues of competition law. The committee has also been vested with the authority to issue non-binding opinions[511].

S. 1501 of the North American Free Trade Agreement (NAFTA) requires the Parties to adopt or maintain measures to proscribe anti-competitive conduct. Furthermore, it commits the Parties to co-operation among enforcement authorities and to mutual assistance in national enforcement. In this regard, the Working Group on Trade and Competition established under s. 1504 of the NAFTA may be cited. Although competition provisions relating to investment and services do exist and state monopolies are being dealt with, the regime es-

508 A. D. Melamed, *ibid.*

509 For information on the ECA Working Groups, compare: http://www.oft.gov.uk/ECA/Working+groups.htm (17.05.2005).

510 Commission Notice on cooperation within the Network of Competition Authorities [Official Journal C 101 of 27.4.2004], available at: http://europa.eu.int/eur-lex/pri/en/oj/dat/2004/c_101/c_10120040427en00430053.pdf (14.05.2005).

511 Compare paras. 58 et sqq of the Commission Notice.

tablished under the NAFTA is comparably weaker than the corresponding provisions in the EC. There is also no rerence to a common "acquis"[512]. Notably, the competition provisions of the NAFTA are also not subject to the general bilateral dispute settlement provisions.

Enhanced regional co-operation must certainly be regarded as an efficient means to address shortcomings under the existing unilateral approaches. Although "regional" cannot generally be equalled to geographical vicinity[513], regional initiatives typically come about through factors which appear to facilitate co-operation, such as historical, economical, political or cultural proximity. At least where such proximity is converted into preferential trade agreements qualifying as a Regional Trade Agreement under Article XXIV of the GATT[514] with its "substantially all the trade" requirement, one would additionally expect that a certain alignment in competition matters would already form part of this underlying agreement. Assuming that trade and competition policy are complementary[515], a maximum co-operation in competition matters as well as a certain degree of convergence would be the logical consequence and an efficient means to address regional competition issues as a supplement to any existing regional competition rules. As will be further elaborated below, various regional initiatives[516] have indeed developed some convergence of competition rules, the European Union being the prime example.

Nevertheless, with regard to their external relations, regional co-operation initiatives do not even aim at overcoming the shortcomings arising from international competition. External effects harmful to other states, international procedural assistance or international capacity building remain non-addressed. Thus, in light of global product markets and, consequently, restrictive practices or mergers with an international dimension, regional co-operation will always have to be supplemented by additional bilateral or multilateral initiatives[517]. Regional co-operation must therefore be rated an efficient tool to overcome shortcomings *inter partes* within a geography or among member states of a Re-

---

512 S. Woolcock, *ibid.*

513 P. Hilpold, *International Competition Law and Regional Trade Agreements,* in: 2(3) Manchester Journal of International Economic Law 2005, 88.

514 Article XXIV of the GATT requires in particular that the respective duties and other restrictive regulations be eliminated with respect to "substantially all the trade" between the countries at issue, compare para 8 lit (a) and (b) of Article XXIV of the GATT.

515 For more details, compare Chapter IV.A.

516 Consider Chapter 15 of the *NAFTA* Agreement as an example. Also, under the *Free Trade Agreement for the Americas (FTAA),* certain co-operation mechanisms have been established, focusing also on capacity building and technical assistance. Recently, however, a further step toward convergence was produced by the third draft chapter of the FAA on competition. According to this draft, the Parties are required to adopt or maintain competition law regimes and certain minimum standards as well as enforcement authorities, compare Article 6 of the 3rd Draft, available at: http://www.ftaa-alca.org/FTAADraft03/ChapterXIX_e.asp (09.08.2005).

517 This is supported by the example of the European Union, which has already concluded additional bilateral co-operation agreements with several states, compare the table published by the EC Directorate General Competition, available at: http://europa.eu.int/comm/competition/international/bilateral/bilateral.html (26.06.2005).

gional Trade Agreement. At the same time, regional co-operation is at best a selective method to overcome shortcomings resulting from international restrictive practices.

2.2.2. *International initiatives*

At the international level, several initiatives have emerged. The OECD, for example, has been an important factor for capacity building in international competition policy through co-operation but also substantive work. In particular, the OECD Council has adopted various non-binding recommendations on competition law and policy. As early as in 1967, a first recommendation on co-operation between the member countries was issued, by which countries were encouraged to engage in bilateral or plurilateral negotiations[518]. Focussing also on the impact of competition policy on international trade, this recommendation was revised in 1995 and now also covers the treatment of mergers. It addresses mutual notification by Member States, exchange of information, co-ordination of action and consultation as well as conciliation mechanisms where proceedings bear implications for other Member States[519]. Where accommodation cannot be achieved, the Competition Law and Policy Committee is to act as a conciliator towards the achievement of a settlement[520]. Thus, the OECD has introduced certain elements of positive comity, although they are non-binding and lack a certain degree of effectiveness. In particular, only selected Member States have made use of the conciliation provisions or engaged in notification on a regular basis[521]. However, the OECD provisions have promoted transparency and the development of international dialogue in competition policy matters. In particular, the OECD hosts the Global Forum on Competition on an annual basis, which provides an important forum of communication for Member States in competition policy matters. Most recently, the participation of Non-Members in the Forum and also in the Competition Committee has been emphasized[522], which must certainly be rated a positive development in light of the Forum's objective of extended international dialogue. Nevertheless, the efforts undertaken by the OECD have been criticized in light of an alleged

518 OECD, *Recommendation of the Council concerning Co-operation between Member Countries on Restrictive Business Practices affecting International Trade*, C(67)53(Final), October 10, 1967.

519 OECD, *Recommendation of the Council concerning Co-operation between Member Countries on Anticompetitive Practices affecting International Trade*, C(95)130/FINAL, available at: http://webdomino1.oecd.org/horizontal/oecdacts.nsf/Display/C0FF10F530824A7BC12570830076B27A?OpenDocument (14.08.2005).

520 Compare para. 8 of the OECD's revised *Recommendation of the Council concerning Co-operation between Member Countries on Anticompetitive Practices affecting International Trade*, 27.7.1995, ibid.

521 Thus, while the US and the European Union were major users of the notification provisions, other Member States have been rather reluctant in this regard, compare S. Woolcock, *International Competition Policy and the World Trade Organisation, Paper for the LSE Global Dimensions/Federal Trust Forum on the 'Singapore Issues' in the WTO, March 25-27th 2003, London School of Economics*, available at: http://www.lse.ac.uk/collections/globalDimensions/tradepolicy/papers/woolcock.htm (24.02.2005).

522 Compare the Agenda for the *Global Competition Forum 2006*, available at: http://www.oecd.org/document/60/0,2340,en_2649_34715_2732220_1_1_1_1,00.html (12.08.2005).

lack of financial backbone[523]. In addition, the fact that membership to the OECD must be regarded as being limited to developed countries stands in vast contrast to the Global Forum on Competition's objective of global dialogue[524].

In contrast to the OECD, the United Nations Conference on Trade and Development (UNCTAD) has a very diverse membership and has been deployed by developing countries to forward their specific concerns with regard to international competition policy. In 1980, the UNCTAD adopted the UN Set of Multilaterally Agreed Equitable Principles and Rules for the Control of Restrictive Business Practices[525], which was last reviewed and reaffirmed in 2000[526]. It contains non-binding guidelines for private firms as well as states, addressing *inter alia* anti-competitive conduct, governmental co-operation, technical assistance, international capacity building and preferential or differential treatment for developing countries. Lately, further emphasis is being put on the possibility of formulating a model agreement on co-operation in competition law matters[527]. Although the UN Set does contain few concrete provisions and does not impose any binding obligations on Member States[528], it can nevertheless be regarded as a major catalyst and facilitator of intergovernmental co-operation in competition policy matters through reciprocal knowledge exchange. Developing countries in particular have benefited from special training and advice provided by UNCTAD[529]. For instance, UNCTAD has also produced a Model Law, which provides a valuable basis for new adoptions[530].

Furthermore, the International Competition Network (ICN) must be mentioned. Based on the recommendations of the 2000 Report of the International Competition Policy Advisory Committee (ICPAC)[531], the ICN is an informal network of enforcement authorities from both developed and developing countries focussed very much on practical issues of the actual enforcement process itself

[523] Compare U. Böge, *Konvergenz kartellrechtlicher Normen und deren Anwendung auf globale Sachverhalte*, in: 10 Wirtschaft und Wettbewerb 2001, 927.

[524] A list of the thirty OECD Member States can be obtained from http://www.oecd.org/document/58/0,2340,en_2649_201185_1889402_1_1_1_1,00.html (24.08.2005).

[525] *UN Set of Multilaterally Agreed Equitable Principles and Rules for the Control of Restrictive Business Practices*, UN General Assembly, Resolution 35/63 (December 5, 1980), available at: http://r0.unctad.org/en/subsites/cpolicy/docs/CPSet/cpsetp4.htm (12.08.205).

[526] United Nations Conferences to Review All Aspects of the Set, *Fourth Review Conference* (25-29 September 2000), resolution (TD/RBP/CONF.5/15 of 4 October 2000), available at: http://www.unctad.org/en/docs/tdrbpconf5d15.en.pdf (12.08.2005).

[527] P. Brusick, *UNCTAD's role in promoting Multilateral Co-operation on Competition Law and Policy*, in: 24(1) Journal of World Competition 2001, 25 et sqq.

[528] S. Woolcock, *ibid.*, 6.

[529] Compare P. Brusick, *ibid.*, 28 et sqq.

[530] UNCTAD, *Model Law on Competition* (2004), TD/B/RBP/CONF.5/7/Rev.2, available at: http://r0.unctad.org/en/subsites/cpolicy/docs/Modelaw04.pdf (13.09.2005).

[531] International Competition Policy Advisory Committee to the Attorney General and Assistant Attorney General for Antitrust, *Final Report 2000 (ICPAC-Report)*, available at: http://www.usdoj.gov/atr/icpac/forward.pdf (24.09.2005).

through the fostering of procedural and also substantive convergence[532]. Particular attention has been given to mergers in a multi-jurisdictional context, where the need for co-operation was perceived to be essential. To that end, a merger working group has been established, focussing on *(i)* merger notification and review procedures, *(ii)* investigative techniques of merger review and *(iii)* merger review analysis[533]. Given the ICN's complementary role to other international organizations dealing with international competition policy, its sole focus on competition policy and its practical and project oriented approach, the ICN must certainly be regarded a promising forum. Nevertheless, potential shortcomings can be identified. First, comparable to the OECD, the ICN appears to be dominated by developed countries' interests[534]. This impression is supported by the requirement to have an adopted competition law in place in order to become a member to the ICN in the first place[535]. Developing countries in the process of adoption are thereby excluded. Second, although the lack of institutional framework can facilitate dialogue, it deprives the recommendations of some of their effectiveness[536]. Third, a considerable proportion of the ICN's work pertains to the development of substantial convergence[537]. However, the ICN's organizational structure which lacks "institutionalism" and the non-binding nature of its recommendations stand in vast contrast to that goal.

2.3. Interim summary

Inter-governmental co-operation must certainly be regarded as one valuable means to address the international dimension of competition policy and enforcement in a global market place. The actual value of inter-governmental co-operation will, however, depend on the degree of legal integration between the co-operating parties on the one hand; the value of co-operation rising with the degree of legal integration. On the other hand, the value of co-operation will be perceived differently by individual market participants as opposed to state actors.

---

532 *Memorandum on the Establishment and Operation of the International Competition Network*, available at: http://www.internationalcompetitionnetwork.org/mou.pdf (13.08.2005).

533 Compare the *Recommended Practices for Merger Notification and Review Procedures* as an example, which are available at: http://www.internationalcompetitionnetwork.org/mnprecpractices.pdf (13.09.2005). *Inter alia*, with a view to facilitating convergence, this set addresses *(i)* sufficient nexus between the transaction's effects and the reviewing jurisdiction; *(ii)* clear and objective notification thresholds; *(iii)* flexibility in the timing of merger notification; *(iv)* merger review periods; *(v)* requirements for initial notification; *(vi)* conduct of merger investigations; *(vii)* procedural fairness; *(viii)* transparency; *(ix)* confidentiality; *(x)* interagency coordination; *(xi)* remedies; *(xii)* competition agency powers; and *(xiii)* review of merger control provisions.

534 M. Todino, *International Competition Network. The State of Play after Naples*, in: 26(2) Journal of World Competition 2003, 283 et sqq.

535 Memorandum on the Establishment and Operation of the International Competition Network, *ibid.*

536 M. Todino, *ibid.*

537 For instance, substantive tests for merger review have been a major aspect in the discussion, compare M. Todino, *ibid.*, at 296 at sqq.

Generally speaking, co-operation primarily aims to overcome the "symptoms" of the current friction due to co-existing diverse domestic competition laws and enforcement regimes, but not to eliminate the underlying causes. For an individual competitor seeking to realise a transaction affecting several jurisdictions, co-operation will - without underlying convergence of substantive laws - ease the disadvantages and risks implied by multi-filings, divergent legal requirements and extraterritorial application of domestic laws where the states at issue adhere to a regime of positive comity, and achieve little else. Different from "mere" negative comity according to which states are to restrict the application of their domestic laws in the case of colliding foreign interests[538], states are less likely to apply their domestic competition law to situations taking place abroad under a system of Positive Comity. Rather, states will rely on other states to enforce the other states' respective domestic laws if so requested[539]. However, the reach of co-operation agreements and thus Positive Comity is limited by the fact that a request to enforce foreign competition law is generally not binding for the state receiving that request, and that such a request does not transfer any sovereign power of disposition[540]. Moreover, Positive Comity does not resolve the problem of deliberate exemptions such as export cartels[541]. In addition, the majority of co-operation agreements are bilateral ones. Furthermore, even if multilateral co-operation led to a comprehensive network of positive comity and to an extended coverage of domestic competition laws due to capacity building, co-operation would not necessarily entail convergence of substantive rules. Therefore, from an individual competitor's perspective, co-operation as opposed to convergence will only provide a sub-optimal and limited remedy, as international transactions or proceedings nevertheless entail increased compliance costs and legal uncertainty.

In comparison, from an individual state's perspective, inter-governmental co-operation appears to be a preferred method to overcome international competition policy issues as this method is the one least restrictive of domestic jurisdiction and national sovereignty[542]. However, co-operation commitments generally do not prevent states from extraterritorially applying their domestic law to situations taking effect in another state. Thus, there is still potential for conflict due to domestic exemptions or unilateral measures. Nevertheless, co-operation does provide a discussion forum and certainly bears a positive influence on diplomacy in competition law matters. However, in order for co-operation to work efficiently it is necessary that the states or jurisdictions at issue have a

[538] U. Immenga, *Comment: The Failure of Present Institutions and Rules to Respond to the Globalization of Competition*, in: 49 (II/III) Aussenwirtschaft 1994, 203. The GE/Honeywell Case can be cited as one example for the consequences of the disregard of Negative Comity obligations.

[539] H. Wins, *ibid.*, 87.

[540] H. Wins, *ibid.*, 88.

[541] H. Wins, *ibid.*

[542] U. Immenga, *ibid.*

common understanding and perception of the anti-competitiveness of a restraint and attach similar priority to enforcement in that case[543].

A "horizontal" approach to international competition issues is based on the assumption that such issues can be best solved at the national and nation-to-nation level, i.e. by unilateralism and bilateral or regional co-operation[544]. The horizontal approach is particularly relevant when the states at issue share common aspects in their substantive approaches or when they are legally integrated. Taking the European Union as an example which has adopted binding competition rules and Community jurisdiction for situations with a community dimension, co-operation could certainly be regarded an efficient means even before Regulation 1/2003. However, where nations do not have well-resourced enforcement agencies, co-operation will bring about neither efficient results nor any incentives for binding commitments for the parties involved. Therefore, co-operation in terms of administrative assistance may be helpful for developed countries, but it is not so helpful for developing countries with poor resources or little bargaining power. This argument is supported by the current member structure of the existing co-operation initiatives, which either are largely comprised by industrialized states at a similar stage of economic development, or comprise a broader membership but focus on capacity building and discussion rather than a straightforward obligation to mutual administrative assistance. Thus, from an "internationalist's"[545] perspective, the prevailing system of co-operation initiatives can be regarded as a mere starting point meriting further development.

3. Convergence of Domestic Competition Laws

The term "convergence" can have several meanings, ranging from procedural alignment to some "co-ordination" of minimum requirements to total harmonization of substantive laws. For an individual market participant, substantive convergence in terms of total procedural and substantive harmonization appears to be the preferred approach, as it would minimize the costs of legal advice and facilitate compliance in multiple jurisdictions[546]. From that perspective, further simplification could be achieved where there was only a single authority to enforce competition law.

From a state's perspective, the preferred approach is to keep as much sovereignty in competition law matters as possible. Competition policy is a sensitive policy area where economical rationales are combined with additional specific

---

543 Compare E. Fox, *International Antitrust and the Doha Dome,* in: 43 VA.J.INT'L L. 2003, 921.

544 E. Fox, *ibid.*, 912.

545 E. Fox, *ibid.*, 912.

546 Compare C. S. Goldman/J. F. Rill, *The Internationalization of Competition Law and the Need for Global Convergence,* available at: http://www.europe-canada.org/en/CD-Rom/pdf/BIAC.pdf (15.09.2005).

public policy goals[547]. Thus, the individual policy goals vary to a considerable extent, and states are reluctant to cede any sovereignty in that area. Therefore, it is difficult to perceive of an appropriate international authority that could impose binding convergent procedural and substantive competition rules. This is supported by the fact that enforcement of competition law requires a distinct degree of discretion and judgement. For instance, the majority of cases involve the application of discretion and not the assumption of *per se* violations. Thus, at the international level, the viability of harmonized rules must be questioned[548]. Furthermore, there are considerably divergent interests concerning competition policy among industrialized countries on the one hand and developing countries on the other. From a "pure" competition policy perspective, therefore, material international convergence of substantive competition laws is a political illusion that could conceivably be considered a threat from an individual domestic competition policy maker's point of view. In short, "one size does not fit all"[549] unless it is forming part of a general process of "deep integration" in terms of the attempt to adopt a common regulatory regime[550].

Thus, while binding competition rules at the multilateral level have been discussed in the context of international trade policy, and although multilateral competition rules do exist in the context of the WTO Agreement today, they are fragmentary and lack a systemic approach[551]. Rather, empirical evidence shows that the existing examples of sophisticated multilateral convergent competition laws are integrated in what could generally be referred to as "regional integration zones"[552].

There are several approaches to classify what has generally been referred to as "regionalism". Regionalism is typically incentivized by economic rationales supplemented by an existing higher degree of integration in terms of economical, political, institutional and cultural similarities. Potential economic gains and these similarities is what may justify a limitation of national sovereignty through regional alignment. Typically, sorted by increasing degree of scope and intensity of the underlying legal integration, the possible approaches are Free

---

547 Compare Chapter II.C. abvove.

548 B. Hoekman/P. C. Mavroidis, *Economic Development, Competition Policy and the World Trade Organization*, in: 3(1) Journal of World Trade 2003, at 6.

549 WTO, Working Group on the Interaction Between Trade and Competition Policy to the General Council, *Report 2000*, WT/WGTCP/4, 30 November 2000 (00-5169), available at: http://www.wto.org/english/tratop_e/comp_e/wgtcp4.doc (22.03.2003), at para. 28.

550 B. Hoekman, *Free Trade and Deep Integration. Antidumping and Antitrust in Regional Trade Agreements*, World Bank Policy Research Paper 1950 (July 1998), available at: http://wdsbeta.worldbank.org/external/default/WDSContentServer/IW3P/IB/1998/07/01/000009265_39809 28162543/Rendered/PDF/multi0page.pdf (27.09.2005). Hoekman opposes "deep integration" as the attempt to deal with "behind the border policies" as opposed to "shallow integration", which focuses on the elimination of "at the border measures" or the abolition of discrimination against foreign competitors so as to ensure market access for importers. The GATT has originally focused on "shallow integration".

551 See Chapter IV.C.1. below.

552 Compare P. Hilpold, *Regional Integration According to Article XXIV GATT – Between Law and Politics*, in: 7 Max Planck UNYB 2003, at 224.

Trade Areas, Customs Unions, Common Markets and Monetary Unions[553]. Many of these Regional Trading Agreements are only aimed at the achievement of "shallow integration" through abolition of at-the-border measures and granting national treatment to imported products so as to eliminate discrimination. Shallow integration can also extend to factors in production such as labour and capital. "Deep integration" envisages the abolition of contingent protection through governmental action to reduce the market-segmenting effects of differences in domestic regulatory regimes regarding products, producers, production processes but also natural persons[554]. Deep integration will require either a system of mutual recognition or harmonization in certain policy areas.

Thus, convergence of competition policy can be one aspect of deep integration. The inclusion of competition policy in Regional Trade Agreements may be motivated by the potential welfare or distribution gains that can be achieved through coordination of competition law regimes, while the institutional framework of a Regional Trading Agreement allows reaping these benefits. Alternatively, it may be argued that the benefits of trade liberalization cannot fully be achieved without common competition law regimes[555]. The individual approaches to such integration of competition policy in Regional Trade Agreements vary.

Arguably, the European Union is a *sui generis* example for a particularly highly integrated Regional Trade Agreement. It is unique in that it involves the complete liberalization of trade in goods, services, labour and capital. Furthermore, competition policy has been attributed a major role for the creation of the Single Market and certain policy goals[556], such as the protection of SMEs or the creation of "equal competitive opportunities"[557]. The European Union has imposed supranational competition rules for anti-competitive practices affecting trade between Member States with supranational enforcement by Community bodies. The individual rules as well as the existing co-operation mechanisms have already been discussed in detail above. Notably, the European Union has not formally imposed any obligation to harmonize domestic competition laws despite being highly legally integrated and despite regarding competition policy as one major aspect for the achievement of the Single Market[558] . Still, the current draft of a European Constitution foresees the exclusive competency of the European Union in competition matters affecting the Common Market[559], which underlines its importance from an institutional point of view as well.

---

553 For a comprehensive classification of these forms compare P. Hilpold, *ibid.*, 224 et sqq.
554 B. Hoekman, *ibid.*, 4 et sqq.
555 B. Hoekman, *ibid.*, 5 et sqq.
556 For a brief summary of policy goals pursued so far compare Chapter II.C. above.
557 B. Hoekman, *ibid.*, at 15.
558 B. Hoekman, *ibid.*
559 *Treaty Establishing a Constitution for Europe*, Article I-13, available at: http://europa.eu.int/constitution/en/lstoc1_en.htm (14.09.2005).

The approach adopted in the EEA has equally been described above[560]. It is worth noting the entire "Acquis" of the European Union in competition policy matters is applied to all EFTA members. However, although the EFTA Members have accepted a common set of competition law, they have not accepted a supranational jurisdiction of the EC Commission. Rather, an EFTA Surveillance Body has been established. Note, however, that the competition provisions of the EEA have accommodated different national competition jurisdictions within a single market, as one and the same law is applied by two implementing authorities, namely the EC Commission and the EFTA Surveillance Body[561]. Markedly, the EEA is not a Customs Union, but a Free Trade Agreement. A common trade policy with regard to Third Parties is therefore not required *per se*. Consequently, from a legal point of view, the EEA is clearly less integrated than the European Union. Therefore, the EEA's approach to competition appears to be clearly motivated by its effective proximity to EC competition policy due to congruent membership.

Another highly integrated and interesting example for competition provisions in a Regional Trade Agreement is the Australia-New Zealand Closer Economic Relations Trade Agreement (ANZCERTA). Its Article 12(1)(a) requires the Members to "examine the scope for taking action to harmonize requirements relating to restrictive trade practices". Indeed, New Zealand has harmonized its competition law with that of Australia[562], and both states are applying their domestic competition laws in parallel to each other. Arguably, the quest to realize free trade in a single market comparable to the European Common Market was the motivation behind this harmonization approach[563]. This is supported by the fact that ANZCERTA has adopted free movement of labor and has achieved a considerable liberalization of the trade in services.

As illustrated above, competition policy is also addressed in the North American Free Trade Agreement (NAFTA) albeit in a less comprehensive approach. S.1501 merely commits the Parties to adopt and *maintain* measures to proscribe anti-competitive private business conduct and to take appropriate action in this regard[564]. S.1501 also commits the Parties to co-operation in enforcement. Notably, however, neither Party may have recourse to NAFTA dispute settlement in competition matters[565]. Thus, from a legal point of view, convergence of the Parties' competition regimes is clearly less pronounced than in the other examples. Although trade and investment have undergone substantial liberalization

---

[560] Compare Chapter IV.D.2.2..

[561] S. Woolcock, *ibid.*, Section 4.

[562] B. Hoekman, *ibid.*, at 21 et sqq.

[563] B. Hoekman, *ibid.*, at 23.

[564] Thus, Mexico was obliged to adopt a comprehensive competition law which it did not have before accession to NAFTA.

[565] Compare M. J. Trebilcock/R. Howse, *The Regulation of International Trade*[3] (2005), at 595.

and despite the efforts undertaken by Canada[566], NAFTA apparently does not attempt to apply common competition rules to intra-NAFTA trade. This may be ascribed to the underlying material differences between the respective approaches to substantive competition law and enforcement of the US and Canada[567].

In light of the above, the author concludes that Regional Trade Agreements provide significant potential for convergence in competition policy and legal instruments. However, regional integration initiatives come about through the interaction between both economic and political rationales[568]. Thus, the divergent approaches among Regional Trade Agreements to competition policy show that even at the regional level, convergence is impeded by differences in individual domestic legal regimes and policy goals. Convergence in competition policy will, therefore, always imply a trade-off between potential welfare gains associated with such convergence against the potential costs and risks entailed through systemic change and policy concessions thereby required for an individual state.

It can also be concluded from the above that the higher the degree of economic and institutional integration prevailing in a Regional Trade Agreement, the more importance is attributed to some alignment of competition policy. Yet, states are still very reluctant to advance substantive convergence in competition policy. Rather, convergence must be seen as the result of a trade-off on a case-to-case basis. This is even more true for a potential cessation of national jurisdiction to a supranational authority. Consider the fact that the European Union is the only example of a Regional Trade Agreement with a supranational enforcement authority enforcing supranational competition provision. Thus, although there are several examples of Regional Trade Agreements in the context of which some alignment has been considered beneficial if not required for the attainment of the specific goals pursued by that regional initiative, total harmonization or a complete cessation of national jurisdiction and enforcement by a supranational body must certainly be regarded as the exception to the rule.

In sum, regional experience shows that convergence of competition policy and legal instruments is possible and potentially bears positive welfare implications at the international level. At the same time, it must be acknowledged that the multifaceted examples for competition provisions within Regional Trading Agreements by their very nature may not be simply transposed to the multilateral level. Without a specific incentive to cede national sovereignty in competition policy matters, individual states will be unlikely to agree to such cessation in order to bring about further convergence in competition laws.

566 In particular, Canada was seeking common disciplines for competition policy in order to have them replace anti-dumping and countervailing duties within NAFTA, compare S. Woolcock, *ibid.*, Section 4.

567 B. Hoekman, *ibid.*, at 24.

568 Compare P. Hilpold, *Regional Integration According to Article XXIV GATT – Between Law and Politics*, in: 7 Max Planck Yearbook of United Nations Law 2003, 222 et sqq.

E. Conclusion

It has been demonstrated that the current approach of co-existing divergent domestic competition laws is fragmentary and imperfect and may imply negative welfare implications, in particular for developing countries. Currently, industrialized states predominantly rely on the extra-territorial application of their domestic competition laws or bilateral co-operation agreements. Although convergence has partly proven successful at the regional level, a potential case for convergence at the international level is multifaceted and complex from a competition policy perspective.

Convergence can have several meanings from procedural alignment with co-operative elements to some co-ordination of minimum requirements to total substantive harmonization. From an individual competitor's perspective, the current situation is time-consuming and expensive in terms of resources, and certainly merits improvements with regard to the legal uncertainty prevailing. From the perspective of an individual state, the as-is situation of extra-territorial application combined with some inter-governmental co-operation may be working quite well where the state is an industrialized and well-resourced developed country. If the state is not a developed one, that case might not be so clear. Governmental interests in competition policy matters are diverse and complex. Outside the ambit of Regional Trading Agreements, mutual consent on convergent competition policy is a political illusion unless there is a supranational incentive for further convergence.

So is there such a supranational incentive? The goals pursued by international trade policy and the WTO Agreement in particular might provide an answer to that question. In the following, therefore, the case for additional international competition rules shall be discussed from a trade policy perspective.

IV. The Case for International Competition Rules from a Trade Policy Perspective

A. The Complementary Nature of Trade and Competition Policy

Competition laws aim at the promotion of free competition. For some, this already suggests the importance of competition laws to international trade[569]. On closer examination, trade and competition policy intersect when anticompetitive restraints hamper the ability of potential competitors to compete in foreign markets. Such restraints may result from the behaviour of firms, governments or a combination of these two.

When private parties are, for example, permitted by the national legislator to restrain trade between states through anti-competitive price-fixing or market-sharing agreements, such practices can in effect substitute governmental barriers to trade that the international trading regime intends to limit[570]. Vice versa, where the international trading regime allows for a departure from the principles of free trade, for instance by tolerating inefficient producers to be protected from free competition, the policy goals of national competition or antitrust law may be frustrated[571].

Thus, the interaction between competition and trade policies has been internationally recognized as early as in the 1920s[572]. From that point, it was argued repeatedly that[573] restrictive business practices could bear a significant influence on the functioning of international markets and consequently, that international trade policy should be concerned with such practices. At the same time, trade policy measures resulting in barriers to international trade might detriment domestic market structures by diminishing competition.

Nevertheless, a majority has left anticompetitive practices to the field of national competition law. This is why the nine articles in the draft ITO Charter which dealt with restrictive business practices were never adopted in the GATT. In light of the reduction of formal governmental barriers to trade, however, attendance of "trade advocates" has shifted from traditional "at-the-border"-measures to internal measures possibly affecting international trade[574]. Anti-competitive practices can constitute such internal measures. In particular,

569 Jackson/Davey/Sykes, *ibid.*, 1110.

570 Jackson/Davey/Sykes, *ibid.*, have pointed out that these considerations must be recognized as a main aspect with regard to the purpose of the competition rules established by the EC Treaty, compare the early case law of the ECJ, e.g. Cases 56&58/64 *Consten & Grundig v Commission* [1966] ECR 299.

571 Jackson/Davey/Sykes, *ibid.*

572 For instance, the League of Nations has identified international cartels as "an enemy of world trade", see E. Iacobucci, *The Interdependence of Trade and Competition Policies*, in 21(2) Journal of World Competition 1997, at 5.

573 Compare OECD, *Competition and Trade Policies: Their Interaction* 87, 112-13 (1984).

574 Compare *ICPAC Report 2000*, Executive Summary, available at: http://www.usdoj.gov/atr/icpac/execsummary.htm (01.10.2004), at 24.

it has been argued that there is substantial evidence that the international marketplace is more and more hindered by private practices or transactions, which come neither under international trade rules nor under national competition laws[575]. In the following, therefore, the author shall first explore the relationship between competition and trade policy in order to establish as to whether there is a need to supplement the rules regulating the international trading regime by competition rules from a trade policy point of view. To that end, the author shall compare the underlying policy objectives as well as the target groups addressed, and consider possible intersections or contradictions.

1. Objectives of competition policy

First and most notably, competition law has traditionally been a set of rules with a domestic focus, primarily dealing with the market behaviour of private corporate and business entities operating on national or domestic markets, coming about "within the border"[576].

Moreover, as discussed above, competition laws are usually based on the premise that while the goal of free market behaviour is generally desirable, some interference in the market is necessary to maintain and nourish the competitive pressures and to promote competition amongst producers[577]. The aims of competition policy are determined by the individual national appreciation of three basic factors, which are *(i)* economic considerations, *(ii)* political considerations, and *(iii)* institutional aspects.

The basic economic goal behind these considerations is the assumption that the maximal welfare gain by the most efficient allocation of resources can be achieved through the maintenance and promotion of free competition. By curtailing and steering private market power, competition law aims to protect consumer interests from firms engaging in anti-competitive conduct by raising the prices of their products above the competitive price level[578].

As illustrated above[579], competition law may also be used to implement other policy aims. For instance, the European Union has traditionally used competition law as a means to realize the creation of the Single Market. For purely integrationist motives, the EC competition law instruments have been applied by the European authorities so as to foster the protection of individual competitors and, in particular, small and medium sized businesses. Moreover, public policy

575 For many, compare J. Epstein, *The Other Side of Harmony: Can Trade and Competition Laws Work Together in the International Marketplace?* 17 American University International Law Review 2002, 345 (citing the ICPAC Report 2000, 211-226).

576 A. D. Mitchell, *ibid.*

577 Compare A. D. Mitchell, *Broadening the Vision of Trade Liberalisation. International Competition Law and the WTO,* in 24(3) Journal of World Competition 2001, 345.

578 A. D. Mitchell, *ibid.* The instruments typically used for that purpose have been discussed in Chapter II.D.

579 Compare Chapter II.C.2.

considerations have borne a considerable influence on competition policy[580]. For example, Article 81 EC case law has admitted considerations relating to employment policy, industrial policy or environmental policy as well as to factors related to consumer health and safety[581]. Moreover, competition policy will depend on the particular type of enforcement authority a country establishes. Competition policy can be enforced by either administrative bodies or courts. Depending on its type, an enforcement authority will typically be equipped with a certain amount of discretion by the legislator. The ultimate amount of discretion afforded may, however, bear a considerable influence on the actual decision-taking process, the factors considered within that process and the remedies available[582].

2. *Objectives of international trade policy*

International trade policy has been pursued in view of trade liberalisation. Trade liberalisation refers to the process of facilitating and increasing trade in goods, services, technology, ideas and knowledge between two or more states[583]. However, the economic and political case for international trade liberalisation has always been controversial[584].

The school of mercantilism in the 17th and 18th century argued for close government regulation of international trade in order to *(i)* maintain a favourable balance of trade through aggressive export but restrictive import policies, and *(ii)* promote the production of raw materials in the home country due to autarky and employment considerations[585]. These considerations were based on the concern that international trade might entail an inadequate supply of means of payment due to a balance of payment deficit. Moreover, in light of the colonization efforts then prevailing, it has been argued that a transfer of *specie* abroad might be unwise from a political point of view[586].

In 1752, *David Hume* was the first to demonstrate that international trade was prone to maintain equilibrium in the balance of payments. He argued that a surplus currency would entail a rise in domestic prices with regard to prices of foreign commodities, while a shortage of currency would attract foreign currency through a fall of domestic prices. Subsequently, *Adam Smith* in the Wealth of Nations (1776) argued that the case for specialization in domestic economic

---

580 See G. Monti, *Article 81 and Public Policy*, 39(5) Common Market Law Review 2002, 1057 et sqq.

581 Compare the decisions in *Metro I* [1977] ECR 1875, *DSD* [2001] OJ L319/1, *Asahi* [1994] OJ L354/87, see comments under II.C. above.

582 Compare Chapter II.C.3.

583 A. D. Mitchell, *ibid.*

584 The most commonly cited counterarguments have been the alleged negative influence on wages and employment, on national security and self sufficiency, on social policy and cultural diversity, compare. M. J. Trebilcock, *The Regulation of International Trade* (2002), 12 et sqq; Jackson/Davey/Sykes, *ibid.* 18 et sqq.

585 See M. J. Trebilcock, *The Regulation of International Trade* (2002), 2 et sqq.

586 This concern also explains the colonization efforts

activities likewise applied to specialization in international trade. He concluded that unilateral trade liberalisation would be an advantageous trade policy for a state if other states have absolute advantages with regard to particular products or services[587].

Subsequently, in 1817, *David Ricardo* formulated his theory, which has been referred to as the "Theory of Comparative Advantage"[588]. It is based on the assumption that a state should specialize in the production and exportation of the goods in which it is most efficient, and, thus, enjoys the greatest advantage in comparison to other states, and should import goods in which its comparative disadvantage is most pronounced. That way, all states would benefit as they could use their resources more efficiently. Although partly reformulated and refined[589], the Theory of Comparative Advantage still constitutes the main economic rationale for the proponents of international trade liberalisation today. Thus, the major economic rationale behind trade liberalisation is that by focusing its production on the goods and services where a state has a comparative advantage, the global output will increase, which entails global welfare implications for consumers and also efficiency gains.[590] To that end, international trade laws also aims at the promotion of open ("contestable") markets und undistorted competition.

The competitiveness of a given state in international trade will be determined by natural[591] and financial production factor endowments as well as production costs. Yet, a state's individual approach to legal and economic regulation can be viewed as "created factor endowments" which will affect that state's competi-

---

587 For a comprehensive summary see, M. J. Trebilcock, *ibid.*, or J. H. Jackson/W. J. Davey/A. O. Sykes, *Legal Problems of International Economic Relations* (2002), 7 et sqq.

588 *David Ricardo* used a simple arithmetic example to demonstrate his theory: His calculation was based on the assumption that country A could produce a given quantity of cloth with the labour of 100 men, and another given quantity of wine with 120 men. Country B, in turn, could produce the same quantity of cloth with 90 men, and wine with 80 men. Although B enjoys an absolute advantage over A, *Ricardo* argued that trade was still mutually advantageous to both countries. This was due to the fact that where A exported the cloth produced by 100 men to B in exchange to wine produced by 80 men in B, A imported wine that would have required the labour of 120 men in A. At the same time, B would gain by its 80 men's labour cloth that would have taken 90 of its men to produce. Consequently, both countries were able to take advantage of the trade. For a comprehensive analysis, see J. H. Jackson/W. J. Davey/A. O. Sykes, *Legal Problems of International Economic Relations* (2002), 7 et sqq.

589 For instance, *Ricardo*'s theory was based on the assumption of constant costs at all levels of production. Later, account was taken of increasing opportunity costs, which has been formulated in the *Factor Proportions Hypothesis* or *Heckscher-Ohlin Theorem*: According to that theory, countries will usually enjoy comparative advantages when they produce goods that use their abundant factors of production rather than their scarce ones. Given the specialization prevailing in modern industrialized economies and countries commonly specializing in different segments of like product markets, the *Factor Proportions Hypothesis's* static notion that all production factors are exogenously determined cannot be fully endorsed, however. Rather, a lot of endogenous variables like financial factors (e.g. capital accumulation rates), human resources, state investment in research and development or public infrastructure (e.g. transports, communications) will also bear a substantial influence on the patterns of specialization and comparative advantage. Thus, the notion of *Comparative Advantage* has been held to be a very flexible one, rather than being static as endorsed by the *Factor Proportions Hypothesis*, compare M. J. Trebilcock, *ibid.*, 5 et sqq.

590 A. D. Mitchell, *ibid.*

591 E.g. Natural resources, commodities, climate.

tiveness in international trade. In light of the various different national factor endowments and preferences, every state will have a different regulatory optimum[592]. Thus, national regulatory systems compete with each other in regard to production costs and mobile production factors, such as international capital, investments, or technology, which has been referred to as "regulatory competition"[593].

Unlike competition law, trade laws and policies traditionally operate in an international context. They focus on the liberalisation of *governmental* measures restricting or distorting international trade. Such restrictions may come about either through border regulation like tariffs and quantitative restrictions, internal regulation like discriminatory taxes or through government participation in trade[594]. Consequently, trade liberalisation instruments have been negotiated by states, and are addressed to states[595]. This traditional emphasis of trade policy on governmental market access barriers is based on the assumption that governmental measures constitute more important barriers to trade than private ones[596]. It has to be borne in mind, however, that the GATT rules were originally expected to be supplemented by a set of international competition rules and, therefore, based on the assumption that trade would occur "under fully competitive conditions"[597].

Staying with the GATT as the most comprehensive source of international economic law today, it is important to note that besides the focus on governmental market-access barriers, the second characteristic feature of the GATT is the continued expansion of its scope from traditional trade policy instruments such as discriminatory governmental treatment of imports or exports, but also to internal policy instruments, such as non-discriminatory technical regulations or standards. This expansion should not be too much of a surprise given that such considerations were already pursued as early as during the negotiations for the

---

592 Compare E.-U. Petersmann, *International Competition Rules for Governments and for Private Business. The Case for Linking Future WTO Negotiations on Investment, Competition and Environmental Rules to Reforms of Anti-Dumping Laws,* in: 30(3) Journal of World Trade 1996, at 11 et sqq).

593 Compare E.-U. Petersmann, *International Competition Rules for Governments and for Private Business. The Case for Linking Future WTO Negotiations on Investment, Competition and Environmental Rules to Reforms of Anti-Dumping Laws,* in: 30(3) Journal of World Trade 1996, at 12.

594 Compare E. U. Petersmann, *Proposals For Negotiating International Competition Rules In The GATT-WTO World Trade And Legal System,* in: 49 (II/III) Aussenwirtschaft 1994, 233.

595 From a practical point of view, however, international trade is directly expanding the contract opportunities for private economic actors, who are, thereby, the intermediate beneficiaries. Ultimately, however, the welfare benefits accrued through curtailing state intervention in international trade are accorded to consumers, compare M. J. Trebilcock, *ibid.*, at 4.

596 This has been justified by the fact that the gains from further liberalisation of government measures such as tariffs, non-tariff border measures, technical regulations, standards, rules of origin, antidumping, subsidies, and the like are arguably higher than the gains from supplementary international rules for private restraints of competition, compare E. U. Petersmann, *International Rules for Governments and for Private Business,* 30(3) Journal of World Trade 1996, 18.

597 See GATT 1947 Article VII:2 (b). Compare E. U. Petersmann, *Proposals For Negotiating International Competition Rules In The GATT-WTO World Trade And Legal System,* in: 49 (II/III) Aussenwirtschaft 1994, 235.

Havana Charter[598]. Since the foundation of the WTO, a particular focus on broader and integrated market-access guarantees can be observed. Arguably, such approach corresponds more accurately to the globalization of production and markets, and provides for additional opportunities to promote economic welfare and liberty through reciprocal "package deals" in the ambit of the WTO[599]. Moreover, this development must be seen in line with the intended increase of international economic integration between the WTO Member States as envisaged by them at the point of ratification.

In regard to individual amendments, private anti-competitive practices potentially affecting the trade in goods, services and intellectual property have been addressed in various WTO instruments. Examples commonly cited are *(i)* the Agreement on Technical Barriers to Trade (TBT), *(ii)* the General Agreement on Trade in Services (GATS), *(iii)* the Agreement on Trade-Related Intellectual Property Rights (TRIPS), or *(iv)* the Agreement on Trade-Related Investment Measures (TRIMS)[600]. By laying down these additional rules to the "core" principles in trade policy, such as the principles of Non-Discrimination, Most Favoured Nation Treatment, the prohibition of quantitative restrictions, or Reciprocity (for example through mutual granting of tariff concessions), it has been recognized that trade liberalisation policy must be co-ordinated with other areas of law in order to maximize global welfare.

This recognition is based on the consideration that even if all governmental barriers to international trade were removed, some markets would still be foreclosed to new market entrants because of anti-competitive conduct if complementary regulation of competition were absent. It has been argued in this regard that these private barriers could eventually replace the public barriers to market access that have been removed by international agreements[601].

Outside the WTO Agreement, similar trends can be discerned. Various younger regional free trade area and customs union agreements are based on a broader concept of "competition rules", in that both governmental as well as private practices are understood to potentially affect trade liberalisation[602]. The European experience may serve as an illustrative and early example in this regard. Already in 1957, the Treaty of Rome creating the European Economic Community provided detailed as well as binding measures to control anti-competitive practices affecting trade between the Member States. According to its Article 2, the Treaty was aimed at "establishing a common market [...]". To

---

598 P. Mardsen, *A Competition Policy for the WTO (2003)*, 46.

599 E. U. Petersmann, *International Rules for Governments and for Private Business,* 30(3) Journal of World Trade 1996, 18.

600 Compare E. U. Petersmann, *International Rules for Governments and for Private Business,* 30(3) Journal of World Trade 1996, 19 et sqq. These examples shall be elaborated in more detail below.

601 A. D. Mitchell, *ibid.*

602 E. U. Petersmann, *Proposals For Negotiating International Competition Rules In The GATT-WTO World Trade And Legal System,* in: 49 (II/III) Aussenwirtschaft 1994, 235.

that end, Article 3 para 1 (g) EC-Treaty called for the "institution of a system ensuring that competition in the internal market is not distorted"[603]. Thus, the ultimate objective of welfare enhancement for the Member States was intended to be realized by ensuring free trade through market integration, and private barriers to trade liberalisation were the main distortion to be prevented[604]. Arguably, this underlying intention of achieving an uncompromised economically integrated "Common Market" fast and efficiently required this extension to private practices and a most rigid pursuit on part of the EC authorities enforcing the respective competition rules.

To sum up, international trade policy aims at the enhancement of global welfare. By opening up national markets to international trade and, thereby, making them more competitive, international trade policy aims at an improved allocation of resources through liberalisation, so as to promote economic efficiency and consumer welfare[605]. In addition, however, it may be observed that the greater the intended degree of economic integration, the more likely will the core focus on governmental access barriers be extended to complementary areas of regulation and to private market-access barriers.

3. *Commonalities and Conflicts*

From the above, we may, first of all, discern that international trade policy and competition policy share certain common objectives. At the same time, however, conflicts can be distinguished. In the following, we shall discuss these commonalities and conflicts in light of *(i)* economics, *(ii)* market access, *(iii)* regulatory competition, and *(iv)* institutional aspects.

3.1. Economics

From an economic theory point of view, both competition policy and international trade policy are aimed at the enhancement of consumer welfare through the promotion of efficiency in production and consumption in the long term[606]. Thus both are intended to improve the ultimate economic output for consumers through competition while considering both long-term benefits and political feasibility of short-run measures[607]. More concretely, trade law is concerned with the protection of consumers from higher prices due to the distorting effects of primarily public barriers to trade, whereas competition law is *inter alia* concerned with the protection of consumers from anticompetitive behaviour of pri-

603 For a summary see P. Mardsen, *A Competition Policy for the WTO (2003)*, 51.

604 European Commission, *Report on Competition Policy* (1972), 10.

605 R. Weinrauch, *Competition Law in the WTO. The Rationale for a Framework Agreement* (2004), 55 et sqq.

606 A. D. Mitchell, *ibid.*, 346.

607 R. Weinrauch, *ibid.*

vate firms exercising market power[608]. In this regard, it is also important to note that trade policy is operating in an international context, while competition policy has evolved in a national context, regulating the economic activity within the borders of a specific jurisdiction.

It has been brought forward that in practice, trade policy is substantially grounded in a government's efforts to promote its particular exporting industries, irrespective of the fact as to whether the targeted foreign markets are workably competitive from an economic point of view. In comparison, competition policy targets industry structures in general, without any preference for a specific sector. It seeks to prevent industry structures and practices which afford excessive market powers to sellers, enabling them to raise prices above or reduce output below competitive level. Therefore, it has been argued that while trade policy is aimed at the promotion of the interests of individual competitors, competition policy is more concerned with the promotion and sustaining of competitive market structures[609].

However, it has been argued above that the policy objectives underlying competition policy are not necessarily restricted to purely economic considerations. Rather, individual domestic public policy considerations may be integrated in competition law instruments, as has been illustrated by the European Union, for example[610]. Consequently, competition policy must be regarded as based on economic considerations as a means and foundation for imbedding additional policy goals of purely domestic interest. In comparison, international trade law appears to be oriented toward the enhancement of global welfare. Being an instrument of inter-state agreement and a result of a diplomatic process, the final agreement will have to be restricted to general principles, benefiting the majority if not all of the negotiating parties. Otherwise, an agreement would not be feasible in practice. Therefore, international trade policy appears to be confined to the formulation of general economic principles in a more "straightforward" way. The fact that there are no such general international principles or standards in competition law also favors such an interpretation[611].

---

608 A. D. Mitchell, *ibid.*, 347. The acceptance of this convergence in the underlying policy goals by Economic Theory is founded in the rather recent recognition that increased competition is a precondition for more rapid total factor productivity increases. This, in turn, is due to the realization that the main driver for efficiency gains in the medium to long run is not the reallocation of resources in a static sense, but rather the enhancement of total factor productivity. This line of argument is to some extent in conflict with *Joseph Schumpeter's* theory that a firm must have market power as a prerequisite for any innovation, compare E. M. Graham, *The Relationship Between International Trade Policy and Competition Policy*, in Z. Drabek (ed.), *Globalization Under Threat: The Stability of Trade Policy and Multilateral Agreements* (2001), 227 et sqq.

609 See D. K. Tarullo, *Norms and Institutions in Global Competition Policy*, in: (94) The American Journal of International Law 2000, 483. Compare however the criticism raised with regard to the European Union allegedly pursuing an approach of favouring individual competitors or groups of competitors against others.

610 Compare Chapter II.C.

611 E. M. Graham, *ibid.*, 236. This is in line with the argument above that competition policy may embody very national and individual policy goals, which is why agreement on common principles is so hard if not impos-

3.2. Market access

Competition policy intersects with international trade policy if anti-competitive conduct on a given market hinders foreign market participants from entering this market[612]. Therefore, it has often been argued that unregulated anti-competitive practices can prevent market access for foreign producers. Consequently, it has been feared that this could undermine the policies of comparative advantage and, thus, inhibit the policy goals justifying international trade liberalisation. Certainly, liberal trade policies include the notion that competition will promote efficiencies among different producers, in particular if they are located in different countries[613]. From a market access perspective, therefore, trade liberalisation and measures to increase domestic competition appear to serve a similar end. Trade liberalisation serves to introduce new sellers into markets abroad, whereas competition policy serves to enlarge the number of the individual competitors. In either case, the decisive factor is the contestability of the market, i.e. whether or not new (domestic or foreign) entrants are able to penetrate a market.

Barriers to entry may consist in governmental border measures, such as quantitative restrictions or tariffs. Yet, barriers to entry may also be created by purely private measures, such as restrictions of access to essential distribution or retailing facilities. In the latter case, competition policy could therefore be regarded as the main remedy, while trade policy rather servers as an adjunct to competition policy[614]. Given the significant progress in trade liberalisation and the removal of public barriers to market access, this latter consideration would partly explain the notable shift of public attendance toward private measures.

In light of the above, it has been a common argument that international trade policy and competition law are consistent with each other, as both promote open markets and more choice for consumers[615]. However, it has also been argued that although some congruencies may be recognized, the existing ambiguities should be considered in more detail. For instance, Tarullo pointed out that discussions on the alleged congruence of competition policy and international trade policy would often merge private anticompetitive practices with public laws or policies, impeding competition in themselves[616]. In this regard, he has argued that remarkably few of the examples for private market access

---

sible to achieve. This is still true although there appears to be growing consensus on certain hard-core restrictions among industrialized states.

[612] D. K. Tarullo, *Norms and Institutions in Global Competition Policy,* in: (94) The American Journal of International Law 2000, 483.

[613] J. H. Jackson, *Alternative Approaches for Implementing Competition Rules in International Economic Relations,* 49 (II/III) Aussenwirtschaft 1994, 186.

[614] E. M. Graham, *ibid.*

[615] Compare in this regard the results of The Working Group on the Interaction between Trade and Competition Policy, *Report to the General Council,* WTO Document WT/WGTCP/2 (1998), 7-8; OECD Joint Group on Trade and Competition, *Complementarities Between Trade and Competition Policies,* COM/TD/DAFFE/CLP(98)98/FINAL (1999).

[616] D. K. Tarullo, *ibid.*

barriers cited by the WTO Working Group on the Interaction between Trade and Competition Policy provided persuasive evidence of being tied to competition policy as such, and that only distribution systems could be rated as a genuine example of this interaction[617].

Moreover, some argue that although both international trade policy and competition policy are concerned with market access in the broader sense, trade policy promotes market access for individual competitors of a particular industry of a given state, whereas competition policy is more apprehensive of sustaining competitive market structures in order to ensure consumer welfare in general[618]. Yet, the admissibility of this line of argument must be examined in light of the different competition laws prevailing. For instance, when looking at the United States, this argument can be fully accepted. For the European Union, on the other hand, the argument cannot be acknowledged that easily. Rather, in line with certain public policy considerations relating to the dominance of small and medium-sized undertakings in the Common Market, the European Union would appear to endorse an approach of protecting individual competitors in addition to market structure considerations[619]. Thus, the degree of congruence between trade and competition policy in terms of market access will also differ from state to state, depending on the individual policy considerations.

3.3. Regulatory competition

The author has demonstrated that the individual domestic approach to economic or legal regulation constitutes one factor to determine a given state's competitiveness in international trade[620]. Similarly to competition among firms,

---

[617] D. K. Tarullo, *ibid.*, 484. The *Kodak-Case* may illustrate the market access issues raised for distribution systems in Japan, for instance. The history of the Japanese industry has demonstrated a close and complex interaction of governmental and private conduct, which allegedly foreclosed certain essential distribution channels to foreign companies and, thereby, denied access to the Japanese product market at issue. The trade policy-related aspects of that conflict have mainly stemmed from the involvement of the Japanese government in the distribution systems at issue through statutory enactments and administrative guidance. Ultimately, this non-violation claim was dismissed, however, as a sufficient impact of the alleged influence of the governmental measures on the competitive relationship between foreign and domestic producers could not be established. Private measures were not considered by themselves.
The non-applicability of GATT Article XXIII to private business practices was formalised by the GATT in 1960, and this principle equally applies under the WTO Agreement, see E. M. Graham, *ibid., at Note 9.]* Compare WTO Case *Japan – Measures affecting Consumer Photographic Film and Paper,* WTO/DS44/R, with comments in Jackson/Davey/Sykes, *ibid.*, 277 et sqq. In this regard, see also D. K. Tarullo, *ibid.*, 484 et sqq. In that case, the United States claimed that through the application of three broader categories of liberalisation "countermeasures", the Japanese Government had inhibited the distribution and sale of imported consumer photographic film and paper in Japan. These three categories included distribution measures, restrictions on large retail stores with regard to alternative distribution channels, and promotion measures allegedly disadvantaging imports. The US claimed that these measures nullified or impaired certain benefits in the meaning of Article XXIII:1(b) GATT 1947 and that the distribution measures were infringing Article III:4 of the latter agreement. The panel rejected the claim.

[618] D. K. Tarullo, *ibid.*

[619] A. Jones/B. Sufrin, *ibid.*, at 34.

[620] Compare comments under Chapter III.B.3. above.

competition among governments has been said to increase information and mutual learning, freedom of choice, a more efficient allocation of resources as well as technological innovation. Consequently, the question of possible market failures through misallocating productive resources at the international level has also been raised. Moreover, there are concerns with regard to a possible "race to the bottom" or a sub-optimal level of lenient regulation through competition among rules[621].

Thus, competition policy clearly intersects with international trade policy where regulatory differences in competition law constitute an "unfair distortion" of international trade. "Unfair regulatory differences" have been defined as involving market failures or governmental failures with trans-national trade distorting effect[622]. Such unfair distortions have been regarded to be suboptimal, mainly if there are cross border external effects or international public goods are concerned[623].

However, as *Petersmann* pointed out, it may be difficult in practice to challenge a government's perception as to what constitutes a "market failure", a need for governmental intervention or the necessity to supply public goods[624]. In addition, economic theory does not provide precise guidelines for identifying governmental failures or legitimate political trade-offs. Thus, international rules are required, as the various views among sovereign states on how to differentiate between "legitimate comparative advantages" and "unfair regulatory differences" may vary considerably[625].

The GATT generally does not prevent diverging domestic policies and regulatory competition, provided they do not cause harmful trans-national external effects. Nevertheless, the general GATT principles do address unfair regulatory differences to a certain extent[626]. GATT dispute settlement practice has also consistently construed the GATT rules as protecting the legitimate "expectations on the competitive relationship between imported and domestic products", and, consequently, as incorporating competition rules for governments. As such, according to GATT legal practice, there is no need to demonstrate a substantial damage to trade in order to file a successful claim for "nullification or impairment of benefits accruing under the GATT". Such "non-violation" complaints reflect the idea that the GATT could be frustrated by governmental

621 E.-U. Petersmann, *International Competition Rules for Governments and for Private Business. The Case for Linking Future WTO Negotiations on Investment, Competition and Environmental Rules to Reforms of Anti-Dumping Laws*, in: 30(3) Journal of World Trade 1996, at 12 et sqq.

622 E.-U. Petersmann, *ibid.*

623 In this regard, the example of cross-border pollution has been used to illustrate the phenomenon of trans-national market failure as an externality and governmental failure in terms of State responsibility for cross-border pollution, see E.-U. Petersmann, *ibid.*, 15.

624 E.-U. Petersmann, *ibid.*

625 E.-U. Petersmann, *ibid.*

626 See in particular Articles II, III, VI, XVII, XVII-XXI and XXIII of the GATT, compare E.-U. Petersmann, *Proposals for Negotiating International Competition Rules in the GATT-WTO World Trade and Legal System*, in 49(II/III) Aussenwirtschaft 1994, at 240.

measures even when they are consistent with the Agreement[627]. In addition, the WTO approach of extended and integrated market access guarantees for goods, services, trade-related intellectual property rights and investments certainly reflects an increased awareness of the influence of regulatory competition on international trade. Nevertheless, in this regard, it has been argued that a more consistent and systematic approach should be pursued[628].

3.4. Institutional aspects

While the goals of competition policy and international trade policy do certainly share common aspects in light of the above, their respective processes of implementation or underlying institutional aspects could not be more different[629]. In this regard, institutional aspects comprise at least two factors. On the one hand, the term "institution" can be used to refer to a set of rules[630]. On the other hand, it can also be used to refer to an organization[631]. Both aspects shall be considered here.

To begin with, the process of rule making is substantially different for competition policy as opposed to international trade policy. Competition policy is primarily the result of a – at least in theory – democratic decision-making process at the national level. It results in a rule-based system, which is very much dependent on substantial fact finding and seeks to limit the discretion of enforcement bodies, which rely on the consideration of market structures and processes in order to determine whether a given conduct has to be rated as being anticompetitive[632]. In addition, competition enforcement authorities are generally vested with the powers to act *ex officio*.

In comparison, international trade policy is the result of a process of lobbying, consultation and diplomacy. In theory, states are free to adopt a protectionist approach for their trade policy, unless they have voluntarily committed themselves to a binding agreement not to do so. States have this right or ability even though from an economic perspective, a liberal trade policy would appear to be in the state's unilateral interest. Strictly speaking, multilateral negotiations should, therefore, not be required. However, given the political power of domestic producers, governments often do not achieve a unilateral opening of their markets[633]. Therefore, trade laws can be regarded as being less an instru-

---

627 E.-U. Petersmann, *ibid.*

628 E.-U. Petersmann, *International Competition Rules for Governments and for Private Business. The Case for Linking Future WTO Negotiations on Investment, Competition and Environmental Rules to Reforms of Anti-Dumping Laws*, in: 30(3) Journal of World Trade 1996, at 12 et sqq.

629 E. M. Graham, *ibid.*

630 For a summary of the different institutional setups prevailing in this regard, compare J. Epstein, *The Other Side of Harmony: Can Trade and Competition Laws Work Together in the International Marketplace?* In: (17) American University International Law Review 2002, 360 et sqq.

631 Compare D. K. Tarullo, *ibid.*

632 R. Weinrauch, *Competition Law in the WTO. The Rationale for a Framework Agreement* (2004), 57.

633 E. M. Graham, *ibid.*, at 233.

ment of "law" in a strict sense, but rather a "policy" instrument on their own. Consequently, the decision-making process for international trade laws is characterized by avoiding confrontation and limiting time-consuming fact finding. The amount of discretion available in the enforcement of international trade laws is more confined than it is in competition cases. In addition, at least under WTO law[634], the mandate to examine international trade law issues will depend on a claim by one of the contracting parties or member states of the agreement at issue; there is no enforcement *ex officio.* Arguably, this feature can be explained by the nature of international trade law, being the result of a negotiating process among states. In such a process, any concessions in terms of national sovereignty will usually be limited to what is absolutely mandatory to reach a given goal, and not beyond that. Therefore, a supranational authority enforcing international trade law *ex officio* cannot be regarded a realistic picture, as will be explored in more detail below. However, this second aspect of "institution leads up with the discussion of the various roles of organizations in the implementation process of competition and international trade policy.

With regard to organizational differences, the main difference consists in enforcement. Competition policy instruments are enforced by national enforcement authorities established by the national legislator. These authorities may be administrative bodies or courts, vested with the statutory powers to investigate and sanction private and, to a lesser extent, public anti-competitive behaviour. By contrast, the enforcement of international trade law instruments is based on the agreement of the negotiating sovereign parties to it. Thus, they voluntarily submit themselves under a given regime. This also implies that the enforcement powers of the established authorities will be limited to the exact scope the individual parties will agree to. In the case of the GATT, this is public, i.e. governmental behaviour only[635]. Generally speaking, therefore, private behaviour affecting international trade will be subject to international trade law instruments and sanctions only when brought about by or allowed for through governmental measures or acquiescence.

4. Conclusion

Competition policy and international trade policy do share the primary objective of welfare enhancement. In addition, both competition and trade policy are concerned with market access. Nevertheless, although traditionally concerned with domestic regulation only, it appears that competition policy has a wider policy focus than trade policy. In particular, ensuring market access for potential competitors is only one among many goals of competition policy which is

---

[634] Compare Article 3:7 of the *Understanding on Rules and Procedures governing the Settlement of Disputes (DSU).*

[635] The non-applicability of GATT Article XXIII to private business practices was formalised by the GATT in 1960, and this principle equally applies under the WTO Agreement, see E. M. Graham, *ibid.*, at Note 9.

aimed to ensure the free and competitive operation of markets. In comparison, the provision of market access for potential foreign competitors in order to enhance global welfare through a more efficient allocation of resources is the main purpose of international trade law. In addition, competition policy may pursue various other public policy goals, which are not necessarily related to considerations of market access and efficiency. Moreover, while trade and competition policy pursue the same objective in the long term, their respective *modi operandi* are very different, in particular with regard to market access. Moreover, the processes of implementation of competition policy and international trade policy vary to a considerable extent.

Consequently, not all international competition issues are similarly relevant to international trade law[636]. Rather, a given practice could be endorsed by national competition law, while it could be rated as adversely impacting international trade flows at the same time[637]. Generally, the borders of where international trade policy ends and where competition policy begins are hard to define[638]. Rather, international trade policy cannot be fully separated from competition policy. Various examples of overlaps between trade and competition policy, and of how these policy issues are influenced by market failures due to anti-competitive behaviour have been cited[639].

In conclusion, although they share the same long-term objective, competition and trade policy cannot be held to be fully congruent. All the same, welfare economics have indicated that efficient economic outcome will occur only where both free flows of international trade and competitive market conditions are maintained[640]. In this regard, competition policy has been referred to as a "non-trade policy instrument", which can influence international trade patterns significantly[641]. Thus, competition policy and international trade policy must be held as being complementary means to a common end, as far as general welfare

---

636 Compare ICPAC Report 2000, Executive Summary, at: http://www.usdoj.gov/atr/icpac/execsummary.htm (01.10.2004), at 25, and also Chapter 5 of the ICPAC Report for a more detailed analysis.

637 In the Report, the Advisory Committee takes advantage of the example of vertical restraints so as to illustrate that different ratings could be possible from a competition policy point of view on the one hand and a trade policy point of view on the other hand. For instance, a given vertical restraint could be regarded as efficiency-enhancing with regard to local market participants. Nevertheless, the same restraint could be rated as impeding international trade flows, as market access of potential foreign competitors could be prevented through that practice.

638 D. Fritz-Aßmus, *Zum Ordnungsrahmen einer internationalen Wettbwerbspolitik*, in: D. Fritz-Aßmus/E. Tuchtfeldt (Eds.), *Beiträge zur Wirtschaftspolitk (Vol. 66): Die Ordnung des Welthandels: A. Ghanie Ghaussy zum 65. Geburtstag* (1997), at 206.

639 J. H. Jackson, *Alternative Approaches for Implementing Competition Rules in International Economic Relations*, 49 (II/III) Aussenwirtschaft 1994, 184 et sqq. Examples that have been cited in this regard include "buy-national" policies; anti-dumping laws; intellectual property issues; product standards; private cross-border arrangements such as the development of agencies, subsidiaries or tying arrangements; state trading enterprises; commodity trade; subsidies; or the individual domestic approach to antitrust policy in general.

640 A. D. Mitchell, *ibid.*, 346.

641 G. Koppmann, *Internationalisierung der Wettbewerbspolitik: Korrelat zur internationalen Handelspolitik?* In: 56(II) Aussenwirtschaft 2001, 161.

enhancement and market access are concerned[642]. One could therefore argue that enhanced coordination of international trade policy with competition policy could be welfare-enhancing in the long term.

This complementarity of trade and competition policy is also supported by the fact that various provisions of the WTO instruments are already integrating competition rules directed at governments and private actors into the WTO Agreement. In the following, therefore, the existing legal instruments in the WTO Agreement shall be examined in some more detail.

B. Existing Legal Instruments Addressing Competition in the 1994 Agreement Establishing the World Trade Organization

1. Integrated competition rules for governments

As compared to the obligations under the GATT 1947, the 1994 Marrakesh Agreement establishing the World Trade Organization (in the following "WTO Agreement") has introduced a stricter and more integrated approach with regard to governmental anticompetitive practices in trade in goods, trade-related investments and intellectual property rights[643]. In fact, most WTO agreements and associated documents can be regarded as relating to competition, as they limit the sovereignty of governments to impose trade measures that would directly or indirectly constrain or distort competition – in particular with regard to foreign competitors – in markets for goods or services[644]. In the following, the most prominent provisions among them shall be examined in so far as they relate to competition policy.

1.1. The prohibition of discriminatory internal regulation (National Treatment)

The prohibition of discriminatory internal regulation is one aspect of the fundamental principle of Non-Discrimination in the WTO Agreement[645], and is formulated in various provisions of the WTO Agreement.

---

642 J. Drexl, *International Competition Policy after Cancun: Placing a Singapore Issue on the WTO Development Agenda*, in: 27(3) Journal of World Competition 2004, 424.

643 E.-U. Petersmann, *Proposals For Negotiating International Competition Rules In The GATT-WTO World Trade And Legal System*, in: 49(II/III) Aussenwirtschaft 1994, at 247.

644 World Trade Organization, Report (1998) of the Working Group on the Interaction Between Trade and Competition Policy to the General Council, WT/WTGCP/2, Dec. 8, 1998. at para. 58.

645 The Principle of Non-Discrimination consists of the obligation for National Treatment, e.g. Article III GATT 1947, and the Most-Favoured Nation Clause, e.g. in Article I GATT 1947.

1.1.1. General Agreement on Tariffs and Trade (GATT) 1947[646]

The primary provision is Article III GATT 1947, the beneficiaries of which are the producers of importing states[647]. Arguably, Article III. 4 of the GATT 1947 is most relevant to the area of competition policy, and Dispute Settlement Panels have endorsed a rather wide scope of this provision. In particular, the wording "affecting the internal sale" has been held not to be limited to measures focusing on the conditions of trade, but rather to apply to "any laws or regulations which might adversely modify the conditions of competition between [...] domestic and imported products on the internal market"[648]. For instance, written and legally binding purchase and export undertakings submitted by potential investors were held to be covered despite their voluntary submission[649]. In any case, the practices of state trading enterprises have been held to be subject to the provisions of Article III of the GATT 1947 insofar as they concern internal laws, regulations or requirements affecting the imposition of a minimum price for the sale of imported products, special packing requirements for imported products, practices regarding the listing and de-listing of products by state-operated liquor stores or regulations affecting internal transportation[650].

Notably, however, while Article III protects imported goods, it does not apply to the governmental treatment of goods destined for the supply to foreign markets through exportation[651].

The "no less favourable treatment" standard of Article III of the GATT 1947 has been interpreted extensively. Thus, it has been held to require the equality of competitive opportunities between domestically produced and imported products. In particular, it has been held to protect expectations rather than specific outcomes, and to prohibit measures that might adversely affect the internal

646 Article III of the GATT 1947 reads: "1. The contracting parties recognize that internal taxes and other internal charges, and laws, regulations and requirements affecting the internal sale, offering for sale, purchase, transportation, distribution or use of products, and internal quantitative regulations requiring the mixture, processing or use of products in specified amounts or proportions, should not be applied to imported or domestic products so as to afford protection to domestic production." [...] "4. The products of the territory of any contracting party imported into the territory of any other contracting party shall be accorded treatment no less favourable than that accorded to like products of national origin in respect of all laws, regulations and requirements affecting their internal sale, offering for sale, purchase, transportation, distribution or use. The provisions of this paragraph shall not prevent the application of differential internal transportation charges which are based exclusively on the economic operation of the means of transport and not on the nationality of the product."

647 See the WTO Dispute Panel's decision in *Canada – Foreign Investment Review Act (FIRA)*, para. 6.5, BISD 30S/140, L/5504, adopted on Feb. 7, 1984.

648 Compare the early Panel decision in *Italian Discrimination against Imported Agricultural Machinery*, para. 12, BISD 7S/60, L/833, adopted on 23 October 1958, which was subsequently upheld by later decisions, compare for example the Panel Report on *EC – Regime for the Importation, Sale and Distribution of Bananas*, para. 7.175, WT/DS27/R.

649 WTO Dispute Panel's decision in *Canada – Foreign Investment Review Act (FIRA)*, para. 5.4, BISD 30S/140, L/5504, adopted on Feb. 7, 1984.

650 WTO Working Group on the Interaction between Trade and Competition Policy, *The Fundamental WTO Principles of National Treatment, Most-Favoured-Nation Treatment, Background Note by the Secretariat*, WT/WGTCP/W/114, of 14 April 1999, at para. 24.

651 WTO Working Group on the Interaction between Trade and Competition Policy, *ibid.*, at para. 20.

market's conditions of competition for imported products compared to domestically produced products[652]. Moreover, the existence of a "like product" has notably been interpreted very similarly to the common market definition analysis based on substitutability generally deployed by competition laws[653].

In addition to the general security exceptions as stipulated in Article XXI, the main exceptions to Article III can be found in Article XX, which allows trade restrictions necessary to protect certain public policy objectives. These exceptions are subject to the requirement that measures taken pursuant to them are not applied in a manner constituting a means of "arbitrary or unjustifiable discrimination between countries where the same conditions prevail" or a "disguised restriction on international trade".

1.1.2. General Agreement on Trade in Services (GATS)

Under the GATS, the beneficiaries of the obligation of National Treatment are the individual service providers. The beneficiaries can therefore be natural persons. However, the individual benefit to National Treatment as stipulated in Article XVII of the GATS will depend on whether or not an individual commitment to National Treatment has been made[654]. National Treatment is to be granted "in respect of all measures affecting the supply of services". The scope of "measures", which are defined generously in Article XXVIII of the GATS already, has been construed equally broad than for trade in goods under Article III.4 of the GATT 1947.[655]

Under the GATS, the interpretation of the no less favourable treatment standard as no less favourable conditions of competition can explicitly be found in the Agreement itself. In this regard, paragraph 3 of Article XVII of the GATS states that "[...] treatment shall be considered to be less favourable if it modifies the conditions of competition in favour of services or service suppliers of the Member compared to like services or service suppliers of any other Member."

The general exception to National Treatment under the GATS can be found in Article XIV, which is based on its GATT 1947 counterpart in Article XX. The GATT 1947 also serves as an example for GATS in that GATS similarly does not apply to services destined for exportation to foreign markets[656].

---

652 This interpretation of early panels has been upheld by later decisions; compare the WTO Appelate Body's Report in *Japan – Taxes on Alcoholic Beverages II*, p. 27, WT/DS8/AB/R, WT/DS10/AB/R, WT/DS11/AB/R, Nov. 1, 1996, where it stated that "... Article III protects expectations not of any particular trade volume but rather of the equal competitive relationship between imported and domestic products".

653 Compare Panel Report in *Korea – Taxes on Alcoholic Beverages*, pp. 171-192, WT/DS75/R.

654 Compare Article XIX of the GATS.

655 Compare Report of the Appellate Body in *EC – Regime for the Importation, Sale and Distribution of Bananas*, para. 220, WT/DS27/AB/R.

656 WTO Working Group on the Interaction between Trade and Competition Policy, *ibid.*, at para. 20.

1.1.3. Agreement on Trade-Related Aspects of Intellectual Property Rights (TRIPS)

As far as intellectual property is concerned, National Treatment has always been the cornerstone of international agreements in that area, like the Paris and Berne Conventions[657]. It is also of fundamental importance to the TRIPS. According to Article 3 of the TRIPS, National Treatment shall be granted to nationals of other Member States with regard to the "protection" of intellectual property rights, thereby referring to their availability, acquisition, maintenance, enforcement and use[658]. Similarly to the GATT, Article 3 of the TRIPS affords the "no less favourable treatment" standard[659].

This rather comprehensive scope of the National Treatment obligation under the TRIPS is outweighed by the fact that where exceptions to this principle have been made under the main pre-existing intellectual property conventions, they are also permitted under the TRIPS Agreement[660].

1.1.4. National Treatment in other Multilateral Agreements

The National Treatment obligation of the GATT 1994 is supported by various other Multilateral Agreements under the WTO Agreement. For instance, the Agreement on Trade-Related Investment Measures (TRIMs) provides clarification in its Annex of the obligation under Article III.4 not to "apply any TRIM that is inconsistent with the provisions of Article III or Article XI of the GATT 1994"[661]. The Agreement on Technical Barriers to Trade (TBT) further strengthens the prohibition of discriminatory internal regulation not justified by public policy objectives under Article XX of the GATT 1994 by ensuring that technical regulations and standards as well as related testing and certification procedures do not create unnecessary obstacles to international trade, and that "no less favourable" treatment is afforded to like products of other Member States. Member States remain with a certain amount of discretion to impose higher or lower standards[662]. Nevertheless, this discretion is limited by the fact that it must be based on a legitimate object, of which Article 2.2. TBT provides a demonstrative list. The "prevention of deceptive practices" may be cited as an

---

[657] Compare Article 2 of the *Paris Convention for the Protection of Industrial Property* and Article 5 of the *Berne Convention for the Protection of Literary and Artistic Works*.

[658] Compare Footnote #3 to Article 3 TRIPS.

[659] Article 3 TRIPS reads: "1. Each Member shall accord to the nationals of other Members treatment no less favourable than that it accords to its own nationals with regard to the protection (3) of intellectual property, subject to the exceptions already provided in, respectively, the Paris Convention (1967), the Berne Convention (1971), the Rome Convention or the Treaty on Intellectual Property in Respect of Integrated Circuits. [...] 2. Members may avail themselves of the exceptions permitted under paragraph 1 in relation to judicial and administrative procedures, including the designation of an address for service or the appointment of an agent within the jurisdiction of a Member, only where such exceptions are necessary to secure compliance with laws and regulations which are not inconsistent with the provisions of this Agreement and where such practices are not applied in a manner which would constitute a disguised restriction on trade."

[660] WTO Working Group on the Interaction of Trade and Competition Policy, *ibid.*, at para. 37.

[661] Article 2 of the TRIMs.

[662] Compare Recital 6 to the TBT: "[...] at the level it considers appropriate [...]".

example related to competition law in a broader sense. Likewise, the Agreement on Sanitary and Phytosanitary Measures (SPS) enumerates the "necessity" and "non-discrimination" standards of the GATT.

1.2. Most Favoured Nation Principle (MFN)

The Most Favoured Nation Principle is *inter alia* laid down in Article I of the GATT 1994[663], in Article II of the GATS and in Article 4 of the TRIPS, but also in various other Multilateral Agreements of the WTO Agreement. It constitutes the major cornerstone of the multilateral nature of the WTO Agreement and maximizes the scope of application for the WTO Agreement's important underlying economic rationale of the Theory of Comparative Advantage.

Relating to competition policy, the main function of the MFN principle is the extended prohibition of discrimination. Unlike the principle of National Treatment which applies to internal taxes and regulations, the MFN principle is extended to border measures as well[664].

The scope of Article I GATT 1994 has been construed widely by the Panel, which held that advantages could only be conditional on criteria directed to the actual imported product[665]. With regard to Article II of the GATS, the scope was held to be equally broad as under the National Treatment obligation, thus requiring no less favourable conditions of competition[666].

Apart from the general exceptions and security exceptions discussed above, an important exception to the MFN principle can be found in Article XXIV of the GATT 1994, which deals with Regional Trading Agreements, and preferences in favour of and between developing countries through the "Enabling Clause"[667]. Likewise, the GATS and the TRIPS provide for additional specific exceptions.

---

663 Article I of the GATT 1994 reads: "1. With respect to customs duties and charges of any kind imposed on or in connection with importation or exportation or imposed on the international transfer of payments for imports or exports, and with respect to the method of levying such duties and charges, and with respect to all rules and formalities in connection with importation and exportation, and with respect to all matters referred to in paragraphs 2 and 4 of Article III,* any advantage, favour, privilege or immunity granted by any contracting party to any product originating in or destined for any other country shall be accorded immediately and unconditionally to the like product originating in or destined for the territories of all other contracting parties. [...]"

664 WTO Working Group on Trade and Competition Policy, *ibid.*, para. 44.

665 WTO Panel, *Indonesia – Certain Measures affecting the Automotive Industry*, WT/DS54, 55, 59, 64/R, adopted on July 23, 1998.

666 WTO Panel Report on *European Communities – Regime for the Importation, Sale and Distribution of Bananas* WT/DS27/R/USA, paras. 7.298 to 7.304. This finding was upheld by the Appellate Body, albeit on different grounds, compare Report of the Appellate Body on *European Communities – Regime for the Importation, Sale and Distribution of Bananas*, WT/DS27/AB/R.

667 GATT Contracting Parties, *Decision of 28 November 1979 on "Differential and More Favourable Treatment, Reciprocity and Fuller Participation of Developing Countries"*, BISD 26S/203.

1.3. Transparency

The concept of transparency comprises obligations concerning *(i)* the publication of all relevant regulations prior to enforcing them, and *(ii)* the notification of the other Member States of certain forms of governmental actions. This principle is *inter alia* laid down in Article X of the GATT 1994, in Article III of the GATS as well as in Article 63 of the TRIPS. Article X of the GATT also contains provisions on the uniform, impartial and reasonable administration of trade measures and the right of review of action taken pursuant to them.

The underlying goals, among others, are the creation of a rule-based approach ensuring impartial enforcement and the maximum economic gain out of the advantages granted by the WTO Agreement, such as market access or the protection of intellectual property[668].

1.4. Antidumping and Countervailing Duties

Article VI of the GATT 1994 condemns dumping by which "material injury" is caused or threatened to an established industry, or by which the establishment of a domestic industry is "materially retarded"[669]. Although specified by the Agreement on Implementation of Article VI of the General Agreement on Tariffs and Trade 1994, the concrete determination of "dumping" and "injury" continues to be rather vague. Arguably, this discretion can encourage protectionist abuses by petitioners and antidumping authorities at the expense of exporters and domestic consumers. Thus, it has been argued that this regime might actually lessen competition and foreclose markets[670].

1.5. Prohibition of export subsidies and discriminatory subsidies

Articles III and XVI:B of the GATT 1994 together with the Agreement on Subsidies and Countervailing Measures have introduced a more rule-based and ar-

---

[668] WTO Working Group on Trade and Competition Policy, *ibid.*, para. 57.

[669] Article VI of the GATT 1994 reads: "1. The contracting parties recognize that dumping, by which products of one country are introduced into the commerce of another country at less than the normal value of the products, is to be condemned if it causes or threatens material injury to an established industry in the territory of a contracting party or materially retards the establishment of a domestic industry. For the purposes of this Article, a product is to be considered as being introduced into the commerce of an importing country at less than its normal value, if the price of the product exported from one country to another *(a)* is less than the comparable price, in the ordinary course of trade, for the like product when destined for consumption in the exporting country, or, *(b)* in the absence of such domestic price, is less than either *(i)* the highest comparable price for the like product for export to any third country in the ordinary course of trade, or *(ii)* the cost of production of the product in the country of origin plus a reasonable addition for selling cost and profit. Due allowance shall be made in each case for differences in conditions and terms of sale, for differences in taxation, and for other differences affecting price comparability.* 2. In order to offset or prevent dumping, a contracting party may levy on any dumped product an anti-dumping duty not greater in amount than the margin of dumping in respect of such product. For the purposes of this Article, the margin of dumping is the price difference determined in accordance with the provisions of paragraph 1.* [...]"

[670] Compare E.-U. Petersmann, *Proposals For Negotiating International Competition Rules In The GATT-WTO World Trade and Legal System,* 49 (II/III) Aussenwirtschaft 1994, 250 et sqq.

guably more predictable and "justiciable"[671] subsidy regime compared to the situation under the GATT before Uruguay. From a competition policy point of view, this provision addresses governmental involvement in potentially anti-competitive practices on export markets.

1.6. Article XI of the GATT 1994

Article XI of the GATT 1994 prohibits any non-tariff border measures, whether made effective through "quotas, import or export licenses or other measures"[672]. In light of the effects doctrine, Article XI of the GATT 1994 may be relevant when Member States take action against foreign measures having detrimental effects in their domestic markets. In particular, Article XI is relevant for export cartels[673].

Arguably, this prohibition of non-tariff border measures has been further reinforced by the Uruguay Round[674]. For example, the Understanding on the Balance-of-Payments Provisions" requires Member States to prefer "price-based measures" over quantitative restrictions[675]. In addition, the Understanding in Respect of Waivers of Obligations under the GATT 1994 requires "waivers" to be phased out progressively[676]. Furthermore, the Agreement on Agriculture stipulates the obligation of "tariffication" of non-tariff border restrictions[677].

1.7. Article XVII of the GATT 1994

The principle of Non-Discrimination through internal taxation and regulation in Article III is supplemented by Article XVII of the GATT 1994, which specifies the obligation of non-discrimination for the business activities of state trading enterprises[678]. Accordingly, purchases or sales should be made in accordance

---

[671] E.-U. Petersmann, *ibid.*, 249 et sqq.

[672] Article XI of the GATT 1994 reads: "1. No prohibitions or restrictions other than duties, taxes or other charges, whether made effective through quotas, import or export licences or other measures, shall be instituted or maintained by any contracting party on the importation of any product of the territory of any other contracting party or on the exportation or sale for export of any product destined for the territory of any other contracting party. [...]"

[673] B. Hoekman, B./P. C. Mavroidis, *Economic Development, Competition Policy, and the World Trade Organization*, World Bank Policy Research Paper 2917, October 2002, available at: http://wdsbeta.worldbank.org/external/default/WDSContentServer/IW3P/IB/2002/11/22/000094946_02111404425138/Rendered/PDF/multi0page.pdf (04.06.2005), at 15 et sqq.

[674] E.-U. Petersmann, *Proposals For Negotiating International Competition Rules In The GATT-WTO World Trade and Legal System*, 49 (II/III) Aussenwirtschaft 1994, 248.

[675] *Ibid.*, para. 2.

[676] *Ibid.*, para. 2.

[677] *Ibid.*, Article 4 para. 2.

[678] Article XVII of the GATT 1994 reads: 1. (a) Each contracting party undertakes that if it establishes or maintains a State enterprise, wherever located, or grants to any enterprise, formally or in effect, exclusive or special privileges,* such enterprise shall, in its purchases or sales involving either imports or exports, act in a manner consistent with the general principles of non-discriminatory treatment prescribed in this Agreement for governmental measures affecting imports or exports by private traders. (b) The provisions of subparagraph (a) of this paragraph shall be understood to require that such enterprises shall, having due regard

with commercial considerations, and enterprises of other contracting parties shall be afforded adequate opportunity to compete, in accordance with customary business practices[679]. Since the Understanding on the Interpretation of Article XVII, strengthened notification and review procedures have been imposed so as to ensure the efficient surveillance of state-trading enterprises.

1.8. Prohibition of discriminatory safeguard measures

Article XIX of the GATT 1994 as interpreted by the Agreement on Safeguards has experienced considerable strengthening as opposed to GATT 1947. In particular, the Agreement provides for rules on investigation procedures, the non-discriminatory nature and diminishment of safeguard measures as well as a maximum duration. Moreover, certain "grey areas measures", such as voluntary export restraints, are explicitly prohibited[680].

1.9. GATS

Despite the GATS extending to "any service in any sector except services supplied in the exercise of governmental authority"[681], its Annexes provide for several sector-specific deviations and exemptions from the MFN principle, which tolerate, for example, market-sharing agreements in air and maritime transport services. Monopolies and exclusive service suppliers are permitted subject to consistent acting with the MFN obligation under Article II GATS and specific commitments.

Most prominently, and different from the GATT, Article IX of the GATS explicitly recognizes that "certain business practices of service suppliers, other than those falling under Article VIII, may restrain competition and thereby restrict trade in services"[682]. Article IX:2 provides for a consultation mechanism to eliminate such practices.

Another very explicit rule addressing competition is contained in Article XVI:2,a of the GATS, which stipulates that market access commitments entail a prohibition to limit the number of service suppliers through the use of monopolies and exclusive service suppliers.

Finally, the GATS' function to promote non-discriminatory conditions of competition can be read from Article XVII GATS which declares that "formally

to the other provisions of this Agreement, make any such purchases or sales solely in accordance with commercial considerations,* including price, quality, availability, marketability, transportation and other conditions of purchase or sale, and shall afford the enterprises of the other contracting parties adequate opportunity, in accordance with customary business practice, to compete for participation in such purchases or sales. [...].

679 WTO Working Group on Trade and Competition Policy, *ibid.*, para. 44.

680 Article 11 of the Agreement on Safeguards.

681 Article I GATS.

682 Article IX para. 1 of the GATS.

identical or formally different treatment shall be considered to be less favourable if its modifies the conditions of competition in favour of services or service suppliers of the Member compared to like services or service suppliers of any other Member".

1.10. TRIPS

The TRIPS Agreement is explicitly directed at the reduction of trade distortions and impediments, which are being caused by the inadequate protection of intellectual property rights. According to its Preamble, it pursues these objectives by implementing "adequate standards and principles concerning the availability, scope and use of trade-related intellectual property rights", by establishing a means of enforcement of intellectual property rights and by providing for effective and expeditious procedures for dispute settlement among governments. Thus, the Agreement arguably also enhances the transferability and international competition of intellectual property rights[683].

With regard to intellectual property, the issue of international exhaustion has been very controversial, as it can imply a restriction of competition through absolute territorial protection by means of import or export bans[684]. The TRIPS has not clarified this issue.

Under Article 40 of the TRIPS, Member Sates are entitled to exercise a certain amount of control over anticompetitive practices in contractual licensing. In particular, Member States are permitted to specify certain licensing practices or conditions for their respective jurisdictions, which might constitute an abuse and therefore, have an adverse effect on competition in the relevant market.

Likewise, Member States can arrange for compulsory licensing. Where they do, they must adhere to the conditions stipulated in Article 31 of the TRIPS. In any case, compulsory licensing can be used "to remedy a practice determined after judicial or administrative process to be anti-competitive"[685]. Moreover, Member States may take into account the need to correct "anti-competitive practices" for the determination of remuneration of compulsory licenses.

2. *Competition rules addressing private anticompetitive practices*

Different from the GATT 1947, the WTO Agreement has endorsed broad market access guarantees and integrated them into the Agreement. Consequently,

---

683 E.-U. Petersmann, *ibid.*, 251 et sqq.

684 For an overview of the EC Case Law on the issue of exhaustion refer to ECJ in Case C-355/96 *Silhouette* [1998] ECR I-4799; ECJ in Case C-173/98 *Sebago* [1999] 2 CMLR 1317; CFI in Case T-198/98 *Micro Leader* [1998] ECR II-3989; ECJ in *Javico International and Javico AG* v. *Yves Saint Laurent Parfums SA* Case C-306/96 [1998] ECR I-1983; ECJ in Cases C414-416/99 *Zino Davidoff SA* v. *A & G Imports Ltd. And Levi Strauss and Co. and Others* v. *Tesco Stores Ltd. And Others* [2000] ECR I-8691.

685 Article 31 (k) of the TRIPS.

various WTO provisions explicitly address private market-access barriers. However, given the fact that WTO law only creates obligations at the state level and not for private parties[686], the WTO approach toward private market-access barriers has been called imperfect[687]. Nevertheless, the current approach arguably corresponds better to increasingly global markets and affords the choice among alternative export strategies, foreign investment strategies, or licensing strategies to undertakings engaging in cross-border business activities[688]. Notably, many WTO provisions explicitly call for complementary WTO rules on private anti-competitive practices. In the following, the author shall briefly examine the current regulatory regime for private practices under the WTO Agreement.

2.1. GATS

Certain provisions in the GATS are designed to ensure that "monopolies and exclusive service suppliers" do not nullify or impair obligations and commitments under the GATS. For example, Members must ensure that in the course of competition a monopoly supplier does neither directly nor via a subsidiary abuse its dominant position[689].

The control of monopolistic abuses of dominant positions by existing competitors also constitutes a major aspect of ongoing negotiations in the services, such as in the telecommunications sector. These negotiations are based on the "specific commitments" as regulated in Articles XVI to XVIII of the GATS. Consequently, some of these market-access commitments amount to an internationalization of competition policy, and may imply the need to adopt more general competition rules for the countries subject to the individual concessions granted under the GATS[690].

Moreover, the GATS explicitly recognizes that "certain business practices of service suppliers [...] may restrain competition and thereby restrict trade in services"[691]. Member States are required to enter into consultations so as to eliminate such practices[692].

---

686 Compare Article II of the 1994 Marrakesh Agreement in relation with its Article XI, where it is stipulated that *Members* of the WTO are the GATT Contracting Parties (and thus states) and the European Communities.

687 E.-U. Petersmann, *International Competition Rules for Governments and for Private Business. The Case for Linking Future WTO Negotiations on Investment, Competition and Environmental Rules to Reforms of Anti-Dumping Laws*, in: 30(3) Journal of World Trade 1996, at 18.

688 E.-U. Petersmann, *ibid.*

689 Compare Articles VIII:1 and VIII:2 of the GATS:

690 Compare E.-U. Petersmann, *ibid.*, 19 et sqq.

691 Article IX:1 of the GATS.

692 Article IX:2 of the GATS.

2.2. TRIPS

In the area of intellectual property, there is general tension between the protection of intellectual property as an incentive for innovation and, therefore, a precondition of competition on the one hand, and the inherent risk of restraints on competition due to too far-reaching protection of exclusive intellectual property rights on the other[693]. Unlike the GATS, therefore, the TRIPS Agreement does not only focus on market access, but also establishes "unfair trade rules".

For instance, its Article 17 addresses the "fair use of descriptive terms" as a possible limited exception to the rights conferred by a trademark. Articles 22 et sqq. of the TRIPS focus on "misleading" use of geographical indications or use constituting an "act of unfair competition". Article 39 of the TRIPS stipulates that "in the course of ensuring effective protection against unfair competition", Member Sates shall protect undisclosed commercial information against "unfair commercial use".

However, the existing regulatory regime of the TRIPS on the delimitation of the potential "abuse of intellectual property rights by right holders" and the potential resort to "practices which unreasonably restrain trade or adversely affect the international transfer of technology"[694] against legitimate incentives for innovation must still be considered fragmentary[695]. The TRIPS has introduced rather virulent provisions such as Article 31 on patent uses without authorization of the right-holder to "correct anti-competitive practices"[696] through compulsory licensing. Article 40, which regulates the control of anti-competitive practices in contractual licences through exclusive grant-back conditions, conditions preventing challenges to validity and coercive package licensing may serve as another example for a rather stringent regime. Yet, the TRIPS has deliberately omitted any commitments concerning the vexed issue of international exhaustion of intellectual property rights[697].

In any case, the TRIPS entails a need for domestic competition laws not only for developing countries who have not yet adopted one, but also for developed countries whose competition laws merit a more systemic approach to the protection of competition among intellectual property rights as opposed to their potential abuse[698].

---

693 E.-U. Petersmann, *ibid.*, 20.

694 Article 8 of the TRIPS.

695 E.-U. Petersmann, *ibid.*

696 Article 31, (k) of the TRIPS.

697 Article 6 of the TRIPS reads: "[...] nothing in this Agreement shall be used to address the issue of the exhaustion of intellectual property rights."

698 E.-U. Petersmann, *ibid.*

2.3. Other Multilateral Agreements

Private anti-competitive practices are addressed in various other Multilateral Agreements of the WTO Agreement.

For instance, the TBT lays down a detailed regime intended to guarantee the least trade-restrictive approach for the preparation, adoption and application of technical regulations and standards, as well as the related conformity assessment procedures by non-governmental bodies[699].

The Agreement on Preshipment Inspection regulates the activities of private pre-shipment inspection entities[700]. The Agreement on Implementation of Article VI of the General Agreement on Tariffs and Trade 1994 regulates in detail private injurious dumping and price undertakings. In particular, for the determination of injury, the Agreement inter alia refers to "trade-restrictive practices of and competition between the foreign and domestic producers"[701].

Private practices are addressed in the Agreement on Subsidies, which regulates market displacement and price undercutting in an industry[702], as well as the possibility of voluntary undertakings of an exporter to revise its prices so as to suspend or terminate proceedings under the Agreement[703].

Moreover, the Agreement on Safeguards prohibits voluntary export restraints and orderly marketing arrangements or similar measures, such as compulsory import cartels, or discretionary exporting or importing licensing schemes which would afford protection[704]. In addition, it requires the Member States not to "encourage or support the adoption or maintenance by public and private enterprises" of non-governmental measures equivalent to these latter practices[705].

C. Traditional Arguments for Additional International Competition Rules from a WTO Perspective

1. Inconsistency and lack of systemic approach to competition under current WTO Law

The complementarity of trade and competition policy as illustrated above merits a more consistent approach of WTO law toward competition than currently contained. Both policy areas pursue the same economic objective of increasing welfare. This relationship between competition and trade policy has been ac-

[699] Compare Articles 3, 4 and 8 of the Agreement on Technical Barriers to Trade.
[700] Article 2 of the Agreement on Preshipment Inspections.
[701] Compare Article 3.5 of the Agreement on Implementation of Article VI of the GATT 1994.
[702] Compare Article 6 of the Agreement on Subsidies and Countervailing Measures.
[703] *Ibid.*, Article 18.
[704] Article 11.1 of the Agreement on Safeguards, with a reference to Note #4 to it.
[705] Article 11.3 of the Agreement on Safeguards.

knowledged as early as the 1920s, when international cartels were identified as "an enemy of world trade" by the League of Nations[706]. Subsequently, the importance of competition to multilateral trading agreements has been recognized in the draft ITO Charter.

In light of the success of the liberalisation of traditional at-the-border measures such as tariffs or other governmental non-tariff trade barriers, the past approach of predominance of trade policy over competition policy should be reconsidered. It is widely recognized that in the absence of a sound competition law regime, the maximum possible benefits from trade liberalisation and regulatory reforms in the course of FDI cannot be achieved.[707] In particular, successful liberalisation has increased the relative significance of private market barriers and privately initiated market distortions where no competition law is in force. Likewise, lenient enforcement of domestic competition laws could undermine the effects of liberalisation. Existing domestic legal instruments addressing unfair trade practices can only imperfectly deal with international anti-competitive business practices. Consequently, an increasing number of trade disputes have a competition dimension[708].

Currently, a number of provisions can be found in the WTO Agreement, which are addressing competition among governments as well as competition among private actors. The current approach is imperfect, however, as competition is addressed only in a non-systematic and fragmentary manner[709].

For instance, both GATT and GATS acknowledge the possibility of "nullification" or "impairment" of the competitive benefits afforded under the WTO Agreement by private market-access barriers[710]. At the same time, the existing obligations are predominantly result-oriented. Arguably, the introduction of additional conduct-oriented competition rules would enhance the efficiency of the WTO Agreement[711].

Another important example for the inadequacy of the current system is the TRIPS Agreement. The TRIPS Agreement can be considered as affording rather strong minimum standards for worldwide protection, or more concretely the availability, scope, use and enforcement, of private intellectual property

---

706 E. Iacobucci, *The Interdependence of Trade and Competition Policies*, in 21(2) Journal of World Competition 1997, at 5.

707 I. G. Bercero/S. D. Amarasinha, *Moving the Trade and Competition Debate Forward*, in: Journal of International Economic Law 2001, 481.

708 E. M. Graham, *The Relationship Between International Trade Policy and Competition Policy*, in Z. Drabek (ed.), *Globalization Under Threat: The Stability of Trade Policy and Multilateral Agreements* (2001), at 228 et sqq, referring for instance to the Case *Japan – Measures Affecting Consumer Photographic Film and Paper* (DS44).

709 I. G. Bercero/S. D. Amarasinha, *Moving the Trade and Competition Debate Forward*, in: Journal of International Economic Law 2001, at 481.

710 Compare Chapter IV.A.3.3. above.

711 E.-U. Petersmann, *International Competition Rules for Governments and for Private Business*, in: 30(3) Journal of World Trade 1996, at 22.

rights to their holders. These rights holders are predominantly located in developed countries as the major knowledge "producers"[712]. In Article 40:1, the TRIPS Agreement recognizes that certain practices might restrain competition, distort trade and can impede the transfer and dissemination of technology. Accordingly, Article 40:2 of the Agreement stipulates that "nothing in this Agreement shall prevent Members from specifying in their legislation licensing practices or conditions that may in particular cases constitute an abuse of intellectual property rights having an adverse effect on competition in the relevant market". Yet, while TRIPS lists some potentially abusive practices such as exclusive grant-back conditions or coercive package licensing, no minimum standards are imposed for domestic competition law. Likewise, compulsory licensing is laid down on a high-level basis only[713]. Thus, central questions remain unanswered, such as the concrete practices that should be treated as abuses, appropriate standards of review or remedies[714]. Most importantly, however, the issue of exhaustion should be clarified[715]. Depending on the level of exhaustion at the national, regional or international level, the title holder can prevent a third party from importing protected goods. The application of exhaustion at the national level bears most potential for protectionism, as imports in other countries can be totally banned. The TRIPS Agreement completely excludes this question from its scope, and thus allows for national exhaustion. In light of developing countries being major knowledge importers, it is important to clarify this issue so as to outweigh the existing imbalance caused by the transfer of payments from developing to developed countries as knowledge producers.

It has been illustrated above that under the current system of co-existing domestic competition laws, certain practices cannot be handled adequately by unilateral extraterritorial application of domestic competition law. The acknowledged complementarity of the economic policy objectives supports additional international competition rules within WTO law where such rules cannot be achieved at the level of domestic competition laws.

In light of the various WTO provisions calling explicitly for an examination of the implications relating to competition policy[716], it must be concluded that this examination is still incomplete[717]. Consequently, subject to a comprehensive analysis and implementation of its results, the current approach might be suboptimal.

---

[712] J. Drexl, *ibid.*, at 440.

[713] Compare Article 31 of the TRIPS.

[714] R. Anderson/P. Holmes, *ibid.*, at 549.

[715] E.-U. Petersmann, *Proposals For Negotiating International Competition Rules In The GATT-WTO World Trade and Legal System*, 49 (II/III) Aussenwirtschaft 1994, at 259.

[716] E.g. Article 9 of the Agreement on Trade-Related Investment Measures; Article 6 of the Agreement on Preshipment Inspection.

[717] This is so despite the work of the WTO Working Group on the Interaction of Trade and Competition Policy, which is also supported by the fact that negotiations on the Singapore issue of trade and competition policy have been dropped at the WTO Cancún Ministerial Conference of September 2003.

In addition, competition laws differ from multilateral trade agreements by the greater focus of competition laws on non-discriminatory treatment, equal opportunities for all market participants, protecting the individual rights of domestic citizens, judicial review, and the promotion of basic consumer interests as opposed to interests of certain other (industry) groups in the country[718]. Thus, it has been argued that institutionalizing the links between competition and multilateral trade rules would help to overcome the existing protectionist elements in international trade law and to strengthen the protection of individual rights. Consequently, adding additional international competition rules to the WTO Agreement could contribute to the "constitutionalizing" of the equal rights of domestic citizens and prevent the protectionist abuse of discretionary trade policies[719].

2. *Risk of protectionism through insufficient addressing of international anti-competitive practices by private actors*

Certain shortcomings identified from a competition policy perspective are not outweighed by current WTO law to a sufficient extent. This leads to detrimental welfare effects and supports the case for additional international competition rules from a trade policy perspective as illustrated below.

2.1. *Practices affecting market access for importers – Weak competition rules as Trade Barries*

It has been illustrated above that private market access impediments can result from various practices, such as vertical restraints, import cartels, market sharing agreements, predatory behaviour against importers, certain exclusive or special privileges or monopolies[720]. The potential substitution of governmental market access barriers by private ones has been a major concern among the promoters of additional competition rules for WTO law, and has also brought about the famous Chapter V of the Havana Charter.

The *Kodak/Fuji* case[721] is a classical example for the inherent difficulties of the approach toward private market access impediments under the WTO Agreement. In light of a complaint of the US film producer Kodak that the Japanese government would encourage anti-competitive practices at the manufacturing, distribution and retails levels, the US filed a complaint against Japan. This non-violation complaint was based on Articles III, X as well as XXIII:1, b of the

---

[718] E.-U. Petersmann, *Proposals For Negotiating International Competition Rules In The GATT-WTO World Trade and Legal System*, 49 (II/III) Aussenwirtschaft 1994, at 263.

[719] E.-U. Petersmann, *ibid.*

[720] Compare Chapter III.B.

[721] WTO Panel Report, *Japan – Measures Affecting Consumer Photographic Film and Paper* (DS44).

GATT 1994[722]. This last provision has been interpreted as being based on the idea that "the improved competitive opportunities that can legitimately be expected from a tariff concession can be frustrated not only by measures proscribed by the GATT but also by measures consistent with that Agreement." Consequently, the main value of a tariff concession was held to be the fact that it provides an assurance of better market access through improved price competition[723]. The Panel explained that most non-violation cases in GATT history concerned the introduction of a GATT-consistent subsidy after the grant of a tariff concession on that product. It explained, however, that the application of Article XXIII:1, b to other governmental actions, such as strengthening the competitiveness of certain industry sectors through non-financial assistance, could not *a priori* be ruled out. Consequently, it accepted that a Member State's industrial policy could under certain circumstances "upset the competitive relationship in the market place between domestic and imported products"[724]. Albeit the Panel was ready to apply a rather broad definition of the term "measures" which could also comprise certain non-binding actions providing certain incentives for private parties to act in a particular way, the complainant must also prove a causal *de iure* or *de facto* discrimination with regard to domestic competitors[725]. Due to a lack of evidence as to the actual effects of the "measures" deployed, the claim was dismissed and not appealed. Later case law similarly suggests that Article XXIII:1(b) should be approached with caution and remain an exceptional remedy[726].

Thus, it has been confirmed that WTO law only creates obligations for Member States, but not for private actors. Consequently, WTO rules can be used to challenge private practices which anti-competitively impede market access only if the complaining party can demonstrate that the practices at issue are encouraged or supported by a state authority. In any case, the possibilities of retaliation must be considered limited in light of the findings in *Kodak/Fuji*, as any subsequent introduction of countermeasures were held to very probably constitute an infringement of Article II or Article XI of the GATT 1994[727]. Consequently, when the importing country does not have or does not enforce a com-

---

[722] Article XXIII:1,b reads: "1. If any contracting party should consider that any benefit accruing to it directly or indirectly under this Agreement is being nullified or impaired or that the attainment of any objective of the Agreement is being impeded as the result of [...] or (b) the application by another contracting party of any measure, whether or not it conflicts with the provisions of this Agreement, or [...], the contracting party may, with a view to the satisfactory adjustment of the matter, make written representations or proposals to the other contracting party or parties which it considers to be concerned. Any contracting party thus approached shall give sympathetic consideration to the representations or proposals made to it."

[723] Panel Report in *Japan – Measures Affecting Consumer Photographic Film and Paper*, WT/DS44/R, at para. 10.35; by reference to the earlier *Oilseeds* case.

[724] Panel Report in *Japan – Measures Affecting Consumer Photographic Film and Paper*, WT/DS44/R, at para. 10.38.

[725] *Ibid.*, paras. 10.49, 10.85.

[726] *European Communities – Measures Affecting Asbestos and Asbestos-Containing Products*, WT/DS135/AB/R (March 12, 2001).

[727] F. Amato, *International Antitrust: What Future?* In: 24(4) Journal of World Competition 2001, at 454.

petition law, no remedy might be available under the WTO Agreement against the access impediments.

Given the reasoning in *Kodak/Fuji,* the limited total number of non-violation cases and given also the fact that there has only been one single successful non-violation claim since the 1950ies[728], the application of the GATT 1994 to private anti-competitive measures which do not entail a violation of an existing agreement appears to be difficult in practice[729].

Hauser and *Schoene* brought forward in light of the above that a more aggressive use of non-violation complaints should be endorsed under Article XXIII:1,b of the GATT 1994[730]. This implies the yet unanswered question as to whether passive toleration of a restrictive business practice could amount to governmental support subject to a "legitimate expectation"[731], which might in turn lead to difficulties with regard to consensus. Rating weak or non-existent competition policies as market access barriers distorting trade implies the risk of an obligation to adopt competition laws. Therefore, the excessive focus on market access for competition policy has been criticized by developing countries[732]. In particular, concerns have been raised that such obligation might be detrimental to the establishment and strengthening of domestic industries in light of free competition with more efficient foreign producers.

These concerns are legitimate in light of the general principle under GATT law that each Contracting Party is free to adopt non-discriminatory internal taxes and regulations (Article III GATT 1947), production subsidies (Articles III:8 and XVI:1 of the GATT 1947) or other trade restrictions if they are "necessary" to achieve certain specified public policy purposes as specified by Articles XVII to XXI of the GATT 1947, for example. Consequently, although the introduction of competition law must generally be considered in the interest of each country, no *prima facie* obligation to do so can be derived from current WTO law.

Nevertheless, in light of the incomplete coverage of domestic competition law as illustrated above, a potential need to adapt current WTO law and its interpretation to a changed environment can be identified. However, any potential solution in terms of amending the Agreement would depend on the developing countries' consent, and would have to be fitted accordingly between the principles of non-discrimination and competition among regulatory systems on the one hand, and any legitimate expectations under WTO law on the other.

---

728 GATT decision in *EEC – Payments and Subsidies Paid to Processors and Producers of Oilseeds and Related Animal-Feed Proteins,* compare J. Jackson/W. Davey/A. Sykes, *ibid.*, 284.

729 R. D. Anderson/P. Holmes, *ibid.*, 551.

730 H. Hauser/R.E. Schoene, *Is There a Need for International Competition Rules?* In: 49(II/III) Aussenwirtschaft 1994, at 209.

731 WTO Panel Report, *Japan – Measures Affecting Consumer Photographic Film and Paper* (DS44), at para. 10.61.

732 R. D. Anderson/P. Holmes, *ibid.*, at 540.

2.2. Practices affecting international markets with similar effects for several countries

The major example of such restraints is the problem of international cartels[733]. From a competition policy perspective, despite certain achievements with regard to enforcement in developed countries, international cartels can not yet be considered as fully overcome[734]. The current WTO regime does not have a specific mechanism in place to deal with such practices[735]. Rather, the only possible remedy is a non-violation complaint under Article 26 of the Understanding on Rules and Procedures Governing the Settlement of Disputes (DSU), which does not entail any obligation to withdraw the measure at issue[736].

While it has been questioned that international cartels are a "trade issue" *per se*, international cartels can affect trade policy goals. This is due to the fact that although a complete coverage of strong antitrust laws is a key factor in addressing international cartels, it may also undermine the benefits from trade liberalisation[737]. Consequently, a need for additional rules for international cartels can be supported from a trade policy point of view.

2.3. Practices having a differential impact on national markets – Weak competition policies as strategic Industrial Policy

The widely cited example for a practice having a differential impact on national markets is the export cartel[738]. It has already been illustrated that export cartels are particularly problematic from a competition policy perspective, as they are generally not addressed by domestic competition law due to the lack of anti-competitive effects on the home market[739]. Based on a strict application of the effects doctrine, domestic competition law therefore pursues a "beggar-thy-neighbour" policy. This promotes the competitiveness of domestic undertakings at no social costs, as only foreign consumers are harmed[740].

Arguably, current WTO law even "invites" undertakings to implement export cartels by means of the market access guarantees affords[741]. Still, Article XI of the GATT 1947 can be relevant provided that sufficient governmental in-

733 WTO Working Group on the Interaction of Trade and Competition Policy ("WGTCP"), *Report 1998*, WT/WGTCP/2, available at: http://docsonline.wto.org/DDFDocuments/t/WT/WGTCP/2.doc (23.3.2003), at para. 87.

734 Compare Chapter III.B.1.2.1. In particular, countries are only concerned with international cartels as long as they bear a detrimental effect in their home markets, compare R. D. Anderson/P. Holmes, *ibid.*, 544.

735 WTO WGTCP, *Report 1998*, at para. 62.

736 Article 26:1,(b) DSU.

737 R. D. Anderson/P. Holmes, *ibid.*, 544.

738 WTO WGTCP, *Report 1998*, at para. 89.

739 Compare Chapter II.D.6.2.

740 J. Drexl, *International Competition Policy After Cancún: Placing a Singapore Issue on the Development Agenda*, in: 27(3) Journal of World Competition 2004, at 430.

741 J. Drexl, *ibid.*

volvement can be established. In the *Japan – Semiconductors* case[742], the panel adopted a "but for" test to measure the extent the practice at issue would have occurred without governmental involvement. In that case, the panel did not specify as to whether mere "tolerance" of a cartel would suffice. In light of the wording "restriction", which is wider than "law", "regulation" or "requirement", an extensive interpretation would appear to be possible[743]. Still, a recent Panel suggests that Article XI does not impose a duty of due diligence on Member States to prevent the existence of export cartels[744]. Arguably, a legislative initiative would bring legal certainty to this situation.

So far, therefore, the most promising remedy available to WTO Member States to protect their home markets has been the adoption of competition laws. However, as illustrated above, the adoption of competition law itself is not sufficient in light of procedural and jurisdictional difficulties connected with cross-border investigations. Moreover, pro- and anticompetitive effects of an export cartel may be divided unequally among states. This unequal distribution can imply discriminatory application of domestic competition law if potential negative effects abroad are not taken into consideration[745].

The economic effect of an export cartel is a rise in export prices and, consequently, a terms-of-trade gain for the exporting country[746]. However, given that export cartels usually harm consumers in the export market more than they benefit the colluding firms in the exporting countries, they do not merely constitute a transfer of wealth but a global welfare and efficiency loss[747] which cannot adequately be prevented or dealt with by domestic competition law. Thus, weak competition policies can be used as strategic industrial policy which can potentially bring about protectionist and trade distorting effects[748].

Arguably, the export cartel exemption in the GATT 1994 is contrary to the general obligation of non-discriminatory treatment in international commerce[749] and contrary to the WTO Agreement's underlying policy objective of raising global welfare while allowing for an optimal use of resources[750]. Moreover, this exemption also contravenes the development objectives introduced by the

742 GATT Panel decision, *Japan – Trade in Semi-Conductors*, BISD 36S/345.

743 B. Hoekman/P. C. Mavroidis, *Economic Development, Competition Policy and the World Trade Organization*, in: 37(1) Journal of World Trade 2003, at 13,

744 WTO Panel Report, *Argentina – Measures Affecting the Export of Bovine Hides and the Import of Finished Leather*, WTO Doc. WT/DS155/R (Dec. 19, 2000). Compare A. Alvarez-Jiménez, *ibid.*, at 478.

745 J. Drexl *ibid.*, 431. For instance, under the new EU Merger Regulation 139/2004, a merger can only be declared "incompatible with the Common Market" where it substantially impedes competition "in the Common Market", compare Article 2(2) of Reg. 139/2004.

746 A. Mattoo/A. Subramanian, *Multilateral Rules on Competition Policy – A Possible Way Forward*, in: 31(5) Journal of World Trade 1997, at 103.

747 F. Amato, *ibid.*, 455.

748 A. Mattoo/A. Subramanian, *ibid.*

749 Compare para 3 of the Preamble to the GATT 1947.

750 Compare para 1 of the Preamble to the *Marrakesh Agreement Establishing the World Trade Organization*.

WTO regime[751], because developing countries as common net importers are prime targets of such practices, but often not in the position to effectively enforce domestic competition law.

Other than export cartels, exemptions of co-operative R&D ventures from domestic competition law or the lenient application of domestic merger regulations to "domestic champions" have been cited as examples for practices affecting foreign markets[752]. With regard to the first, the exemption of such ventures to increase the incentive for R&D can confer benefits on domestic rivals. With regard to the latter, the underlying rationale is the promotion of large domestic firms against foreign rivals. Arguably, the second example is more prone to discriminatory behaviour and, thus, more problematic than the first one, as general exemptions for R&D would equally be afforded to foreign entities acting in the jurisdiction at issue.

It can be inferred from these examples that domestic exemptions to competition law do have the potential for negative international spill-over effects. The promotion of competitiveness of domestic undertakings can bring about welfare gains for the state at issue. At the same time, the exemptions leave situations of imperfect competition unimpeded. Consequently, potential welfare gains could occur at the expense of other states. In light of the classical "prisoner's dilemma", a country might be better off individually. Yet, if all countries deployed the same strategy, all of them would be worse off[753]. In sum, a need for supplementing the existing WTO law by additional international competition rules can be established in light of practices having a differential impact on national markets.

3. *Protectionism trough Anti-dumping Laws*

Since Canada adopted the first antidumping regime through its Customs Tariff in 1904, many other predominantly industrialized countries have followed. Generally, these laws provide for sanctions against exporting countries "dumping" goods into domestic markets, thereby causing material injury to domestic producers of the "like product". For the WTO Member States, these laws must be in conformity with the anti-dumping regime under the GATT 1994 and the Agreement on Implementation of Article VI of the GATT 1994 since 1994 at the latest[754]. The GATT 1947 allows for anti-dumping duties in order to offset or prevent dumping, provided that material injury for domestic producers can

[751] Compare for example Preamble to the 1994 *Marrakesh Agreement*.

[752] A. Mattoo/A. Subramanian, *ibid.*

[753] A. Mattoo/A. Subramanian, *ibid.*, 103 et sqq.

[754] Before the foundation of the WTO with the underlying "Single Package Idea", Canada and the USA have not considered them bound by Article VI of the GATT 1947, arguing that their domestic antidumping laws predated the GATT in light of "grandfather rights" under the *Protocol of Provisional Application*.

be positively proved[755]. Based on this intergovernmental source of legitimacy, domestic antidumping laws generally seek to prevent the allegedly detrimental effects of pricing below cost and discriminatory pricing. But do these two effects economically justify the existence of antidumping laws?

With regard to predatory pricing below cost, the economic justification is that systematically pricing below cost with a view to eliminating rivals from the market is particularly harmful to competition in the export markets as it lets the foreign competitor reap any monopoly profits thereby created. Consequently, overall efficiency is being compromised[756]. Yet, the case is not as clear for selling below-cost in order to gain market share or as a short-term measure preferred to a total shortfall of sales. Accordingly, there is no economic rationale to penalize most short-term sales below-cost, as long as marginal costs do not exceed marginal revenues. Moreover, there is no economic rationale in protecting one set of competitors against another as long as efficient competition in the relevant market is not restricted[757].

As far as discriminatory pricing is concerned, the economic case appears to be equally uncertain. Market power and barriers to entry to prevent arbitrage are a prerequisite for charging different prices for the same product in separate markets. Although the existence of market power and barriers to entry indicates that competition in the relevant market is not of optimum efficiency, it must not necessarily follow that overall welfare is affected to the negative[758]. First, with regard to the effects of discriminatory pricing on the exporting country, the two prominent arguments in favour of prohibiting domestic price discrimination are *(i)* a possible decrease in output and *(ii)* social costs due to market segregation and certain incentives to seek monopoly[759]. These arguments appear inconclusive and only allow for the conclusion that although a detrimental effect of dumping on the exporting country cannot be established on balance, the exporters' gains would in the end have to be borne by the consumers[760].

Nevertheless, the case for anti-dumping laws must be justified by the effects of exports at discriminatory prices to the importing country deploying its anti-dumping laws. There is general agreement that consumers in the importing country will benefit from the lower prices of the dumped products, whereas producers will be harmed through a loss of market share to the dumper. Arguably, anti-dumping action is legitimate only where the consumers' benefits would not outweigh the damage to the producers in the long term.

---

755 WTO, *Agreement on Implementation of Article VI of the General Agreement on Tariffs and Trade 1994,* Article 3.1.
756 M. J. Trebilcock, *ibid.*, 182.
757 W. J. Davey, *Antidumping Laws: A Time for Restriction?* In: 1988 Fordham Corp. L. Inst., at 8-1 et sqq.
758 W. J. Davey, *Antidumping Laws: A Time for Restriction?* In: 1988 Fordham Corp. L. Inst., at 8-1 et sqq.
759 M. J. Trebilcock, *The Regulation of International Trade*, at 177 et sqq.
760 W. J. Davey, *ibid.*, at 8-1 et sqq.

This is mainly the case if the dumper is engaging in predatory conduct so as to drive domestic competitors out of the market in order to subsequently raise its prices to monopolistic level. However, in this regard, it is important to note that according to economic theory, predatory dumping is hardly ever to occur in light of the information *ex ante* required for successful predation of market share[761].

Alternatively, anti-dumping action may be legitimate if the dumping is the reaction to a temporary market condition, and if the dumping implies substantial re-adjustment costs for domestic producers upon reactivation of their plants once the dumper leaves their market[762]. Consequently, two inherent questions must be answered. First, is the dumper likely to leave the domestic market? Second, in case it does, will the domestic producer raise its prices so as to offset the consumers' benefits from the dumped prices? In light of empirical evidence, the answer to both questions is negative[763].

Consequently, the only legitimate economic justification for the application of anti-dumping laws may be predatory dumping, which rarely occurs. Rather, dumping might be efficiency enhancing[764]. Thus, economic analysis alone does not justify the imposition of anti-dumping duties in order to offset non-predatory price discrimination or non-predatory below-cost sales, as they are currently applied by various countries. However, efficiency considerations might not reflect the full political grasp of anti-dumping laws[765]. In fact, a major proportion of the discussion concerning their legitimacy is based on arguments not relating to efficiency, but to "fairness" instead, in that low-priced foreign imports are perceived as an "unfair" trading practice. Nations have agreed (first in bilateral and then in multilateral agreements such as the GATT) that unilateral responses to certain trade practices deemed objectionable should be permitted under international trade rules.

However, "fairness" is a "difficult concept"[766] in international economic relations. This is in particular true where the underlying legal framework only provides limited guidance as to what is considered "unfair". Article VI.2 of the GATT 1994 allows for unilateral measures in form of anti-dumping duties by a Contracting Party so as to respond to dumping which causes or threatens material injury to an established domestic industry or materially retards the establishment of a domestic industry. Thus, the Contracting Parties are entitled to

---

[761] In fact, in order to be successful, the predator would have to know in advance *(i)* the price level required to drive domestic producers out of the market, and *(ii)* if it could afterwards raise its prices sufficiently high so as to compensate for the losses through the previously predatory prices, compare W. J. Davey, *ibid.;* Compare also M. J. Trebilcock, *The Regulation of International Trade*, at 178.

[762] W. J. Davey, *ibid.*

[763] W. J. Davey, *ibid.* For a dissenting analysis compare EC Commission, *Eleventh Annual Report on the Community's Anti-Dumping and Anti-Subsidy Acitivities*, at paras. 2.2. et sqq.

[764] H. Wins, *ibid.*, at 56.

[765] M. J. Trebilcock, *The Regulation of International Trade*, at 186.

[766] M. J. Trebilcock, *ibid.*

adopt internal legislation to that effect, according to the requirements set out in the Agreement on Implementation of Article VI of the GATT 1994.

For instance, para 2.4 of the Agreement introduces the ambiguous requirement of a "fair comparison" between export price and normal value of a given product. In addition, while the general MFN obligation of Article I GATT 1994 would equally apply to anti-dumping duties[767], the Contracting Parties appear to have at times interpreted a certain amount of discretion into the Agreement[768]. In light of this discretion, the complex calculations and the multifaceted procedures of taking evidence, there is increased criticism that the use of anti-dumping duties may have become a disguised form of protectionism. This criticism is further reinforced by the fact that the alleged "unfairness" of business practices relating to dumping is not so convincing where similar behaviour taking effect only within the domestic jurisdiction is subject to less restrictive regulation than foreseen by the domestic anti-dumping law[769].

In this regard, it should also be noted that this criticism has first evolved at a point where the main users of anti-dumping duties were large industrialized Contracting Parties such as the US, the EC, Canada or Australia, who mainly imposed anti-dumping against developing countries. Today, various newly industrialized countries as well as developing countries are regularly making use of anti-dumping duties as well[770], which supports the political importance of anti-dumping measures.

In light of *(i)* the lack of economic justification of applying anti-dumping laws to non-predatory sales below cost or non-predatory discriminatory pricing and *(ii)* the criticism of disguised protectionism in the application of domestic anti-dumping laws, it has been argued that they should be replaced with either multilateral or harmonized domestic competition rules focussing on cross-border

767 Compare Jackson/Davey/Sykes, *ibid.*, 698.

768 See for example the wording of para 9.1 of the *Agreement on Implementation of Article VI of GATT 1994*. In this regard, it is also worth noting that dumping cases in the EU result in very different amounts of anti-dumping duties than in the US, for instance. This is due to the EU authorities' discretion according to para. 9.1. of the *Agreement on Implementation of Article VI of GATT 1994* to impose a lesser duty than the amount of the dumping margin, if it would be sufficient to eliminate the injury to a certain industry. Compare also para. 5.8 of the Agreement which lays down certain *de minimis* rules: "[...] The volume of dumped products shall normally be regarded negligible if [...]".Compare Jackson/Davey/Sykes, *ibid.*, 706.

769 In the United States, domestic price discrimination is addressed by the *Robinson-Patman Act*, which provides for numerous defences to price discrimination but none to dumping. Also, the *Robinson-Patman Act* has been interpreted by the Courts to protect competition rather than individual competitors, compare *Brooke Group Ltd. V. Brown & Wiliamson Tobacco Corp., 509 U.S. 209, 113 S.Ct. 2578, 125 L.Ed.2d 168 (1993)*. The US Antidumping statute, on the other hand, has been interpreted to protect individual competitors, regardless of the overall implications for competition, compare Jackson/Davey/Sykes, *ibid.*, 692. Thus, price discrimination is less condemned domestically within the United States than it is internationally. Similarly, domestically, there is acceptance of below-cost sales in the United States as long as they are not predatory, compare *Brooke Group Ltd. V. Brown & Wiliamson Tobacco Corp.*, 509 U.S. 209, 113 S.Ct. 2578, 125 L.Ed.2d 168 (1993). This is not inline with the approach pursued for dumped imports, compare Jackson/Davey/Sykes, *ibid.*, 692.

770 E.g. Brazil and Mexico have become major users, compare J. Mirandes/R. Torres/M. Ruiz, *The International Use of Antidumping*, in: 32 Journal of World Trade 1998, at 5.

predation. This argument is supported by the fact that various jurisdictions have explicitly chosen the primacy of competition laws over antidumping laws[771]. In addition, research undertaken by the International Trade Commission has demonstrated that removing the antidumping and countervailing duties that were active in the US in 1991 would have meant a welfare gain equivalent to about 0.03 percent of the US GDP in that year[772].

Yet, examples such as the approach adopted by the Australian-New Zealand Closer Economic Co-operation Agreement (ANZCERTA) remain an interesting exception to the rule. In the 1990 Protocol on the Acceleration of Free Trade in Goods to the ANZCERTA, its Member States have agreed to revise their competition laws so as to address anti-competitive conduct affecting trans-Tasman trade in goods. Instead of recourse to anti-dumping actions, the Member States have chosen to extend existing extra-territorial application of their competition laws, while mutually lifting immunity from the application of the other Member States' competition laws within their territory[773].

Rather, the approach generally prevailing is to allow for duties on goods priced at non-predatory level, so that the application of anti-dumping laws presently results in welfare losses. These losses occur through costs for consumers in export markets and costs on foreign producers, which domestic ones do not have to bear[774]. Thus, current anti-dumping laws must be held to be ill-equipped to deal with predation. Rather, anti-dumping laws must be considered the price that had to be paid for a multilateral trading system in which certain industries would not have been prepared to face import competition without a guarantee to this trade remedy[775]. Consequently, the currency for the payment of this price should be changed from anti-dumping laws to integrated competition rules.

4. *Domestic competition policy as unfair regulatory competition among governments*

It has already been illustrated in detail that individual domestic competition law instruments feature considerable differences. As explained above, this is generally legitimate under the GATT in light of the general principle of competition among regulatory systems[776]. In addition, the author has shown that domestic

---

771 Chapters III.B.1.1.2.(ii) and III.C.3.1.2.(ii).

772 J. Tavares de Araujo Jr, *Legal and Economic Interfaces Between Antidumping and Competition Policy*, in: 25(2) Journal of World Competition 2002, at 162.

773 S. Woolcock, *International Competition Policy and the World Trade Organisation, Paper for the LSE Global Dimensions/Federal Trust Forum on the 'Singapore Issues' in the WTO, March 25-27th 2003, London School of Economics*, available at: http://www.lse.ac.uk/collections/globalDimensions/tradepolicy/papers/woolcock.htm (24.02.2005).

774 M. J. Trebilcock, *ibid.*, 189.

775 J. Tavares de Araujo Jr, *ibid.*

776 Compare Chapter IV.A.3.3.

competition laws commonly feature certain exemptions which may lead to negative external or spill-over effects for other countries. In light of the foregoing, therefore, the question must be raised in which boundaries WTO laws allow for regulatory differences among the individual Member States?

Generally speaking, national legal and economic systems must be regarded as created factor endowments affecting a given state's competitiveness in international trade. National regulatory systems are in competition with each other with regard to mobile production factors and production costs. Similar to the economic rationale underlying competition among undertakings, competition among governments brings about welfare enhancements, such as innovation, freedom of choice or a more efficient allocation of resource. However, these beneficial welfare effects can be frustrated through "governmental intervention failures" as market failures[777]. The limits of international regulatory competition may, therefore, be identified per analogy to the theory of market failure. Accordingly, the basic principle is that international regulatory competition among different national competition rules is suboptimal only where international public goods are concerned[778], or where there are cross-border externalities[779]. International public goods shall be discussed in more detail below.

External effects created by national competition rules are not *per se* illegitimate. Rather, they must be assessed in the concrete case, weighing the concrete market failures against the risk of alternative government failures, including the risks inherent in international harmonization of domestic competition laws in disregard of divergent national factor endowments[780]. As a basic rule, "unfair regulatory differences" could be defined as those bringing about cross-border trade-distorting effects. In practical terms, however, individual perceptions of legitimate comparative advantages as opposed to unfair regulatory differences will often (and reasonably) differ. This is supported by the fact that traditional economic theory does not suggest any binding or clear-cut rules to identify governmental failures or to evaluate any inherent political trade-offs[781].

---

[777] E.-U. Petersmann, *International Competition Rules for Governments and for Private Business*, in: 30(3) Journal of World Trade 1996, at 12.

[778] Very broadly, "international public good" are defined as all goods that reduce poverty, compare J. Drexl, *ibid.*, at 438. In economic theory, public goods are defined as being *(i)* non-rival in consumption and *(ii)* having non-excludable benefits, compare I. Kaul/R. Mendoza, *Advancing the Concept of Public Goods*, in: I. Kaul/P. Conceição/K. Le Goulven/R. Mendoza (eds.), *Providing Global Public Goods* (2003), available at:
http://www.undp.org/globalpublicgoods/globalization/toc.html (25.05.2005).

[779] E.-U. Petersmann, *ibid.*, 12 et sqq.

[780] E.-U. Petersmann, *ibid.*, 13.

[781] Such trade-offs could be related to opportunity costs of higher national environmental standards, for example; compare E.-U. Petersmann, *ibid.*

International external effects can be financial[782] or non-financial[783]. For the purpose of this analysis, the first group will be central. According to the economic Theory of Optimal Intervention, domestic market failures should be corrected directly at their source through domestic measures in order to obtain optimal results. Accordingly, international market failures and international external effects due to unfair differences among domestic competition laws should be assessed in light of their particular source, and corrected accordingly. Consequently, where domestic competition laws bring about detrimental external effects for other states such as losses with regard to their terms-of-trade, the legitimacy of these laws should be assessed within the ambit of the multilateral agreements regulating international trade[784].

Consequently, in light of the effects doctrine and the common exemption of those anti-competitive practices which only affect export markets, domestic competition policies can bring about detrimental external effects and, thereby, constitute "restrictive governmental practices". Therefore, a case for assessing the legitimacy of domestic competition rules allowing for these external effects can be established at WTO level. Accordingly, this supports the case for a more consistent and integrated approach to competition policy within WTO law.

D. A Brief Outline of Past Negotiation Efforts

As outlined above[785], past negotiation efforts to incorporate additional competition rules in the WTO Agreement have not led to any substantial agreement. At this point, the author will illustrate the key issues of the respective Ministerial rounds and identify the major stumbling blocks as regards the possible contents of any such agreement.

1. Singapore Ministerial (1996)

The Singapore Ministerial was the first Ministerial within the ambit of the WTO Agreement and, therefore, had a particular emphasis on the implementation of the then recent Urugay Round. In addition, however, the Singapore Ministerial also inaugurated new themes for discussion, such as competition policy, public procurement, environmental and labour policy[786]. Most important, the Singapore Ministerial Declaration was adopted during this Ministerial.

---

[782] In terms of competition laws this could be lower costs of compliance or less opportunity costs due to exemptions under domestic merger regulation, for example.

[783] With regard to unfair regulatory differences among domestic competition laws, non-financial external effects, such as cross-border pollution, will only play a subordinate role.

[784] E.-U. Petersmann, *ibid.*, 13 et sqq.

[785] Compare Sections I. and III.C.1. above.

[786] Compare M. Taylor, *International Competition Law. A New Dimension for the WTO?* 2006, at 398 et sqq.

Decision item 20[787] of the Declaration provided the first mandate to discuss competition policy under the WTO Agreement in that it established the WTO Working Group on Trade and Competition so as to "examine the relationship between trade and investment" and to "study issues raised by Members relating to the interaction between trade and competition policy, including anti-competitive practices, in order to identify any areas that may merit further consideration in the WTO framework".

From a political perspective, the EU, having a specific tradition of and focus on competition policy, had been the mainspring for the consideration of competition policy in the WTO. However, the underlying domestic rationales and interests for the consideration of competition policy within the WTO had been very diverse. For instance, the US strongly opposed any reform of anti-dumping laws in light of their producers' interests. South Korea and Hong Kong supported a more comprehensive approach, also comprising anti-dumping, subsidies, safe-guard measures and investment, while developing countries and India in particular strived to address restrictive business practices of TNCs within the ambit of the WTO[788].

The EU's main proposal was to have potential framework rules examined by the Working Group, so that the WTO Members could agree on procedural and and substantive common principles of competition policy. Subsequently, they would be obligated to adopt and enforce corresponding competition rules in line with these principles. Moreover, the EU proposed to examine to what extent the WTO Dispute Settlement System might be applied to warrant compliance with these principles[789].

Unsurprisingly, this approach was considered too extensive by most Members including the US, who supported a more conservative approach after further examination and consensus building. In particular, the US emphasized that a common approach was infeasible in light of diversy policy interests, that negotiations would entail the risk of "lowest common denominator results", that an agreement on competition might lead to potential governmental misuse of confidential information for trade law measures and that the envisaged review of domestic competition law decisions under the WTO Dispute Settlement System would infringe national sovereignty[790].

The final wording of the Singapore Ministerial Declaration clearly reflects a compromise, in that it mandates further research on the interaction of trade and

[787] For the text of the Singapore Ministerial Declaration refer to Footnote 328.
[788] M. Taylor, *ibid.*, 399.
[789] Compare the later *Communication from the European Community and its Member States to the WTO Working Group on the Interaction between Trade and Competition Policy*, 11 June 1997, available at: http://trade.ec.europa.eu/doclib/docs/2003/april/tradoc_111273.pdf (03.02.2007).
[790] Compare M. Taylor, *ibid.*, 399 et sqq.

competition policy, while taking account of the "development dimension" and also requiring explicit consensus for any future negotiations in this area[791].

2. *Geneva Ministerial (1998)*

By 1998, competition policy in the context of the WTO had assumed an important role in academic discourse and was much discussed[792]. Yet, throughout the Geneva Ministerial, it became even more apparent that the individual national positions on a potential inclusion of competition policy in the WTO Agreement differed to a considerable extent. *Taylor*[793] classified the various positions into the following four main groups:

- The EU advanced the view that the adoption of domestic competition laws should be mandatory in order to ensure non-discriminatory market access. Being a frequent user of trade remedies itself, the EU did not support reforms to anti-dumping laws. This view was *inter alia* supported by Canada, Australia, Switzerland, Norway and Switzerland.
- In contrast, the US only supported competition rules addressing private anti-competitive practices while emphasizing the effectiveness of extraterritorial application of domestic competition laws and other retaliatory measures. Consequently, the US also strongly rejected reforms to existing trade remedies.
- Japan and South Korea, on the other hand, supported a comprehensive approach to competition policy in the WTO. Being strongly export-oriented and frequently subject to retaliatory measures, they also advocated reforms to certain trade measures they considered inconsistent with competition policy, such as the existing anti-dumping regime.
- Developing countries such as India, Malaysia and Kenya, however, had a strong focus on competition rules as a means to protect small enterprises from predatory conduct by TNCs. They also emphasized the importance of the elimination of international export and import cartels for their market access to developed countries' markets.

At the end of the Geneva Ministerial Conference, two Ministerial Declarations were adopted. One concerned the area of global electronic commerce[794] and will, therefore, not be considered in more detail. Probably in light of the diver-

---

[791] See decision item 20, last paragraph, of the Declaration.

[792] As an example for the numerous publications of this period refer to E.-U. Petersmann, *Competition-oriented Reforms of the WTO World Trade System – Proposals and Policy Options*, in: R. Zäch, *Toward WTO Competition Rules. Key Issues and Comments on the WTO Report (1998) on Trade and Competition*, 1999, 42-71.

[793] *Ibid.*, 401 et sqq.

[794] Ministerial Declaration on Global Electronic Commerce of 20 May 1998, WT/MIN(98)/DEC/2, available at: http://www.wto.org/english/thewto_e/minist_e/min98_e/ecom_e.htm.

gent views expressed throughout the Ministerial, the second declaration[795] did not expressly mention competition policy, but only "reaffirmed the commitments and assessments"[796] made at Singapore.

3. Seattle Ministerial (1999)

The Seattle Ministerial was intended to be the starting point for a new "Millenium Round" of trade negotiations among WTO Members[797], centered around negotiations on agriculture and services as the "built-in agenda" [798]. In addition, specific Uruguay Round implementation issues, the question of WTO transparency and assistance to developing countries were on the agenda[799]. Yet, the Seattle Ministerial was a dramatic failure, as the conference was suspended without initiating a new round and without adopting any Ministerial Declaration.

The reasons for this failure were manifold. To begin with, vast disagreement prevailed among the Members regarding the scope of the Ministerial[800]. For example, the draft Seattle Ministerial Declaration comprised more than thirty pages and also contained around 400 items in brackets then unresolved[801]. In particular, substantive disagreement prevailed among developed and developing states with regard to the implementation of the Uruguay Round and competition policy. Developing countries argued that an imbalance had resulted from the fact that the Uruguay Round agreements had brought considerably more economic benefits to developed nations than it had brought to them. They feared an additional agreement on competition policy would aggravate these disadvantages, and, therefore, rejected a focus on competition policy but supported a focus on trade and development aspects[802]. In addition, the then inexperienced leadership team of the WTO was not likely to succeed in accommodating the divergent needs and interests of the increasingly growing WTO Membership[803]. In light of its inherent problems, the sensitivity and complexity of the controversial agenda as well as developing countries' general perception of discrimination, the Seattle Ministerial was considered premature[804].

This prematureness was reinforced by the fact that disagreement not only prevailed between developing and developed countries, but also among important

---

795 Ministerial Declaration of 20 May 1998, available at: http://www.wto.org/english/thewto_e/minist_e/min98_e/mindec_e.htm.

796 Decision item 2 of the Declaration.

797 M. Taylor, *ibid.*, 403.

798 US General Accounting Office, *Seattle Ministerial: Outcomes and Lessons Learned. Testimony Before the Committee on Finance, US Senate*, 10 February 2000, available at: http://www.gao.gov/archive/2000/ns00086t.pdf (05.02.2007).

799 M. Taylor, *ibid.*, 403.

800 US General Accounting Office, *ibid.*

801 M. Taylor, *ibid.*, Footnote 40.

802 M. Taylor, *ibid.*, Footnote 41.

803 US General Accounting Office, *ibid.*

804 For example US General Accounting Office, *ibid.*

developed countries themselves. These differences particularly centered on the issues of agriculture and anti-dumping. On the one hand, the EU's excessive use of agricultural export subsidies was strongly opposed by the US and other important agricultural net exporters, such as Australia, Brazil or Canada[805]. On the other hand, the US was heavily criticized by major trading partners like Japan or Korea for its anti-dumping regime[806]. The US favoured a focus on agriculture and key services, whereas the EU or Japan supported extensive multilateral negotiations, including negotiations on competition policy[807]. Subsequently, the US offered to accept this extensive approach if both the EU and Japan would support agricultural reforms. In light of this offer, Canada, Australia, New Zealand and Brazil as agricultural net exporters would follow the US and give up competition policy for agriculture. Competition policy was, thereby, afforded the status of an important bargaining chip within the international trading regime[808].

4. Doha Ministerial (2001)

The fiasco of Seattle was successfully remedied at Doha, where a new round of multilateral negotiations with a particular focus on the concerns of developing countries was launched.

In view of the opposition to competition policy on part of developing countries at the Seattle Ministerial, the EU now argued in favour of a plurilateral agreement on competition so that developing countries would not be mandated to participate in such agreement. However, this approach was criticized as being a disguised first step towards a stricter multilateral agreement and as potentially undermining the multilateral trading system. Alternatively, the EU suggested to tackle competition issues in the manner introduced by the GATS Agreement, in that individual obligations should be entered into on a voluntary basis, which produced similar concerns[809]. The US, on the other hand, supported negotiations of a more limited and non-binding agreement, focusing on the core principles of WTO law and on transparency. The US rejected the proposal of submitting any such agreement to the WTO Dispute Settlement System, and anticipated continued investigation by the WTO Working Group on Trade and Competition Policy[810].

The consultation and negotiation process produced a first draft of a Doha Ministerial Declaration which contained the options of either starting negotiations

[805] *Ibid.*
[806] US General Accounting Office, *ibid.*
[807] M. Taylor, *ibid.*, 404.
[808] Compare M. Taylor, *ibid.*, 404 et sqq.
[809] M. Taylor, *ibid.*, 405 et sqq.
[810] M. Taylor, *ibid.*, 406.

on competition policy or continuing the studies of the Working Group[811]. The majority of developing countries, however, opposed to the commencement of negotiations on additional WTO competition rules so that the language ultimately deployed in the Doha Ministerial Declaration provided for negotiations to take place after the Cancún Ministerial in 2003 after "explicit consensus" on the modalities of any such negotiations. In addition, it recognized the needs of developing and least-developed countries for enhanced support, capacity-building and "appropriate flexibility" in the area of competition policy[812]. Furthermore, it was agreed in the Doha Ministerial Declaration that the Working Group should continue its studies, focusing on *(i)* the clarification of core principles, including transparency, non-discrimination and procedural fairness, provisions on hard-core cartels, *(ii)* modalities for voluntary cooperation and *(iii)* capacity building for the progressive reinforcement of competition institutions in developing countries.

5. *Cancún Ministerial (2003)*

Despite the successful launch of a new negotiation round at Doha, the subsequent Cancún Ministerial was a further and very substantial setback.

Given the outcome of the previous Ministerials, the Cancún Ministerial was very much focused on agriculture on the one hand and development on the other. In preparation of the Ministerial, the EU and the US jointly proposed a liberalisation scheme for agricultural trade. Yet, this proposal was opposed by the so-called "G20", a group of developing countries led by India and Brazil, which argued that the proposed scheme would lead to disproportionate liberalisation on part of the developing countries while allowing the scheme's advocates to avoid liberalisation of their most protected areas[813].

The G20 also dominated the discussion on a potential agreement on competition policy, and it soon turned out that *(i)* the positions expressed at the Seattle and Doha Ministerials were substantially unaltered and *(ii)* that the issue of competition policy was used as a bargaining chip for concessions in other areas such as agriculture: The G20 strongly opposed the proposal of the EU and Japan for the inclusion of competition policy in the WTO Agreement, while the US reiterated its support being limited to a non-binding soft law instrument on competition policy[814].

In light of these divergent views, the draft Ministerial Declaration again provided for either *(i)* the commencement of negotiations subject to the modali-

---

[811] M. Taylor, *ibid.*
[812] For the complete wording of the Doha Ministerial Declaration refer to Footnote 330.
[813] Compare M. Taylor, *ibid.*, 408.
[814] *Ibid.*

ties[815] set out in the draft Declaration, or *(ii)* the referral of competition policy issues to the Working Group in view of a future agreement on such modalities. Yet, no "explicit consensus" was available due to the complete lack of consensus on part of the G20 group. At the same time, the EU proposed to trade in its requests for competition policy and investment as Singapore issues for the G20's acceptance of the joint EU-US proposal on agriculture. Although the US supported the EU this time, the G20 nevertheless refused this offer and claimed that the EU and the US engaged in the illegitimate use of tactics, thereby yet aggravating any existing reservations[816]. Subsequently, however, even another amended draft providing for the delegation of further studies to the Working Group failed.

In the end, the concluding ministerial statement, therefore, had to acknowledge the setback as no consent could be achieved on the Singapore issues, and only reaffirmed the Doha Declaration[817].

6. *July Package (2004)*

Despite the dramatic political failure of Cancún, the fact that the concluding ministerial statement had reaffirmed the Doha Declaration from a legal perspective implied that future negotiations on competition policy within the WTO were still possible. In light of the hardened positions throughout the previous negotiations, the EU limited its proposal to a plurilateral approach. Yet, even this limited approach was not accepted by developing countries at this point. Rather, least developed countries expressed the view that they would not only reject further negotiations on any Singapore issue, but also plurilateral negotiations on a multilateral issue such as competition policy. In their view, a plurilateral approach on competition policy was prevented by the consensus requirement contained in Art. X:9 of the WTO Agreement.

This hostile attitude towards competition policy within the ambit of the WTO was subsequently expressed by an absolute and formal halt of further negotiations on competition policy: Para. 1 (g) of the "July Decision" adopted by the WTO General Council on 1 August 2004 stipulates that the issue of the interaction between trade and competition policy as mentioned in paragraphs 23-25 of the Doha Ministerial Declaration "will not form part of the Work Programme set out in that Declaration and therefore no work towards negotiations" on this

815 These modalities *inter alia* provided for *(i)* the facilitation and effective voluntary co-operation and technical assistance as negotiation objectives, *(ii)* the elements of negotiations identified in the Doha Declaration and by the Working Group being the relevant ones, *(iii)* no recourse to the WTO Dispute Settlement System but only applications to national authorities, *(iv)* developing country exceptions as well as transitional periods.

816 Ibid., 409.

817 Concluding ministerial statement, WT/MIN(03)/20 (23 September 2003), para 6.

issue will take place within the WTO during the ongoing Doha Round[818]. Accordingly, the Working Group on the Interaction of Trade and Competition Policy is now inactive.

7. *Hong Kong Ministerial (2005)*

The Hong Kong Ministerial Declaration adopted on 18 December 2005 explicitly reaffirmed the General Council's July Decision and, thereby, upheld the total exclusion of competition policy from the negotiations during the ongoing Doha Round.

E. Conclusion

Trade and competition policy pursue complementary goals. From a welfare economics perspective, efficient economic outcome will occur only where both free flows of international trade and competitive market conditions prevail. Successful liberalisation has increased the relative significance of private market barriers. Lenient enforcement of domestic competition laws or the lack of domestic competition laws can undermine the economic benefits resulting from trade liberalisation and lead to detrimental welfare effects. Given the complementarity of trade and competition policy, the shortcomings of domestic competition laws as identified in Chapters III and IV mandate international competition rules.

Although the WTO Agreement provides for certain legal instruments concerning competition policy addressing both governments and private actors, from a systemic and institutional perspective the current approach to competition under the WTO Agreement is fragmentary and non-systematic, and, therefore, not satisfactory from a trade policy perspective. As private practices are replacing former governmental barriers to trade, such approach is no longer justified. Notably, institutionalizing the links between competition and multilateral trade rules would besides reaping economic benefits also help to overcome the protectionist elements in international trade law and to strengthen the protection of individual rights.

Furthermore, the insufficient addressing of international anti-competitive practices by private actors may entail protection, thereby frustrating the underlying policy goals of international trade policy. For instance, weak competition laws may entail global welfare losses through privately created barriers to trade or international cartels for which the existing legal remedies under the GATT appear to be limited. Notably, practices with differential impact may result in welfare losses for other states through strategic beggar-thy-neighbour policy. In

[818] Refer to reference in Footnote 39.

this regard, the current legal regime for export cartels under the GATT particularly merits reconsideration. In addition, the WTO antidumping law regime allows for domestic protectionism, and should therefore be replaced by competition rules. Generally, if no solution can be achieved for international problems at domestic level and these problems bring about negative welfare implications for other states like the extensive application of antidumping laws does, these issues must be solved at an international level.

In light of the foregoing, a clear case for additional competition law rules within the ambit of the WTO can be established from an economic, but also from an institutional perspective. This case has also been well researched by the Working Group on Trade and Competition Policy. Yet, looking at the course of past negotiation efforts on competition policy during the WTO Ministerial Conferences, economics have lately been forced into a role of minor importance. Instead, competition policy has been used as a bargaining chip for mutual concessions in other policy areas like agriculture and services. These policy areas are of particular interest also to developing countries. In light of the very emotional debate, one is sometimes almost tempted to assume that certain developing countries (legitimately or not) consider the issue of competition policy as one of the last fortresses to defend on the road to liberalisation and a particular threat of discrimination or other disadvantages. Consequently, the issue of competition policy in the WTO has been vexed in terms of international consensus.

In light of the established case for additional international competition rules within the WTO Agreement, the author supports the view that further negotiations should be pursued despite the past setbacks. The issue of competition policy is worth a renewed in-depth evaluation, taking into account the resulting benefits for all WTO Member States. Yet, the question of how to accommodate developing countries' interests will certainly have to play a crucial role in any future attempt. In the following chapter, the author shall discuss recent perspectives for the discussion which might provide new insights and incentives for a relaunch of negotiations on competition policy. Thereafter, the author will propose a possible approach to overcome the current deadlock situation.

V. How to Break the Deadlock?

A. Recent Perspectives

1. The development dimension of competition policy

The "development dimension" of competition policy was already acknowledged in the Singapore Ministerial Declaration of 1996[819]. Nevertheless, the text of the Doha Declaration itself but also the political developments both surrounding and after the Cancún Ministerial Conference have shown that a future discussion of additional competition rules in the ambit of the WTO will be politically infeasible without special and intensified consideration of economic development and the special situation of developing countries. Developing countries generally fear that any additional pronounced linkage of trade and competition policy might undermine their comparative advantages with regard to primary goods, and that such linkage might function as disguised discrimination[820]. Developing countries are also concerned that if no special and differential status is afforded to them, they might be obliged to expose domestic industries to foreign competition or acquisition, thereby frustrating the fostering of domestic infant industries[821].

These concerns are highly politically sensitive, as demonstrated in the past. Thus, for an analysis of the relationship of development vis-à-vis competition and, subsequently, their appropriate treatment in the WTO, at least two aspects have to be discussed. First, it is necessary to understand if and how competition contributes to economic development. Second, possible approaches to Special and Differential Treatment (S&D) under the WTO Agreement in the context of additional competition rules must be explored.

1.1. The relationship of competition and development

Economic theory rates a strong antitrust policy as essential for economic growth. In particular, vigorous enforcement of competition laws against horizontal mergers, collusive behaviour and strategic alliances sustains the rate of upgrading in an economy[822]. At the same time, it must be noted that competition policy aims to deter specific abuses such as cartelization, monopolization or anti-competitive mergers having negative welfare effects, on a case-to-case basis. Such practices must usually be condemned independent from their actual effect on development. Moreover, there are some examples of "miracle econo-

[819] For the wording of the Declaration refer to Footnote 328.
[820] S. Cho, *ibid.*, 231.
[821] M. J. Trebilcock/R. Howse, *The Regulation of International Trade*[3] (2005), 609.
[822] M. Porter, *The Competitive Advantage of Nations* (1990), 117.

mies" which developed very well despite the absence of modern competition laws in these countries[823]. Still, empirical evidence has shown that international cartels can bear significant influence on the costs of developing countries' imports from developed countries[824]. Thus, even if one adopts the view that competition is not *per se* suited to foster economic development, it cannot be ignored that private international anti-competitive practices can hamper economic development and that developing countries might be exposed to significant costs and setback due to the lack of competition law or capacity to enforce it[825]. This argument is supported by the fact that more and more developing countries chose to adopt competition laws, independently from the discussions in the WTO. Although this adoption deprives them of a bargaining chip for future negotiations, it also shows that developing countries themselves consider competition laws as beneficial for their economies[826].

Competition policy can also be beneficial for developing countries in that it may underpin related microeconomic reforms. As an example, empirical evidence suggests that privatization may have the effect of simply replacing a public monopoly with a private one where it is not accompanied by policy measures strengthening competition[827]. Likewise, a failure to implement competition policy and related regulatory reforms may prevent countries from the realization of potential gains from external liberalization by preventing an adequate reaction in terms of supply[828].

1.2. Applying Special and Differential Treatment to WTO competition rules

The concept of Special and Differential Treatment (S&D) has been a cornerstone of efforts under the GATT and, subsequently, the WTO to facilitate the integration of developing countries in the multilateral trading system. In light of the Doha Ministerial Declaration, the importance of this concept has been reinforced by the mandate to "take fully into account the principle of special and differential treatment"[829].

Other than Articles XVIII, XVI:4 and XXVIIIbis of the GATT, S&D is based on two core pillars, non-reciprocity on the one hand and enhanced and prefer-

[823] A. Bhattacharjea, *The Case for a Multilateral Agreement on Competition Policy: A Developing Country Perspective*, in: 9(2) Journal of International Economic Law 2006, 316 et sqq.

[824] R. D. Anderson/P. Holmes, *Competition Policy and the Future of the Multilateral Trading System*, in: 5(2) Journal of International Economic Law 2002, 553.

[825] F. Jenny, *Globalization, Competition and Trade Policy: Convergence, Divergence and Cooperation*, in: San/Lo/Hom (eds.), *International and Comparative Competition Law and Policies* (2001), 31-70.

[826] A. Bhattacharjea, *ibid.*, 319.

[827] R. D. Anderson/P. Holmes, *ibid.*, 554.

[828] WGTCP, 1998 *Report of the Working Group on the Interaction between Trade and Competition Policy*, *ibid.*, paras. 34, 229.

[829] Doha Ministerial Declaration, *ibid.*, at para. 50.

ential market access on the other[830]. The first has been substantiated in Part IV "Trade and Development". Notably, Article XXXVI:8 exempts reciprocal tariff concessions as "the developed contracting parties do not expect reciprocity for commitments made by them in trade negotiations to reduce or remove barriers to trade of less-developed contracting parties". Preferential market access on the other hand is secured by the Enabling Clause[831], which created a permanent legal basis for the preferential tariff treatment as accorded by the Generalized System of Preferences. In the various WTO agreements, numerous provisions on S&D can be found[832].

When considering the possible application of S&D in a competition context, it must again be borne in mind that for a large number of WTO Member States, competition laws are a young, potentially still not fully developed and also an inefficient policy area. At the same time, developing countries' markets are prone to high degrees of concentration, state intervention and strong lobbying forces, and therefore rather challenging for competition law enforcement by comparatively young authorities[833]. Likewise, as illustrated above, competition policy is a field where discretion and flexibility is required.

In line with the emphasis advanced by UNCTAD[834], many developing countries have taken the view that any agreement on trade and competition would have to ensure in a more consistent and efficient way the required flexibility in developing countries' competition regimes with regard to their specific development objectives. In particular, the need for concrete and enforceable terms on S&D has been emphasized[835]. In light of that call and also the wording of the Doha Declaration which requires full account of the needs of developing and least-developed countries the author shall now examine ways to introduce S&D in a competition discipline in an adequate manner.

1.2.1. The GATS approach

Arguably, the GATS approach to S&D could serve as a role model for a flexible approach. The GATS' structure differs from other WTO agreements in that it allows for a progressive approach to liberalization based on voluntary concessions relating to particular sectors and has therefore been rated as "develop-

---

830 H. Nottage, *Trade and Competition in the WTO: Pondering the Applicability of Special and Differential Treatment*, in: 6(1) Journal of International Economic Law 2003, at 26.

831 GATT Contracting Parties, *Decision on Differential and More Favourable Treatment, Reciprocity and Fuller Participation of Developing Countries*, available at: http://www.wto.org/english/docs_e/legal_e/enabling1979_e.htm (14.08.2005).

832 WTO Secretariat Note, *Implementation of Special and Differential Treatment Provisions in WTO Agreements and Decisions*, WT/COMTD/W77, available at: http://docsonline.wto.org/DDFDocuments/t/WT/COMTD/W77.doc (12.08.2005).

833 H. Nottage, *ibid.*, at 33.

834 UNCTAD, *Preparing for Future Multilateral Trade Negotiations: Issues and Research Needs from a Development Perspective*, UNCTAD/ITCD/TSB/6, September 1999.

835 H. Nottage, *ibid.*, 34.

ment friendly"[836]. Under Article XIX.2 of the GATS, developing countries are explicitly authorized to liberalize and extend market access selectively. Also, they are entitled to impose conditions subject to the objectives listed in Article IV of the GATS.

However, there are concerns with regard to the enforceability of Article IV of the GATS. Allegedly, the S&D provisions are drafted in a general and broad manner and are, therefore, not legally enforceable[837]. Thus, more precise language would be required if the GATS approach was adopted.

Notably, recent case law has interpreted Article IV of the GATS in an unexpectedly restrictive way. In the *Telmex* decision[838], the Panel rejected the argument that development objectives have to be considered in the assessment of whether a developing country is meeting its GATS commitments. Rather, the Panel suggested that any consideration of S&D is only legitimate until an actual commitment has been made, but not for the interpretation of such commitment. Thus, the "development-friendliness" of the GATS approach has recently been put in question.

1.2.2. A broad framework agreement with exceptions and exemptions

As suggested by the European Union and taken up by the Working Group on Trade and Competition Policy[839], the adoption of a broad framework agreement on competition policy focusing on core principles such as transparency, non-discrimination and hard-core cartels could be another option allowing for the flexibility and the progress required. Notably, current proposals are not favouring harmonization, which leaves room for domestic interpretation and arguably could provide for the flexibility and adaptability required to respond to individual development challenges. Such flexibility and adaptability could in particular be achieved by means of sectoral or non-sectoral exceptions and exemptions[840]. Although there appears to be some acceptance of such an exceptions/exemptions approach on part of developing countries[841], it has also been made clear that individual state should in any case be free to decide which areas were relevant for it[842].

Nevertheless, the question must be raised as to whether a system of exceptions and exemptions would benefit any development efforts in the first place. The

[836] H. Nottage, *ibid.*, 36.

[837] H. Nottage, *ibid.*

[838] WTO Panel Report, *Mexico – Measures Affecting Telecommunications Services* (2004), WTO Doc. WT/DS204/R, para 7.214.

[839] WTO WGTCP, *A Multilateral Framework Agreement on Competition Policy*, 25 September 2000, WT/WGTCP/W/152; WTO WGTCP, *A WTO Competition Agreement and Development*, 26 July 2001, WT/WGTCP/W/140.

[840] H. Nottage, *ibid.*, 37.

[841] H. Nottage, *ibid.*

[842] Intervention of Trinidad and Tobago at the WTO WGTCP as presented in the *Report of the Meeting of 5-6 July 2001*, Note by the Secretariat, 14 August 2001, WT/WGTCP/M/15, para. 9.

underlying concern is that if there was excessive use of such exceptions or exemptions, the intended rise in effectiveness of competition law and enforcement in developing countries could be hampered. This ceased rise in efficiency of competition law enforcement could in turn entail global welfare losses[843]. However, Japan's history appears to suggest that such fears may be unfounded, as competitiveness may also be strengthened by the actual process of competition rather than the deployment of industrial policy measures[844].

Clearly, further research would be required with regard to the actual extent to which exemptions and exceptions under either a sectoral or an unspecific non-sectoral approach may be beneficial to development. This further research is in particular required as sectoral exemptions could conflict with competition policy interests[845].

1.2.3. Remaining issues

Given the lack of consensus concerning a competition agreement for the WTO, alternatives to a multilateral approach may be worth considering. This consideration of alternatives appears to be in line with the agreement in the Doha Ministerial Declaration that the "modalities of negotiations" will be subject to separate decision, while the case for a "multilateral framework" has been explicitly recognized[846]. Notably, there was a proposal by the EC Commission which foresaw the possibility to opt out of the agreement at a subsequent stage[847]. This proposal was not endorsed by developing countries[848]. *Hoekman* recently proposed a "more cooperative approach", with conditional recourse to DSU subject to a development test. In addition, soft law instruments could be used to identify "good practices" from an economic development perspective in order to advance the "graduation effect" and to foster the aspects of learning and assistance[849]. Both proposals would generally raise concerns with regard to the Single Package idea. However, the notion of soft law instruments must be rated a viable approach to development, assistance and dialogue.

Another open issue is the question of differentiation among certain categories of developing countries. Although such differentiation might appear justified in light of flexibility for development purposes, it is unclear which categories

---

843 United States, WTO WGTCP, *Report of the Meeting of 5-6 July 2001*, Note by the Secretariat, 14 August 2001, WT/WGTCP/M/15, para. 30.

844 Communication from Japan, *Competition Policies and Exemption Systems*, WTO WGTCP, 4 July 2001, WT/WGTCP/W177.

845 H. Nottage, *ibid.*, 41.

846 Doha Ministerial Declaration, *ibid.*, paras. 23-25.

847 EC Commission, *State of Play and Strategy fort he New WTO Round*, Note fort he Attention of the 133 Committee, Brussels, 13 December 2000.

848 H. Nottage, *ibid.*, 42.

849 B. Hoekman, *Operationalizing the Concept of Policy Space in the WTO: Beyond Special and Differential Treatment*, in: 8(2) Journal of International Economic Law 2005, 414 et sqq.

should be pursued for such differentiation[850]. Arguably, a state's size might not be decisive for its state of development, while economical parameter might be difficult to establish.

As far as technical assistance and capacity building are concerned, there appears to be general consensus that such efforts will have to supplement any agreement on how to pursue with competition policy in the ambit of the WTO. Nevertheless, concerns have been raised as to the efficiency of such efforts. In particular, case-to-case analysis will be required to adequately respond to specific concerns relating to development[851]. Recent research on Trade-Related Technical Assistance and Capacity Building suggests that although competition has received substantially more resources than other areas such as agriculture or market access, both quality and quantity of such initiatives must be improved for a full reaping of the benefits of liberalisation and for a reduction of poverty[852]. *Hoekman* criticised that there were no mechanisms for linking the WTO provisions relating to technical assistance to the actual provision of development assistance. Although the Hong Kong Ministerial Declaration contained a commitment to the Integrated Framework, a greater coherence of trade and development would be required[853].

Finally, transition periods might be a means to respond to development concerns. Still, the appropriateness of transition periods must be questioned due to difficulties with regard to the coherence or timing in light of the institutional capacity potentially required for the full implementation of a WTO agreement on competition[854].

2. *International competition as global public good?*

In light of the developments[855] around the WTO Cancún Ministerial Conference of September 2003, it has been argued that any approach to additional WTO competition rules needs to be evaluated in light of the debate on globalization[856]. Arguably, this is a promising approach due to the fact that for previous proposals[857] the alleged lack of consideration for the problems emerging in the course of globalization, especially with a view to developing countries, must be considered a major reason leading to their failure at Cancún.

---

850 H. Nottage, *ibid.*, 43.

851 H. Nottage, *ibid.*

852 R. Saner/L. Páez, *Technical Assistance to Least-Developed Countries in the Context of the Doha Development Round: High Risk of Failure,* in: 40(3) Journal of World Competition 2006, 479 et sqq., 490.

853 B. Hoekman, *Operationalizing the Concept of Policy Space in the WTO: Beyond Special and Differential Treatment,* in: 8(2) Journal of International Economic Law 2005, 411.

854 H. Nottage, *ibid.*, 46.

855 E.g. the failure of the Seattle WTO Ministerial Conference in 1999, the emergence of the anti-globalisation movement, the Doha Declaration and its intention to integrate constructive criticism of globalisation.

856 J. Drexl, *ibid.*, at 437. For a comprehensive analysis of "globalization" refer to J. Stiglitz, *Globalization and Its Discontents* (2004), or G. Soros, *On Globalization* (2002).

857 For instance the proposal by the European Community, compare Chapter I.

International competition rules as coordinated action against restrictive practices may provide solutions to the problems of globalization. At the same time, however, it must be kept in mind that inherent obligations for market-access could aggravate these problems[858]. Thus, any competition analysis focussing on the developments of globalization must extend the study beyond purely procedural or jurisdictional issues and their implications to global efficiency and consumer welfare to include the implications of the uneven distribution of efficiency gains between states and societies[859].

On the one hand, economic theory defines "public goods" as being non-rival and non-exclusive, meaning that they may be used by one person without excluding another one, while the person providing the good cannot exclude any person from consumption[860]. On the other hand, "international public goods" have been defined by the World Bank as all goods reducing poverty[861]. The UN Development Program (UNDP) prefers the notion "global public goods". Their definition has been refined from "all goods whose benefits extend to all countries, people, and generations" to those "benefiting more than one country, one people, or one generation"[862]. Arguably, this change in definition leads to an extension in the scope of global public goods, as more goods will qualify under the latter definition. The delimitation of public versus private goods and national versus global goods is crucial, but has to be understood as a flexible one. This is so for private goods can be transformed to public goods and vice versa by individuals or national policy decision or law, and the same applies for national goods as opposed to global ones. Also, the process of globalization itself implies a changing structure through an increase in global public goods and a decrease in national public goods[863]

Public goods give rise to market failures. This is due to the fact that private markets will not provide public goods since consumers cannot be excluded from consumption. Traditionally, states have therefore chosen to provide public goods themselves, or, as an alternative, to transform them into private ones through privatization[864]. At a purely domestic level, these decisions will legitimately be incumbent on the government. At the international level, however, the case may not be so clear.

---

858 J. Drexl, *ibid.*

859 J. Drexl, *ibid.*

860 I. Kaul/R. Mendoza, *Advancing the Concept of Public Goods*, available at: http://www.undp.org/globalpublicgoods/globalization/pdfs/KaulMendoza.pdf (29.05.2005), at 80. Classical examples for public goods are the lighthouse, internal security, free broadcasting vis-à-vis its audience or publicly available knowledge, compare J. Drexl, *ibid.*, 438.

861 J. Drexl, *ibid.*

862 I. Kaul/R. Mendoza, *Advancing the Concept of Public Goods*, available at: http://www.undp.org/globalpublicgoods/globalization/pdfs/KaulMendoza.pdf (29.05.2005), at 95.

863 J. Drexl, *ibid.*

864 J. Drexl, *ibid.*

In light of the theory of global public goods, the economic theory of public goods is afforded an international dimension. As a basic rule, national legislators are to decide on whether to provide goods as public or private ones. However, in a globalized world, such national decisions will inevitably have cross-border effects. With the TRIPS as a role model, *Drexl* has argued that states should decide to provide goods as private ones in order to prevent any free-riding by consumers located abroad. Yet, the privatization of public goods brings about development concerns, as poor people may not be in the position to afford certain goods. Likewise, developing countries may not be in the position to provide such goods. For both aspects, the example of health care has been cited[865]. In any case, the lack of sufficient provision of public goods is a major aspect of the criticism of globalization[866].

The UNDP has *inter alia* listed the stability of financial markets, control of communicable diseases, conservation of biodiversity, management of the provision of knowledge or the internet as a global means of communication as global public goods[867]. Under WTO law, global public goods are protected by Articles XXIII and XXV of the GATT 1947[868]. But does WTO law itself qualify as a global public good? According to UNDP, the multilateral trading system is a global public good in form, but not in substance[869]. This appreciation is argued by claiming that the advantages of trade liberalization benefit all states as well as their citizens, and - at least in theory – nobody can be excluded from these benefits. From a substantial point of view, however, it has been argued that the trading system lacks balance and justice, as developing countries would predominantly have to bear the social costs for the maintenance of today's multilateral trade system.

Drexl argued that in light of the established complementarity of trade and competition policy, it would be more convincing to rate international competition as a global public good, which itself meets the criteria laid down by the UNDP[870]. This argument was held to be supported by the fact that the international protection of competition together with additional competition rules in the ambit of WTO law would promote the provision of private goods, and, thereby, facilitate access to private goods for all consumers and especially citizens of developing

---

865 J. Drexl, *ibid.*, 439.

866 Kaul, I./Conceição, P./Le Goulven, K./Mendoza, R., *Why Do Global Public Goods Matter Today?* Available at:
http://www.undp.org/globalpublicgoods/globalization/pdfs/Overviews.pdf (29.05.2005), at 4.

867 Compare Office of Development Studies (UNDP), *Profiling the Provision of Global Public Goods, An ODS Staff Paper*, December 2002, available at:
http://www.undp.org/globalpublicgoods/globalization/pdfs/background-paper-profiles.pdf (29.05.2005).

868 Compare E.-U. Petersmann, *International Competition Rules for Governments and for Private Business*, in: 30(3) Journal of World Trade 1996, at 15.

869 R. Mendoza, *The Multilateral Trade System: A Global Public Good for All?* In Kaul, I./Conceição, P./Le Goulven, K./Mendoza, R., (eds.), *Providing Global Public Goods* (2003), available at:
http://www.undp.org/globalpublicgoods/globalization/pdfs/Mendoza.pdf (29.05.2005), at 455.

870 J. Drexl, *ibid.*, 440.

countries. Consequently, international competition must be regarded as a global public good, which at the same time promotes the provision of private goods.

WTO law can be regarded as a "symbol of a global decision in favour of private goods"[871]. This is certainly true for the liberalization of trade in goods and services. In addition, this interpretation has been particularly fostered by the approach in the TRIPS Agreement, whereby WTO Members are obliged to transform knowledge as a formerly public good into a private one. Arguably, this approach leads to a transfer of payments from developing countries to developed countries producing the knowledge, and restricts the provision of public goods in developing countries more than in developed states[872]. In light of this WTO emphasis on private goods, it is of particular importance to protect the increased trade against private anti-competitive restraints in order to ensure the full benefits of trade liberalization for all consumers.

As has been illustrated above, international competition is currently insufficiently protected. Countries which have not yet adopted competition laws are not in the position to protect their own markets and consumers against anti-competitive practices from abroad, which can occur legitimately under current WTO law. At the same time, certain export-focussed practices are completely excluded from the scope of domestic competition laws where the exporting country's markets are not affected. Given that developed countries tend to have more experience with competition laws and also more resources, it will commonly be developing countries whose inefficient competition laws allow for wealth transfers from developing countries to developed ones[873].

However, capacity building alone will not be sufficient to achieve an international system reacting to distortions of competition in all, but in particular the poorest countries. Rather, if one acknowledges international competition as a global public good, the WTO would have to act as a "supranational legislator" within the borders of the subject matter accorded to it by its Members, just like a national legislator would for its territory. WTO Members should afford international competition the protection it requires as a global public good so as to correct the potential market failures implied for WTO territory through its non-regulation. In order to balance potential trade-offs through anti-competitive practices in the course of the liberalization of trade with private goods, the WTO should provide international competition to its Members as an international public good with a corresponding regulation in the WTO Agreement[874].

If one were to take up *Drexl's* line of argument, the goal would not be competition rules focussed on market access or harmonized competition rules. Rather,

[871] J. Drexl, *ibid.*, 441.
[872] J. Drexl, *ibid*, 441. The latter argument has been reasoned with the average lack of access to certain public goods, which is aggravated by the regime established under the TRIPS.
[873] Compare J. Drexl, *ibid.*, 445 et sqq.
[874] Compare J. Drexl, *ibid.*, 445 et sqq.

to balance the existing market access guarantees provided by WTO law, the actual "process" of competition before and after accessing a given market in a non-discriminatory manner would be at the core of this approach[875].

In addition to the question of adequate protection of international competition as a global public good, it should be noted that its qualification as such also argues in favour of additional rules for regulatory competition as discussed above. This acknowledges the fact that economic theory has recognized that international regulatory competition will be suboptimal if there are international public goods involved[876]. Thus, another argument to have international competition coordinated at WTO level.

3. Lessons from regionalism?

As the achievement of consensus for additional international WTO competition rules appears increasingly unlikely at the multilateral level, alternative avenues of trade negotiations at the international level like Regional Trading Agreements must be considered. It has already been shown above that Regional Trading Agreements have significant potential for convergence of competition law regimes, which may bear a positive influence on the underlying goal of trade liberalization. Regional Trade Agreements may *inter alia* be incentivized by the reduction of costs of non-cooperation in light of an increasing number of global actors and by the fact that consensus is easier to achieve with fewer partners[877]. In addition, a higher degree of integration at the regional level appears to be more feasible than at the international level. Thus, regionalism could arguably serve as a feasible vehicle for the advancement of convergent competition rules in the WTO. Yet, the fit of Regional Trade Agreements into the WTO legal system merits further analysis.

At first sight, Regional Trading Agreements are inherently preferential and discriminatory vis-à-vis non members, which *prima facie* contradicts the general principle of Non-Discrimination under WTO law. In addition, Regional Trade Agreements have been alleged of bringing about trade diversion and, consequently, a distortion of the global allocation of resources. Notably, para. 4 of Article XXIV of the GATT 1947 is based on the assumption that Regional Trade Agreements "facilitate trade between the constituent territories" rather than create barriers. Thus, Article XXIV of the GATT 1947 provides the most important exception to its Most-Favoured-Nation Principle in that it allows for Free Trade Areas and Customs Unions under certain conditions. This exception is, however, based on certain conditions, the most important one being the re-

---

875 J. Drexl, *ibid.*, 444.

876 E.-U. Petersmann, *International Competition Rules for Governments and for Private Business*, in 30(3) Journal of World Trade 1996, at 13.

877 P. Hilpold, *Regional Integration According to Article XXIV GATT*, 7 Max Planck Yearbook of United Nations Law 2003, 220.

quirement of Article XXIV:8 that the agreement has to provide for the elimination of duties and other restrictive regulations of commerce for "substantially all the trade between the member countries"[878]. Members are generally free to decide *how* to eliminate duties. Thus, they may decide to adopt a common competition regime, but they are by no means required to do so[879]. This has been rated a weakness of the WTO system and has led to a call for a requirement for deeper integration under WTO law[880].

For the purpose of the present analysis, it must be asked how Regional Trade Agreements could be deployed in support of international competition rules for the WTO. Arguably, in line with the theory that regional integration may be conducive to inter-regional integration[881], the adoption of convergent competition rules in Regional Trade Agreements could incentivize the creation of further Regional Trade Agreements with convergent competition rules, and thus help to bring about increased coverage and convergence of competition law regimes at the international level. However, the probability of such an effect is highly questionable. Alternatively, one could argue that in light of the complementarity between trade and competition policy, the "substantially all the trade" requirement in connection with the internal trade requirement should be held to comprise an *obligation* for alignment in competition policy matters between the parties to the Regional Trading Agreement. However, there are at least three arguments against such a scenario. First, it is difficult to define the degree of alignment proscribed, which would have to be assessed on a case-to-case basis. Second, such obligation would be problematic where a state did not have the prerequisite of alignment in the first place, namely an adopted competition law. This may in particular be true for developing countries. Third, leaving aside the problem of practical feasibility, prescribing a further degree of integration for states which are already dissenting from the general GATT regime by joining a Regional Trade Agreement appears to be against the underlying rationale of the GATT, given the fact that the allowance for Regional Trade Agreements under the GATT must clearly be rated an exception to the general rule.

Thus, Regional Trade Agreements are a promising approach toward convergent international competition rules where the states at issue deliberately decide to integrate to that degree. All the same, an obligation to align or even harmonize domestic competition laws cannot be supported under the GATT even if such obligation would reinforce trade liberalization.

---

878 P. Hilpold, *ibid.*, 235.

879 B. Hoekman, *Free Trade and Deep Integration. Antidumping and Antitrust in Regional Trade Agreements*, World Bank Policy Research Paper 1950 (July 1998), available at: http://wdsbeta.worldbank.org/external/default/WDSContentServer/IW3P/IB/1998/07/01/000009265_3980928162543/Rendered/PDF/multi0page.pdf, at 33.

880 B. Hoekman, *ibid.*

881 M. J. Trebilcock/R. Howse, *ibid.*, 197.

4. Recent case law

It has already been mentioned that it is a distinct concern of developing countries that the adoption of additional international competition rules in the WTO would *inter alia* put their Special and Differential Treatment at risk. Therefore, developing countries have so far been reluctant to consent to the adoption of any such agreement. In light of recent case law, however, it can be argued that their Special and Differential Treatment is at risk if developing countries do *not* agree to such agreement so as to clarify the scope of S&D.

The Dispute Settlement Body has of late pursued an increasingly activist approach[882]. In particular, existing ambiguities in term of potential obligation of the Member States to apply domestic competition law have been addressed in unexpected clarity. Thus, Member States have been held to be obliged to ensure the compliance of private market participants with the provisions of the WTO Agreement. Moreover, WTO law has been held to be applicable to domestic competition laws.

Thus, the *Film Report* placed a very heavy burden on the use of non-violation complaints under Article XXIII(1)(b) of the GATT 1994. Since the *Act* decision[883], when both the Panel and the Appellate Body took an activist stance and declared the US Anti-Dumping Act of 1916 inconsistent with WTO law, a new approach to competition matters at the WTO could be discerned.

In particular, the *Telmex*[884] decision could result in a decisive extension of the existing obligations under the WTO Agreement, if these obligations are not clarified by an additional set of rules. This applies in particular to developing countries. The *Telmex* decision is also especially significant because it was the first ruling which was based solely on the provisions of the GATS. The panel adopted an interpretation of Article IV of the GATS which limited these special and differential treatment provisions to the stage of GATS bargaining. According to that decision, the commitments of developing countries will be inter-

---

882 A. Alvarez-Jiménez, *Emerging WTO Competition Jurisprudence and its Possibilities for Future Development*, in: 24(2) Northwestern Journal of International Law & Business 2004, 441 et sqq. Compare WTO Appellate Body's decision in *United States – Anti-Dumping Act of 1916*, WT/DS136/R (31.3.2000); WTO Panel Report, *Argentina – Measures Affecting the Export of Bovine Hide and the Import of Finished Leather*, WT/DS162/R (29.05.2000); WTO Panel Report, *Mexico – Measures Affecting Telecommunications Services*, (2004) WTO Doc. WT/DS204/R: Under Mexico's Rules for the Supply of International Long Distance Services (the "ILD Rules"), Mexican operators are required to apply a uniform settlement rate and to ensure proportionate return of incoming, as compared to outgoing, calls. The uniform settlement rate is implemented through a rule which gives the Mexican operator with the greatest share of outgoing calls to a particular country – in the case of the *US, Telmex* – the sole right to negotiate settlement rates with the operators of that country. The case was *inter alia* based on Articles 5(a) and (b) of the *Annex on Telecommunications* to GATS.

883 WTO Appellate Body, *United States – Anti-Dumping Act of 1916*, WT/DS136/R (31.3.2000).

884 WTO Panel Report, *Mexico – Measures Affecting Telecommunications Services*, (2004) WTO Doc. WT/DS204/R.

preted as strictly as those of any other WTO member, once they have been made[885].

In light of this activist case law and the restrictive interpretation of the existing contractual concessions to developing countries, an additional set of rules could clarify the rights and obligations under existing WTO law and, thereby assure legal certainty for developing countries. Such legal certainty would also appear to be mandated by the Doha Declaration and might constitute a new incentive for the relaunch of negotiations on competition policy.

B. The Proposed Approach

In light of the results of the foregoing analysis, the author supports a relaunch of negotiations on competition policy within the WTO Agreement and proposes the following basic parameters for a future agreement:

1. *Framework agreement with clearly formulated and enforceable exemptions/exceptions*
2. *No substantive harmonisation of domestic competition laws*
3. *No general obligation to adopt a domestic competition law*
4. *Obligation to co-operate and to provide administrative assistance*
5. *Specification of the principles of Non-Discrimination and Transparency*
6. *Obligation to prohibit any measure relating to exports which would be prohibited if the measure's effect came about locally*
7. *Institutionalisation of technical assistance and capacity building*
8. *Integration of the Framework Agreement in the DSU*

This approach is based on the following considerations:

Despite the fact that the question of having additional international competition rules incorporated in the WTO Agreement admittedly appears to be burned out politically, the author considers a relaunch of negotiations a potential benefit to WTO membership in general and developing Member States in particular and, therefore, worth pursuing. This is due to the fact that in addition to the general economic and institutional case of additional international competition rules, competition policy may specifically underpin microeconomic reforms and positively influence supply in developing countries.

As regards to the scope of such framework agreement, the many proposals of substantive convergence and detailed competition rules have dropped from the WTO agenda and do not appear worth the effort to be further pursued at this

[885] Compare para. 7.214 of the cited decision.

point, although a supra-national authority and also maximum harmonisation would be positive from an institutional perspective. The suggested approach is, therefore, generally understood as a minimal approach, which in the author's view fits best the previous negotiations' results, increases the political feasibility and also accommodates the very nature of competition policy as a very sensitive policy area, requiring an extra amount of discretion at domestic level.

In light of the ongoing North-South-friction and in particular the halt of further negotiations on competition policy since the July Package, the central issue for any future agreement on renewed negotiations will be the sufficient accommodation of developing countries' interests without imposing any substantial implementation costs to their governments[886]. For that purpose, Special and Differential Treatment must be considered a major vehicle.

Recent WTO case law has created considerable legal uncertainty by pursuing a rather activist approach, in that it has required Member States to ensure compliance of their private market actors with the provisions of the WTO Agreement. In particular, the *Telmex* decision limited the S&D provisions and resulting benefits to the bargaining stage only, and held that commitments of developing countries where to be considered as strictly as those of any other WTO member, once they have been made. Consequently, it appears in favour of legal certainty for developing countries to agree on one single framework agreement, which clarifies the application of the principles of Non-Discrimination and Transparency under WTO law in the context of competition policy and provides for clearly formulated and thus unambiguous and enforceable exemptions and exceptions addressing the relationship of competition and development. This approach would also be in line with the Single Package idea and foster a common mutual understanding.

Despite certain positive experiences with convergent competition rules in Regional Trade Agreements due to their members' generally high degree of integration and the resulting probability of successful competition law regimes and incentives for the creation of further Regional Trade Agreements with convergent competition laws, no special consideration to Regional Trade Agreements shall be afforded under this framework agreement. Neither shall an obligation to adopt convergent competition rules within a Regional Trade Agreement be introduced. Although the "substantially all the trade" requirement of Article XXIV:8 GATT could be interpreted as also addressing competition, the creation of Regional Trade Agreements should keep its status as an exception to the general GATT rules.

With regard to the past discussions on harmonisation, the author would like to stress that any binding harmonisation of substantive domestic competition laws

[886] B. Hoekman/P. C. Mavroidis, *Economic Development, Competition Policy and the World Trade Organization*, in: 37(1) Journal of World Trade 2003, 3.

of WTO Member States is neither politically feasible nor required. Regulatory competition is in line with the GATT provisions and brings about welfare enhancement.

Accordingly, the author supports the view that there should be no obligation to adopt a domestic competition law. Any obligation to invest into the creation of a domestic competition law regime at a specific point in time potentially inopportune for a particular country would most likely result in the rejection of the proposal. Moreover, any such obligation would be inappropriate in light of the GATT's advocacy of regulatory competition. Rather, the trend prevailing since Singapore that more and more countries are adopting competition laws by themselves will help to achieve this goal without any perceived pressure from the part of developed countries.

Yet, supplementing the Principle of Non-Discrimination, the detrimental spillover effects and protectionist beggar-thy-neighbour policy legitimate under the existing export cartel regime must be eliminated. Therefore, the framework agreement should contain an obligation to afford similar protection to measures taking effect *only* abroad, provided the same mechanism would be prohibited if taking effect on the domestic market. At the same time, such wording must not allow for an inappropriate interference with foreign sovereignty and must, therefore, be formulated narrowly. A possible wording of such obligation could be as follows:

> *Members undertake to apply their competition laws to any anticompetitive practice having a detrimental effect on other Members' markets, provided that:*
>
> 1. *the practice is being exercised by persons or legal entities located in the Member's territory; and*
> 2. *the practice would also be prohibited if it had the same impact on the Member's domestic market.*

In addition, Member States would be obliged to engage in reasonable efforts for mutual assistance and co-operation in competition policy and enforcement, provided they do have a domestic competition law regime in place. This obligation would also apply with regard to the administration of sanctions imposed by domestic competition authorities[887].

Soft law instruments should be created to provide guidance on the underlying policy considerations and application of competition law instruments for those countries in need. Some alignment of procedural provisions in form of soft law instruments would also be helpful for procedural and enforcement cooperation.

[887] Vgl. Drexl, J., *International Competition Policy after Cancun: Placing a Singapore Issue on the WTO Development Agenda*, in; 27(3) Journal of World Competition 2004, S. 453.

In order to agree on the required soft law instruments and guidelines and in order to institutionalise technical assistance and capacity building, a regular forum and/or a special Working Group should be created.

Finally, the framework agreement should acknowledge the dispute settlement system as a central element of a rule-based system, providing security and predictability. Therefore, Member States shall be entitled to request consultations and the establishment of panels upon infringement of the subject framework agreement subject to the conditions of Annex 2 to the Marrakesh Agreement.

Concluding Remarks

The past results of negotiations on the adoption of additional international competition rules within the WTO have not led to any substantial agreement. Yet, the technical and subject-specific aspects of the discussion were at certain times subordinate to emotional debate and bargaining chips other than competition policy.

This book wants to show that there still is an economic and institutional case for additional international competition rules in the WTO, and that this case is worth pursuing for both developed and developing countries. The real challenge, however, is to make a political case.

This book is intended as a small contribution to perpetuate the discussion.

Bibliography

Articles & Individual Publications

- *Abbott, F. M.,* Are the Competition Rules in the WTO TRIPS Agreement Adequate? In: 7(3) Journal of International Economic Law 2004, 687-703.
- *Akbar, Y.*, Grabbing Victory from the Jaws of Defeat: Can the GE/Honeywell Merger Facilitate International Antitrust Policy Co-operation? In: 25(4) Journal of World Competition 2002, 403-422.
- *Akbar, Y.*, Global Antitrust. Trade and Competition Linkages (2003).
- *Albach, H./Rosenkranz, S. (eds.)*, Intellectual Property Rights and Global Competition. Toward a New Synthesis, 1995.
- *Alvarez-Jiménez, A.*, Emerging WTO Jurisprudence and its Possibilities for Future Development, in: 24(2) Northwestern Journal of International Law & Business 2004, 441-511.
- *Amato, F.*, International Antitrust: What Future, in: 24(4) Journal of World Competition 2001, 451-473.
- *Anderson, R. D./Holmes, P.*, Competition Policy and the Future of the Multilateral Trading System, in: (2002) Journal of International Economic Law, 531-563.
- *Anderson, R. D./Wager, H.*, Human Rights, Development and the WTO: The Cases of Intellectual Property and Competition Policy, in: 9(3) Journal of International Economic Law 2006, 707-747.
- *Applebaum, H. M.*, The Interface of the Trade Laws and the Antitrust Laws, in: International Antitrust Law and Policy 1998, 233-245.
- *Areeda, P./Turner, D.*, Predatory Pricing and Related Practices Under Section 2 of the Sherman Act, in 88 Harv. L. Rev. 1975, at 697
- *Arhel, P.*, Dimension internationale du droit de la concurrence, in: 410 Revue du Marché commun et de l'Union européenne 1997, 492-495.
- *Arhel, P.*, Droit international de la concurrence. S'oriente-t-on vers des négociations?, in: 425 Revue du Marché commun et de l'Union européenne 1999, 84-95.

- *Arndt, H.-W.*, Europarecht[5], 2001.
- *Baetge, D.*, Das Verhältnis zwischen Antidumpingrecht und Wettbewerbsrecht im Recht der Europäischen Gemeinschaft, in: (62) Rabels Zeitschrift für ausländisches und internationales Privatrecht 1998, 648-677.
- *Bain, J. S.*, Barriers to New Competition, 1956.
- *Bhattacharjea, A.*, Export Cartels – A Developing Country Perspective, in: 38(2) Journal of World Trade 2004, 331 et sqq.
- *Bhattacharjea, A.*, The Case for a Multilateral Agreement on Competition: A Developing Country Perspective, in: 9(2) Journal of International Economic Law 2006, 293-323.
- *Beckington, J. S.*, The World Trade Organization's Dispute Settlement Resolution in *United States – Anti-Dumping Act of 1916*, in: 34 Vanderbilt Journal of Transnational Law 2001, 199-223.
- *Behrens, P. (Ed.)*, EC Competition Rules in National Courts (VI). Die EG-Wettbewerbsregeln vor nationalen Gerichten (VI), 2001.
- *Bellis, J.-F.*, La politique de la concurrence et l'organisation mondiale du commerce, in: Mélanges en hommage à Michel Waelbroeck *(ii)*. Etudes de droit européen et international 1999, 737-764.
- *Bercero, I. G./Amarasinha, S. D.*, Moving the Trade and Competition Debate Forward, in: (2001) Journal of International Economic Law, 481-506.
- *Bierwagen, R. M.*, Aussenwirtschaftsrecht der Europäischen Gemeinschaften, insbesondere gegen unlauteren Handel gerichtete Schutzmassnahmen und Rechtsschutz, in: Zeitschrift für Völkerrecht 1997/6, 710-720.
- *Bilal, S./Olarreaga, M.*, Competition Policy and the WTO: Is there a need for a multilateral agreement? European Institute of Public Administration Working Paper 98/W/02, available at: http://www.eipa.nl/Publications/Summaries/1997_2000/WorkingPapers/98w02.pdf (04.06.2005).
- *Bishop, W.*, Price Discrimination under Article 86: Political Economy in the European Court, 44 MLR 1981, 28

- *Bishop, S./Walker, M.*, The Economics of EC Competition Law: Concepts, Application and Measurement, 1999.
- *Böge, U.*, Neue Entwicklungen in der Frage der internationalen Zusammenarbeit von Wettbewerbsbehörden, in: Europäische Zeitschrift für Wirtschaftsrecht 1/2001, 1.
- *Böge, U.*, Konvergenz kartellrechtlicher Normen und deren Anwendung auf globale Sachverhalte, in: Wirtschaft und Wettbewerb 10/2001, 922-928.
- *Bork, R. H.*, The Antitrust Paradoxon: A Policy at War with Itself, 1993.
- *Bronckers, M./Quick, R. (eds.)*, New Directions in International Economic Law. Essays in Honour of John H. Jackson, 2000.
- *Brusick, P.*, UNCTAD's role in promoting Multilateral Co-operation on Competition Law and Policy, in: 24(1) Journal of World Competition 2001, 23-39.
- *Cadot, O./Grether J.-M./De Melo, J.*, Trade and Competition Policy. Where do we Stand?, in: 34(3) Journal of World Trade 2000, 1-20.
- *Cho, S.*, A Bridge Too Far: The Fall of the Fifth WTO Ministerial Conference in Cancún and the Future of Trade Constitution, in: 7(2) Journal of International Economic Law 2004, 219-244.
- *Christiansen, A.*, The "more economic approach" in EU merger control – A critical assessment (December 2005), available at: http://www.dbresearch.com/PROD/DBR_INTERNET_EN-PROD/PROD0000000000196093.PDF (03.11.2006).
- *Clark, J. M.*, Toward a Concept of Workable Competition 30 American Economic Review (1940), 241-56.
- *Comanor, W. S.*, Vertical price-fixing, vertical market restrictions, and the new antitrust policy, 98 Harvard Law Review (1985) 983 et. sqq.
- *Conrad, Ch. A.*, Balancing the GATT Antidumping Code, in: 22(2) Journal of World Competition 1999, 123-133.
- *Conrad, Ch. A.*, Strategies to Reform the Regulations on International Competition, in 26(1) Journal of World Competition 2003, 101-121.
- *Conrad, Ch. A.*, Improving International Competition Order. An Institutional Approach, 2005.

- *Davey, W. C.*, Antidumping Laws: A Time for Restriction? In: 1988 Fordham Corp. L. Inst., at 8-1 et sqq.
- *Davidow, J.*, International Implications of US Antitrust in the George W. Bush Era, in: 25(4) Journal of World Competition 2002, 493-507.
- *Davidow, J./Shapiro, H.*, The Feasibility and Worth of a World Trade Organization Competition Agreement, in: 37(1) Journal of World Trade 2003, 49-68.
- *De Leon, I.*, Should We Promote Antitrust in International Trade?, in: 21(2) Journal of World Competition 1997, 35-63.
- *Deacon, D.*, Vertical Restraints under EU Competition Law: New Directions [1995] Fordham Corporate Law Institute 307, paras. 16 and 18.
- *Dhanjee, R.*, The Set of Multilaterally Agreed Equitable Principles and Rules fort he Control of Restrictive Business Practices – an Instrument of International Law?, in: 28(1) Legal Issues of Economic Integration 2001, 71-103.
- *Didier, P.*, The WTO Anti-Dumping Code and EC Practice. Issues for Review in Trade Negotiations, in: 35(1) Journal of World Trade, 33-54.
- *Doherty, B.*, Just What Are Essential Facilities? In: 38 Common Market Law Review 2001, 402 et sqq.
- *Drabeck, Z. (ed.)*, Globalization Under Threat: The Stability of Trade Policy and Multilateral Agreements, 2001.
- *Drexl, J.*, International Competition Policy after Cancun: Placing a Singapore Issue on the WTO Development Agenda, in; 27(3) Journal of World Competition 2004, 419-457.
- *Durand, B./Galarza, A. F./Mehta, K.*, The Interface between Competition Policy and International Trade Liberalisation. Looking into the Future: Applying a New Virtual Anti-Trust Standard, in: 27(1) Journal of World Competition 2004), 3-12.
- *EC Commission*, XXVIIIth Report on Competition Policy 1998, [2000] OJ C394/69.
- *EC Commission*, Green Paper on vertical restraints in competition policy, COM(96) 721.
- *EC Commission*, Guidelines on Vertical Restraints [2000] OJ C291/1.

- *European Courts,* Note on the citation of articles of the Treaties in the publications of the Court of Justice and the Court of First Instance, available at: http://curia.europa.eu/en/content/juris/noteinfo.htm (27.09.2006)
- *Egge, M. G.*, The Harmonization of Competition Laws Worldwide. Remarks, http://www.student.richmond.edu/~rjglb/egge.pdf (12.6.2002).
- *Eilmansberger, T.*, Europarecht, Bd. II, 2000.
- *Eilmansberger, T.*, EG-Wettbewerbsrecht und Internet, in: Wirtschaftsrechtliche Blätter, November 2001, 501-512.
- *Epstein, J.*, The Other Side of Harmony: Can Trade and Competition Laws Work Together in the International Marketplace? In: 17 American University International Law Review 2002, 343-368.
- *Erlbacher, F.*, Die neuen Leitlinien der Kommission für die Vergabe staatlicher Regionalbeihilfen, in Europäische Zeitschrift für Wirtschaftsrecht 17/1998, 517-522.
- *European Commission*, Discussion Paper Trade and Competition (GATT/WTO), http://europe.eu.int/comm/competition/international/wto_discussion_paper_en.pdf (12.6.2002).
- *European Commission*, European Union competition policy. XXXIst Report on competition policy, http://europe.eu.int/comm/competition/annual_reports/2001/competition_policy/en.pdf (12.6.2002).
- *European Commission,* Merger Overview, available at: http://europa.eu.int/comm/competition/publications/special/3_merger.pdf (13.01.2005).
- *European Commission*, Submission from the EC and its Member States to the Working Group on the Interaction Between Trade and Competition Policy, "The Relevance of fundamental WTO principles of national treatment, transparency and most favoured nation treatment to competition policy and vice versa", http://europe.eu.int/comm/competition/international/discfinal_en.pdf (12.6.2002).
- *European Commission*, Communication of 21 September 2000 from the European Community and its Member States to the WTO Working Group, WT/WGTCP/W/152, 25 September 2000, available at: http://docsonline.wto.org/gen_search.asp?language=1 (02.10.2005).

- *European Community,* Communication of 21 September 2000 from the European Community and its Member States to the WTO Working Group, WT/WGTCP/W/152, available at: http://docsonline.wto.org/gen_search.asp?language=1 (18.09.2005).
- *European Courts,* Informative Note on the citation of articles of the Treaties in the publications of the Court of Justice and the Court of First Instance, available at: http://curia.europa.eu/en/content/juris/noteinfo.htm (07.10.2006)
- *Evenett S. et al.*, International Cartel Enforcement: Lessons from the 1999's, available at: http://www.econ.worldbank.org/files/2454_wps2680.pdf
- *Fiebig, A.*, A Role for the WTO in International Merger Control, in: 20 Northwestern Journal of International Law and Business 1999/2000, 233-254.
- *Fikentscher, W.*, Wettbewerb und gewerblicher Rechtschutz. Die Stellung des Rechts der Wettbewerbsbeschränkungen in der Rechtsordnung, 1958.
- *Fikentscher, W.*, Recht und wirtschaftliche Freiheit. Die Freiheit des Wettbewerbs, Bd I, 1992.
- *Forschungsinstitut für Wirtschaftsverfassung und Wettbewerb (Köln)*, Die Bedeutung der WTO für die europäische Wirtschaft, 1997.
- *Fox, E. M.*, Competition Law and the Millenium Round, in: Journal of International Economic Law 1999, 665-679.
- *Fox, E. M.*, The Merger Regulation and its Territorial Reach [1999] ECLR 334.
- *Fox, E. M.*, National Law, Global Markets, and *Hartford*: Eyes Wide Shut, in: 68 Antitrust Law Journal 2000, 73-86.
- *Fox, E. M.*, Competition Law, in: *A.F. Lowenfeld (ed.)*, International Economic Law, Chapter 12 (Oxford 2002).
- *Fox, E.M.*, International Antitrust and the Doha Dome, in: 43 VA. J. Int'l. L. (2003), 911-932, available at: http://www.antitrustinstitute.org/recent2/274.pdf.
- *Fox, E. M.*, The WTO's First Antitrust Case – *Mexican Telecom:* A Sleeping Victory for Trade and Competition, in: 9(2) Journal of International Economic Law 2006, 271-292.
- *Frenkel, M./Bender, D. (Hrsg.)*, GATT und neue Welthandelsordnung. Globale und regionale Auswirkungen, 1996.

- *Fritz-Aßmus, D./Tuchfeld, E. (eds.)*, Die Ordnung des Welthandels: A. Ghanie Ghaussy zum 65. Geburtstag, 1997.

- *Fullerton, L./Mazard, C. C.*, International Antitrust Co-operation Agreements, in: 24(3) Journal of World Competition 2001, 405-423.

- *Gelhorn, E./Kovacic, W.E.*, Antitrust Law and Economics[4].

- *Giardina, A./Beviglia Zampetti A.*, Settling Competition-Related Disputes. The Arbitration Alternative in the WTO Framework, 31(6) Journal of World Trade, 5-27.

- *Ginsburg, D. H.*, International Antitrust: 2000 and Beyond, in: 68 Antitrust Law Journal 2000, 571-576.

- *Ginsburg, D. H./Angstreich, S. H.*, Multinational Merger Review: Lessons from our Federalism, in: 68 Antitrust Law Journal 2000, 219-237.

- *Goldman, C. S./Facey, B. A.*, Antitrust and Trade Policy: International Business Perspectives, in: International Antitrust Law and Policy 1998, 279-297.

- *Goldman, C. S./Rill, J. F.*, The Internationalization of Competition Law and the Need for Global Convergence, http://www.europe-canada.org/en/CD-Rom/pdf/BIAC.pdf (12.6.2002).

- *Gomula, J.*, The Standard of Review of Article 17.6 of the Anti-Dumping Agreement and the Problem of its Extension to Other WTO Agreements, in: 23 Polish Yearbook of International Law 1997-1998, 229-250.

- *Government of Canada,* Recent Developments in International Co-operation in Competition Policy Matters, at http://strategis.ic.gc.ca/SSG/ct00056e.html (26.3.2003).

- *Graham, E. M.,* The Relationship Between International Trade Policy and Competition Policy, in Z. *Drabek (ed.),* Globalization Under Threat: The Stability of Trade Policy and Multilateral Agreements, 2001.

- *Grewlich, A. S.*, Globalisation and Conflict in Competition Law. Elements of Possible Solutions, in: 24(3) Journal of World Competition 2001, 367-404.

- *Grünwald, A./Hauser, W./Reininghaus, P.*, Wirtschaftsrecht, 1997.

- *Guzman, A. T.,* Is International Antitrust Possible? In: 73 New York University Law Review 1998, 1501-1548.

- *Guzman, A. T.*, Antitrust and International Regulatory System, in: 76 New York University Law Review 2001, 1142-1163.
- *Hawk, B. E.*, System Failure: Vertical Restraints and EC Competition Law, 32 CMLR (1995), 973.
- *Hawk, B. E. (ed.)*, International Antitrust Law and Policy, 1996.
- *Hawk, B. E.*, Convergence in International Antitrust Law, WuW 9/2001, available at http://www.canada-europe.org/en/CD-Rom/pdf/BDI.pdf.
- *Herdegen, M.*, Internationales Wirtschaftsrecht[2], 1995.
- *Hilpold, P.*, The Multilateral Agreement on Investment. Are the fears justified? In: 16 Academia 1998, available at: http://www.eurac.edu/Press/Academia/16/Artikel2.asp.
- *Hilpold, P.*, Regional Integration According to Article XXIV GATT – Between Law and Politics, in: 7 Max Planck Yearbook of United Nations Law 2003, 219-260.
- *Hilpold, P.*, International Competition Law and Regional Trade Agreements, in: 2(3) Manchester Journal of International Economic Law 2005, 82-93.
- *Hobe, S./Kimminich, O.*, Einführung in das Völkerrecht[8], 2004.
- *Hoekman, B.*, Competition Policy and the Global Trading System, in: 20 The World Economy 1997, 383-406.
- *Hoekman, B.*, Free Trade and Deep Integration. Antidumping and Antitrust in Regional Trade Agreements, World Bank Policy Research Paper 1950 (July 1998), available at: http://wdsbeta.worldbank.org/external/default/WDSContentServer/IW3P/IB/1998/07/01/000009265_3980928162543/Rendered/PDF/multi0page.pdf (27.09.2005).
- *Hoekman, B./Mavroidis, P. C.*, Economic Development, Competition Policy, and the World Trade Organization, World Bank Policy Research Paper 2917, October 2002, available at: http://wdsbeta.worldbank.org/external/default/WDSContentServer/IW3P/IB/2002/11/22/000094946_02111404425138/Rendered/PDF/multi0page.pdf (04.06.2005).
- *Hoekman, B./Mavroidis, P. C.*, Economic Development, Competition Policy and the World Trade Organization, in: 37(1) Journal of World Trade 2003, 1-27.

- *Hoekman, B.*, Operationalizing the Concept of Policy Space in the WTO: Beyond Special and Differential Treatment, in: 8(2) Journal of International Economic Law 2005, 405-424.
- *Hudec, R. E.*, A WTO Perspective on Private Anti-Competitive Behavior in World Markets, in: 34 New England Law Review 1999/2000, 79-102.
- *Hummer, W./Weiss, F.*, Vom GATT '47 zur WTO '94. Dokumente zur alten und zur neuen Welthandelsordnung, 1997.
- *Iacobcci, E.*, The Interdependence of Trade and Competition Policies, in: 21(2) Journal of World Competition 1997, 5-33.
- *ICC*, Comments on European Commission Proposals for Reform relating to horizontal co-operation, http://www.iccwbo.org/home/statements_rules/statements/2000/ec_proposals.asp (18.2.2002).
- *ICC/BIAC*, Recommended framework for best practices in international merger control procedures, http://iccwbo.org/home/competition/BIACpaper.pdf (19.2.2002).
- *ICC/BIAC;* Comments on report of the US International Competition Policy Advisory Committee (ICPAC), http://www.iccwbo.org/home/statements_rules/statements/2000/report_icpac.asp (19.2.2002).
- *Immenga, U.*, Harmonisierung des Wettbewerbsrechts als Aufgabe? In: Europäische Zeitschrift für Wirtschaftsrecht 15/1997, 449.
- *Immenga, U.*, Trade and Competition: Is there a Need for International Competition Rules? Abstract, ECSA Conference "The WTO after the Seattle Ministerial Conference: Recent Developments and Future Perspectives, Vienna, December 9th and 10th, 1999, available at: http://fgr.wu-wien.ac.at/ecsa/wtoabstr.htm#immenga.
- *International Competition Policy Advisory Committee to the Attorney General and Assistant Attorney General for Antitrust*, Final Report 2000 - Foreword, http://www.usdoj.gov/atr/icpac/forward.pdf (19.2.2002).
- *International Competition Policy Advisory Committee to the Attorney General and Assistant Attorney General for Antitrust*, Final Report, at: http://www.usdoj.gov/atr/icpac/finalreport.htm (28.3.2003).

- *Ismail, F.*, How Can Least-Developed Countries and Other Small, Weak and Vulnerable Economies Also Gain from the Doha Development Agenda on the Road to Hong Kong? In: 40(1) Journal of World Trade 2006, 37-68.
- *Jackson, J. H./Davey, W. J./Sykes, A. O.*, Legal Problems of International Economic Relations. Cases, Materials and Text, 2002.
- Janow, *M. E.*, Public, Private, and Hybrid Public/Private Restraints on Trade: What Role for the WTO? In: 31 Law and Policy of International Business 1999/2000, 977-980.
- *Janow, M. E./Lewis, C. R.*, International Antitrust and the Global Economy: Perspectives on The Final Report and Recommendations of the International Competition Policy Advisory Committee to the Attorney General and the Assistant Attorney General for Antitrust, in: 24(1) Journal of World Competition 2001, 3-21.
- *Jebsen, P./Stevens, R.*, Assumptions, Goals and Dominant Undertakings: The Regulation of Competition Under Article 86 of the European Union, (1995-96) Antitrust Law Journal 443, 487-491.
- *Jenny, F. (Moderator)*, Antitrust and Trade Policy Roundtable, in: International Antitrust Law and Policy 1998, 307-356.
- *Jenny, F.*, Cartels and Collusion in Developing Countries: Lessons from Empirical Evidence, in: 29(1) Journal of World Competition 2006, 109-137.
- *Jones, A./Sufrin, B.*, EC Competition Law. Text, Cases and Materials, 2001.
- *Jones, C. A.*, Toward Global Competition Policy? The Expanding Dialogue on Multilateralism, in: 23(2) Journal of World Competition 2000, 95-99.
- *Jones, C. A.*, Private Antitrust Enforcement in Europe: A Policy Analysis and Reality Check, in: 27(1) Journal of World Competition 2004, 13-24.
- *Jones, C. A./Matsushita, M. (eds.)*, Competition Policy in the Global Trading System, 2002.
- *Jung, Y.*, Modelling a WTO Dispute Settlement Mechanism in an International Antitrust Agreement, in: 34(1) Journal of World Trade 2000, 89-110.
- *Kaul, I./Conceição, P./Le Goulven, K./Mendoza, R. (eds.)*, Providing Global Public Goods, 2003, available at: http://www.undp.org/globalpublicgoods/globalization/toc.html (25.05.2005).

- *Kearns, J. E.*, International Competition Policy and the GATS: A Proposal to Address Market Access Limitations in the Distribution Services Sector, in: 22 University of Pennsylvania Journal of International Economic Law 2001, 285-323.
- *Kennedy, K. C.*, Foreign Direct Investment and Competition Policy at the World Trade Organzation, in: 33 George Washington International Law Review 2000/2001, 585-650.
- *Kiriazis, G.*, Jurisdiction and cooperation issues in the investigation of international cartels, at: http://europa.eu.int/comm/competition/speeches/text/sp2001_010_en.pdf (28.3.2003).
- *Klein, J. I.*, Anticipating the Millenium: International Antitrust Enforcement at the end of the Twentieth Century, in: International Antitrust Law and Policy 1997, 1-12.
- *Klein, M./Meng, W./Rode, R. (Hrsg.)*, Die Neue Welthandelsordnung der WTO. Schriftenreihe Wirtschaftspolitik, Bd I, 1998.
- *Klodt, H.*, Towards a Global Competition Order, 2005.
- *Kobayashi, H.*, The World Trade Organization and Competition Policy, in: The World Trade Organization and Competition Policy, in: International Antitrust Law and Policy 1997, 27-30.
- *Kolalsky, W. J.*, Conglomerate Mergers and Range Effects: It's a Long Way from Chicago to Brussels, 23 Address before the George Mason University Symposium, Washington, D.C. (9 November 2001), http://www.usdoj.gov/atr/public/speeches/9536.htm.
- *Kommission der Europäischen Gemeinschaften,* 3 Competition Policy Newsletter 2001, S. 5-13.
- *Kommission der Europäischen Gemeinschaften*, Evaluierungsbericht der Kommission über die Gruppenfreistellungsverordnung (EG) Nr. 240/96 für Technologietransfer-Vereinbarungen (GFTT), http://europa.eu.int/comm/competition/antitrust/technology_transfer/ (21.2.2002).
- *Kommission der Europäischen Gemeinschaften*, Grünbuch über die Revision der Verordnung (EWG) Nr. 4064/89 des Rates, KOM (2001) 0745.
- *Kommission der Europäischen Gemeinschaften*, Vorschlag für eine Verordnung des Rates zur Durchführung der in den Artikeln 81 und 82 EG-Vertrag niedergelegten Wettbewerbsregeln und zur Änderung der Verordnungen (EWG) Nr. 1017/68, (EWG)

Nr. 2988/74, (EWG) Nr. 4056/86 und (EWG) Nr. 3975/87 („Durchführungsverordnung zu den Artikeln 81 und 82 EG-Vertrag), KOM (2000) 0582.

- *Koopmann, G.*, Wettbewerbspolitische Instrumente der Welthandelsorganisation, 1998.
- *Koopmann, G.*, Internationalisierung der Wettbewerbspolitik: Korrelat zur internationalen Handelspolitik? In: 56(II) Aussenwirtschaft (2001), 159-199.
- *Koppensteiner, H.-G.*, Österreichisches und europäisches Wettbewerbsrecht[3] (1997).
- *Kruse, J./Mayer, O. G. (Hrsg.)*, Aktuelle Probleme der Wettbewerbs- und Wirtschaftspolitik, in: FS Kantzenbach, 1996.
- *Lloyd, P./Sampson, G.*, Competition and Trade Policy: Identifying the Issues after the Uruguay Round, in: *Lloyd, P. J. (ed.)* International Trade Opening and the Formation of the Global Economy: Selected Essays of P. J. Lloyd. Economists of the Twentieth Century Series, 1999, at pp. 435-459.
- *Lukas, M.*, Stand und Perspektiven des EG-Antisubventionsrechts, in: 5/2000 EWS, 203-207.
- *Luz, K.*, The Boeing-McDonnell Douglas Merger: Competition Law, Parochialism, and the Need for a Globalized Antitrust System, in: 32 George Washington Journal of International Economic Law 1999/2000, 155-177.
- *MacLaren, R.*, Two Steps Forward and No Steps Back. Drafting a New Course for Trade and Competition Policy, in: International Business Lawyer 1996, 464-457.
- *Magney, J. S./Anderson, R. C.*, Recent Developments in Criminal Enforcement of US Antitrust Laws, in 27(1) Journal of World Competition 2004, 101 et sqq.
- *Magnus, J. R.*, Joint Export Trade Provisions in Antitrust Laws: A Supporter's Perspective, in: 39(1) Journal of World Trade 2006, 181-184.
- *Malaguti, M.-C.*, Restrictive Business Practices in International Trade and the Role of the World Trade Organization, in: 32(3) Journal of World Trade 1998, 117-149.
- Marschall, R. H., Patents, antitrust, and the WTO/GATT: using TRIPS as a vehicle for antitrust harmonization, in: 28 Law & Policy of International Business 1996/97, 1165-1193.

- *Marsden, P. B.*, Dealing with International Exclusion. The Right Focus for the WTO Working Group on Trade and Competition Policy, in: 21(2) Journal of World Competition 1997,91-110.
- *Marsden, P. B.*, Innovative trade rules with anti-competitive effects? In: 29 International Business Lawyer 2001, 129-132.
- *Marsden, P.*, A Competition Policy for the WTO, 2003.
- *Matsushita, M.*, Reflections on Competition Policy/Law in the Framework of the WTO, in: International Antitrust Law and Policy 1997, 31-51.
- *Mattoo, A./Subramanian, A.*, Multilateral Rules on Competition Policy – A Possible Way Forward, in: 31(5) Journal of World Trade 1997, 95-115.
- *Mavroidis, P.C./Van Siclen, S. J.*, The Application of the GATT/WTO Dispute Resolution System to Competition Issues, in: 31(5) Journal of World Trade 1997,5-48.
- *Meessen, K. M.*, Das Fuer und Wider eines Weltkartellrechts, in: Wirtschaft und Wettbewerb 1/2000, 5-16.
- *Melamed, A. D.*, Antitrust Enforcement in a Global Economy, in: International Antitrust Law and Policy 1998, 1-13.
- *Melamed, A. D.*, International Cooperation in Competition Law and Policy: What Can Be Achieved at the Bilateral, Regional, and Multilateral Levels, in: 2(3) Journal of International Economic Law 1999, 423-433.
- *Mirandes, J./Torres, R./Ruiz, M.*, The International Use of Antidumping, in: 32 Journal of World Trade 1998, 5.
- *Mitchell, A. D.*, Broadening the Vision of Trade Liberalisation. International Competition Law and the WTO, in: 24(3) Journal of World Competition 2001, S. 343-365.
- *Moeschel, W.*, Systemwechsel im Europaeischen Wettbewerbsrecht? Zum Weißbuch der EG-Kommission zu den Art. 81 ff. EG-Vertrag, in: 55(2) Juristenzeitung 2000, 61-112.
- *Monti, G.*, Article 81 EC and Public Policy, 39(5) Common Market Law Review 2002, 1057-1099.
- *Monti, M.*, Antitrust in the US and Europe: a History of convergence, http://europa.eu.int/comm/competition/speeches/index_2001.html (12.6.2002).

- *Monti, M.*, International Cooperation in Antitrust: US/EU and Beyond, in: 69 Antitrust Law Journal 2001-2, 361-367.
- *Mueller, W.*, Stand und Perspektiven des EG-Antidumpingrechts, in: EWS 5/2000, 195-*203.*
- *Murphy, D.*, Interjurisdictional Competition and Regulatory Advantage, in: 8(4) Journal of International Economic Law 2005, 891-920.
- *Nagel, B.*, Wirtschaftsrecht der Europäischen Union. Eine Einführung[3], 2001.
- *Neuhold, H./Hummer, W./Schreuer, Ch. (Hrsg.)*, Österreichisches Handbuch des Völkerrechts[3], Bd I, 1997.
- *Nicolaides, P.*, An Essay on Economics and the Competition Law of the European Community, in: (27) Legal Issues of Economic Integration 2000-1, 7-24.
- *Niels, G./Kate, A.*, Trusting Anitrust to Dump Antidumping. Abolishing Antidumping in Free Trade Agreements Without Replacing it with Competition Law, in: 31 (6) Journal of World Trade 1997, 29-43.
- *Nottage, H.*, Trade and Competition in the WTO: Pondering the Applicability of Special and Differential Treatment, in: 6(1) Journal of International Economic Law 2003, 23-47.
- *OECD,* Competition and Trade Policies: Their Interaction, 1984.
- *OECD,* Recommendation of 27 and 28 July 1995, http://europe.eu.int/comm/competition/international/3a04en.html (13.6.2002).
- *OECD,* Competition Policy and Intellectual Property Rights. Series Roundtables on Competition Policy Nr. 18, JAFFE/CLP(98)18, 1998, at: http://www1.oecd.org/daf/clp/roundtables/IPR-GD.PDF, 25.3.2003.
- *Ohlhoff, S.*, Verbotene Beihilfen nach dem Subventionsabkommen der WTO im Lichte aktueller Rechtsprechung, Europäische Zeitschrift für Wirtschaftsrecht 21/2000, 645-668.
- *Papakrivopoulos, D.*, The Role of Competition Law as an International Trade Remedy in the Context of the World Trade Organization, in 22(3) Journal of World Competition 1999, 45-64.
- *Parkinson, J. E.*, Corporate Power and Responsibility, 1993.

- *Paulweber, M.*, The End of a Success Story? The European Commission's White Paper on the Modernisation of the European Competition Law, in: 23(3) Journal of World Competition 2000, 3-48.
- *Petersmann, E.-U.*, International Competition Rules for the GATT-MTO World Trade and Legal System, 27(6) Journal of World Trade 1993, 35-86.
- *Petersmann, E.-U.;* International Competition Rules for Governments and for Private Business. The Case for Linking Future WTO Negotiations on Investment, Competition and Environmental Rules to Reforms of Anti-Dumping Laws, in: 30(3) Journal of World Trade 1996, 5-35.
- *Petersmann, E.-U.*, Competition-oriented Reforms of the WTO World Trade System – Proposals and Policy Options, in: *Zäch, R.*, Toward WTO Competition Rules. Key Issues and Comments on the WTO Report (1998) on Trade and Competition, 1999, 42-71.
- *Petersmann, E.-U. (ed.)*, International Trade Law and the GATT/WTO Dispute Settlement System, 1999.
- *Petersmann, E. U.*, Legal, Economic and Political Objectives of National and International Competition Policies: Constitutional Functions of WTO "Linking Principles" for Trade and Competition, in: 34 New England Law Review 1999/2000, 145-162.
- *Petersmann, E.-U.*, Challenges to the Legitimacy and Efficiency of the World Trading System: Democratic Governance and Competition Culture in the WTO, in: 7(3) Journal of International Economic Law 2004, 585-603.
- *Pitofsky, R.*, Competition Policy in a Global Economy – Today and Tomorrow, in: 2(3) Journal of International Economic Law 1999, 403-411.
- *Porter, M.*, The Competitive Advantage of Nations, 1990.
- *Posner, R.*, Antitrust Law[2], 2000.
- *Rapp, R.*, Predatory Pricing and Entry Deterring Strategies: the Economics of AKZO, in: [1986] ECLR 233.
- *Rowley, J. W.*, Global Welfare: Competition Policy and Market Access, in: International Business Lawyer 1996, 446-450.

- *Ruttley, P./Macvay, I./George, C. (ed.)*, The WTO and International Trade Regulation, 1998.
- *Sack, R.*, Das internationale Wettbewerbsrecht nach der E-Commerce-Richtlinie (ECRL) und dem EGG-/TDG-Entwurf, in: Wettbewerb in Recht und Praxis 12/2001, 1408-1425.
- *Saner, R./Pâez, L.*, Technical Assistance to Least-Developed Countries in the Context of the Doha Development Round: High Risk of Failure, in: 40(3) Journal of World Trade 2006, 467-494.
- *Schaub, A.*, Konvergenz kartellrechtlicher Normen und deren Anwendung auf globale Sachverhalte, in: Wirtschaft und Wettbewerb 10/2001, 928-933.
- *Schaub, A.*, The Global Competition Forum: How it should be organised and operated, http://europa.eu.int/comm/competition/speeches/txt/sp2001_003_en.pdf (12.6.2002).
- *Scherer, F. M./Ross, D.*, Industrial Market Structure and Economic Performance, 1990.
- *Schoneveld, F. R.*, Cartel Sanctions and International Competition Policy: Cross-Border Cooperation and Appropriate Forums for Cooperation, 26(3) Journal of World Competition 2003, 433-471.
- *Schricker, G./Henning-Bodewig, F.*, Elemente einer Harmonisierung des Rechts des unlauteren Wettbewerbs in der Europäischen Union, in: Wettbewerb in Recht und Praxis 12/2001, 1367-1407.
- *Scott, A.*, Cain and Abel? Trade and Competition Laws in the Global Economy, in: 68(1) The Modern Law Review 2003, 135-155.
- *Sharma, R./Rosychuk, J.*, The Collision of Trade and Competition Law: Assessing the Aftermath of the WTO *Telmex* Decision, available at: http://www.heenanblaikie.com/en/media/pdfs/pdf/20040625_Sharma.pdf (02.06.2005).
- *Siebert, H. (ed.)*, Toward a New Global Framework for High-Technology Competition, 1997.
- *Singham, S. A.*, Is it Time for an International Agreement on Uncompetitive Public Sector Practices, in: 27 Brooklyn Journal of International Law 2001, 35-64.
- *Slot, P. J.*, Case C-367/95 P, Commission v. Chambre Syndicale Nationale (Sytraval), Judgement of the full court of 1998m [1998] ECR I-1719, and Case T-95/96, Gestevi-

sion Telecinco S.A. v. Commission, judgement of the Court of First Instance of 1998, [1998] ECR II-3407, in: 36 Common Market Law Review 1999, 1335-1344.

- *Stirati, Gabriele,* The Appraisal of Collective Dominance and Efficiency Gains under the Substantive Test of the New EU Merger Regulation, in: 1(3) Erasmus Law and Economics Review 2004, 249 et sqq., available at: http://www.eler.org/viewarticle.php?id=12 (03.11.2006)
- *Takigawa, T.,* Harmonization of Competition Laws after Doha, in: 36(6) Journal of World Trade 2002, 1111-1124.
- *Tarullo, D. K.,* Norms and Institutions in Global Competition Policy, in: (94) The American Journal of International Law 2000, 478-504.
- *Tavares de Araujo, J.,* Legal and Economic Interfaces Between Antidumping and Competition Policy, in 25(2) Journal of World Competition 2002, 159-172.
- *Taylor, M.,* International Competition Law. A New Dimension for the WTO? 2006.
- *The International Forum on Globalization (IFG),* Die Welthandelsorganisation (WTO): Unsichtbare Regierung für die Welt des neuen Jahrtausends? Eine Einführung, Analyse und Kritik, 2001.
- *Todino, M.,* International Competition Network. The State of Play after Naples, in: 26(2) Journal of World Competition 2003, 283-302.
- *Trebilcock, M. J.,* Competition Policy and Trade Policy. Mediating the Interface, in: 30 (4) Journal of World Trade 1996, 72 et sqq.
- *Trebilcock, M. J./Howse, R.,* The Regulation of International Trade, 2002.
- *Trebilcock, M. J./Iacobucci, E. M.,* Designing Competition Law Institutions, in: 25(3) Journal of World Competition 2002, 361-394.
- *UNCTAD,* Can developing economies benefit from WTO negotiations on binding disciplines for hard core cartels? UNCTAD/DITC/CLP/2003/3 - 27/01/04, available at: http://www.unctad.org/en/docs//ditcclp20033_en.pdf .
- *UNCTAD, Closer Multilateral Cooperation on Competition Policy: The Development Dimension.* Consolidated Report of 15 May 2002, at: http://r0.unctad.org/en/subsites/cpolicy/gvaJuly/docs/DohaFinal-en.pdf (28.3.2003).

- *UNCTAD,* Model Law on Competition 2000, available at: http://www.unctad.org/en/docs/tdrbpconf5d7.en.pdf.
- UNCTAD, *Model Law on Competition* (2004), TD/B/RBP/CONF.5/7/Rev.2, available at: http://r0.unctad.org/en/subsites/cpolicy/docs/Modelaw04.pdf (13.09.2005).
- *UNCTAD, Trade and Development Board,* Consultations on Competition Law and Policy, Including the Model Law and Studies Related to the Provisions of the Set of Principles and Rules. A preliminary report on how competition policy addresses the exercise of intellectual property rights, TD/B/COM.2/CLP/10, March 30 1999, at: http://www.unctad.org/en/docs/c2clp99d10.pdf, 24.3.2003.
- *UNCTAD,* Word Investment Report 2004. The Shift toward Services, available at: http://www.unctad.org/en/docs/wir2004_fas_en.pdf, 19.03.2005.
- *UNCTAD,* World Investment Report 2003. FDI Policies for Development: National and International Perspectives, available at: http://www.unctad.org/en/docs/wir2003_en.pdf (08.05.2005).
- *UNCTAD*, WTO core principles and prohibition: obligations relating to private practices, national competition laws and implications for a competition policy framework, UNCTAD/DITC/CLP/2003/2 - 27/01/04, available at: http://www.unctad.org/en/docs//ditcclp20032_en.pdf.
- *UNCTAD*, World Investment Report 2000. Cross-border Mergers and Acquisitions and Development, available at: http://www.unctad.org/en/docs/wir2000_en.pdf.
- *UNCTAD*, Preparing for Future Multilateral Trade Negotiations: Issues and Research Needs from a Development Perspective, UNCTAD/ITCD/TSB/6, September 1999.
- *Van Miert, K.*, The WTO and Competition Policy: the Need to Consider Negotiations, Address before Ambassadors to the WTO, 21. 4. 1998, at: http://europa.eu.int/comm/competition/speeches/text/sp1998_038_en.html, 26.3.2003.
- *Varney, C. A.,* Vertical Restraints Enforcement at the FTC, Speech at the ALI-ABA Annual Advanced Course on Product Distribution and Marketing, January 16, 1996, at: http://www.ftc.gov/speeches/varney/varnmg.htm, 30.04.2004.
- *Vermulst, E.*, Adopting and Implementing Anti-Dumping Laws. Some Suggestions for Developing Countries, in: 31 (2) Journal of World Trade 1997, 5-23.

- *Vermulst, E./Komuro, N.*, Anti-Dumping Disputes in the GATT/WTO. Navigating Dire Straits, in: 31(1) Journal of World Trade 1997, 5-43.
- *Vermulst, E./Driessen, B.*, New Battle Lines in the Anti-Dumping War. Recent Movements on the European Front, in: 31(3) Journal of World Trade 1997, 135-157.
- *Vermulst, E.*, EC Countervailing Duty Practice After the Uruguay Round Revisited: "Leges bonae ex malis moribus procreantur", in: 27(3) Legal Issues of Economic Integration 2000, 217-238.
- *Vickers, D./Hay, D.* (eds.), The Economics of Market Dominance, 1987.
- *Von Beibom, W./Geiger, A.*, Ein Weltkartellrecht als ultima ratio, in: Europäische Zeitschrift für Wirtschaftsrecht 9/2002, 261-266.
- *Waller, S. W.*, An International Common Law of Antitrust, in: 34 New England Law Review 1999/2000, 163-172.
- *Warner, M. A. A.*, International Aspects of Competition Policy. Possible Directions for the FTAA, in: 22(1) Journal of World Competition 1999, 1-36.
- *Warner, M. A. A.*, After Seattle: Is There a Future for Trade and Competition Policy Rule-Making? In: 26 Brooklyn Journal of International Law 2000/2001, 307-362.
- *Weinrauch, R.*, Competition Law in the WTO. The Rationale for a Framework Agreement, 2004.
- *Wesseling, R.*, The Commission White Paper on Modernisation of E.C. Antitrust Law: Unspoken Consequences and Incomplete Treatment of Alternative Options, ECLR 1999, 420 et sqq.
- *Wilcox, W. K.*, GATT-based Protectionism and the Definition of a Subsidy, in: 16 Boston University International Law Journal 1998, 129-163.
- *Wils, W. P. J.*, Should Private Antitrust Enforcement Be Encouraged in Europe?, in: 26(3) Journal of World Competition 2003, 473-488.
- *Wins, H.*, Eine internationale Wettbewerbsordnung als Ergänzung zum GATT, 2000.
- *Woolcock, S.*, International Competition Policy and the World Trade Organisation, Paper for the LSE Global Dimensions/Federal Trust Forum on the 'Singapore Issues' in the WTO, March 25-27th 2003, London School of Economics, available at:

http://www.lse.ac.uk/collections/globalDimensions/tradepolicy/papers/woolcock.htm (24.02.2005).

- *WTO General Council,* Decision adopted by the General Council on 1 August 2004 ("July Package"), WT/L/579, 2 August 2004, available at: http://www.wto.org/english/tratop_e/dda_e/draft_text_gc_dg_31july04_e.htm (01.11.2006).
- *WTO,* Singapore Ministerial Declaration, adopted on 13 December 1996, http://www.wto.org/english/news_e/pres96_e/wtodec.htm
- *WTO Working Group on the Interaction Between Trade and Competition Policy to the General Council,* Report 1998, WT/WGTCP/2, 8 December 1998 (98-4914), at: http://docsonline.wto.org/DDFDocuments/t/WT/WGTCP/2.doc (23.3.2003).
- *WTO Working Group on the Interaction Between Trade and Competition Policy to the General Council,* Report 1999, WT/WGTCP/3, 11 October 1999 (99-4245), at: http://docsonline.wto.org/DDFDocuments/t/WT/WGTCP/3.doc, 22. 3. .2003.
- *WTO Working Group on the Interaction Between Trade and Competition Policy to the General Council,* Report 2000, WT/WGTCP/4, 30 November 2000 (00-5169), at: http://www.wto.org/english/tratop_e/comp_e/wgtcp4.doc (22.3.2003).
- *WTO Working Group on the Interaction between Trade and Competition Policy*, The Fundamental WTO Principles of National Treatment, Most-Favoured-Nation Treatment, Background Note by the Secretariat, WT/WGTCP/W/114, of 14 April 1999.
- *WTO Working Group on the Interaction between Trade and Competition Policy*, The Fundamental Principles of Competition Policy - Background Note by the Secretariat, WT/WGTCP/W/127, of 7 June 1999.
- *WTO Working Group on the Interaction between Trade and Competition Policy,* Communication from the European Community and its Member States, 2001, WT/WGTCP/W/175.
- *WTO Working Group on the Interaction Between Trade and Competition Policy to the General Council,* Report 2001, WT/WGTCP/5, 8 October 2001 (01-4871), at: http://docsonline.wto.org/DDFDocuments/t/WT//WGTCP/5.doc (22.03.2003).

- *WTO Working Group on the Interaction between Trade and Competition Policy,* Core Principles, including Transparency, Non-Discrimination and Procedural Fairness, Background Note by the Secretariat, WT/WGTCP/W/209, of 19 September 2002.
- *WTO Working Group on the Interaction Between Trade and Competition Policy to the General Council,* Report 2002, WT/WGTCP/6, 9 December 2002 (02-6787), at: http://docsonline.wto.org/DDFDocuments/t/WT//WGTCP/6.doc (20.03.2003).
- *WTO,* Annual Report 2001, at http://www.wto.org/english/res_e/booksp_e/anrep_e/wto_anrep01_e.pdf, 28.3.2003.
- *WTO,* Annual Report 2002, at http://www.ifcba.org/anrep02_e.pdf, 28. 3. 2003
- *WTO,* Ministerial Declaration of 20 November 2001, WT/MIN(01)/DEC/1, 20 November 2001, No. 23-25, available at: http://www.wto.org/english/thewto_e/minist/min01_emindecl_e.htm (18.09.2004).
- *WTO,* Ministerial Declaration of 18 December 2005, WT/MIN/(05)/DEC, 22 December 2005.
- WTO Secretariat Note, *Implementation of Special and Differential Treatment Provisions in WTO Agreements and Decisions,* WT/COMTD/W77, available at: http://docsonline.wto.org/DDFDocuments/t/WT/COMTD/W77.doc (12.08.2005).
- *Yacheistova, N.,* What may Commonwealth of Independent States expect from Multilateral Competition Rules?, in: 23(1) Journal of World Competition 2000, 51-56.
- *Zaech, R. (ed.),* Toward WTO Competition Rules. Key Issues and Comments on the WTO Report (1998) on Trade and Competition, 1999.

Legal Texts

- *Agreement between the Government of the United States of America and the Commission of the European Communities regarding the application of their competition laws,* OJ L132, http://europa.eu.int/comm/competition/international/bilateral/.
- *EC Commission,* Commission Notice on the definition of relevant market for the purposes of Community competition law [1997] OJ C372/5.

- *EC Commission*, Commission Regulation (EC) No 2790/1999 on the application of Article 81(3) of the Treaty to categories of vertical agreements and concerted practices [1999] OJ L336/21.
- *EC Commission*, Commission Notice – Guidelines on Vertical Restraints [2000] OJ C291/1.
- *EC Commission*, Commission Regulation 2659/2000 on the application of Article 81(3) of the Treaty to categories of research and development agreements [2000] OJ L304/7.
- *EC Commission*, Guidelines on the applicability of Article 81 of the EC Treaty to horizontal cooperation agreements, [2001] OJ C3/02.
- *EC Commission*, Commission Notice on agreements of minor importance [2001] OJ C368/07.
- *EC Commission*, Guidelines on the assessment of horizontal mergers under the Council Regulation on the Control of Concentrations between Undertakings [2004] OJ C31/03.
- *EC Commission*, Commission Regulation (EC) No 802/2004 of April 7 2004 implementing Council Regulation (EC) No 139/2004 on the control of concentrations between undertakings [2004] OJ L133/1.
- *EC Council*, Council Regulation 384/96 (EC) No 384/96 of 22 December 1995 on protection against dumped imports from countries not members of the European Community [1996] OJ L056.
- *EC Council*, EEC Regulation 4064/89 [1990] OJ L257/13 as amended by Council Regulation (EC) No 1310/97 of 30 June 1997 [1997] OJ L180/1.
- *EC Council*, Council Regulation (EC) No 1/2003 of 16 December 2002 on the implementation of the rules on competition laid down in Articles 81 and 82 of the Treaty [2003] OJ L1/1.
- *EC Council*, Regulation (EC) No 1/2003, OJ 2003 L1/1.
- *EC Council*, Council Regulation (EC) No 139/2004 of 20 January 2004 on the control of concentrations between undertakings [2004] OJ L24/1.
- *EWG-Rat*, Verordnung Nr. 17: Erste Durchführungsverordnung zu den Artikeln 85 und 86 des Vertrages, ABl. P 013 (21/02/1962).

- *Federal German Cartel Office,* Guidelines on Domestic Effects of Mergers Completed Abroad (1999), available at: http://www.bundeskartellamt.de/wDeutsch/download/pdf/Merkblaetter/Merkblaetter_englisch/99_Inlandsauswirkung_e.pdf (21.05.05).
- *GATT Contracting Parties,* Decision of 28 November 1979 on "Differential and More Favourable Treatment, Reciprocity and Fuller Participation of Developing Countries", BISD 26S/203, available at: http://www.wto.org/english/docs_e/legal_e/enabling1979_e.htm (14.08.2005).
- *GATT Contracting Parties,* General Agreement on Tariffs and Trade (1994).
- *Havana Charter for an International Trade Organization ("ITO-Charter"),* available at: http://www.wto.org/english/docs_e/legal_e/havana_e.pdf.
- *ICN,* Memorandum on the Establishment and Operation of the International Competition Network, available at: http://www.internationalcompetitionnetwork.org/mou.pdf (13.08.2005).
- *ICN,* Recommended Practices for Merger Notification and Review. available at: http://www.internationalcompetitionnetwork.org/mnprecpractices.pdf (13.09.2005).
- *Kommission der Europäischen Gemeinschaften,* Vorschlag für eine Verordnung des Rates zur Durchführung der in den Artikeln 81 und 82 EG-Vertrag niedergelegten Wettbewerbsregeln und zur Änderung der Verordnungen (EWG) Nr. 1017/68, (EWG) Nr. 2988/74, (EWG) Nr. 4056/86 und (EWG) Nr. 3975/87 („Durchführungsverordnung zu den Artikeln 81 und 82 EG-Vertrag, KOM (2000) 582.
- *Marrakesh Agreement Establishing the World Trade Organisation* (1994).
- *OECD,* Recommendation of the Council concerning Co-operation between Member countries on restrictive business practices affecting international trade, C(67)53(Final), October 10, 1967.
- *OECD,* 1995 Recommendation of the Council concerning Co-operation between Member Countries on Anticompetitive Practices affecting International Trade, available at http://webdomino1.oecd.org/horizontal/oecdacts.nsf/Display/C0FF10F530824A7BC12570830076B27A?OpenDocument (14.08.2005).
- *UN General Assembly,* UN Set of Multilaterally Agreed Equitable Principles and Rules for the Control of Restrictive Business Practices, Resolution 35/63 (December 5, 1980),

available at: http://r0.unctad.org/en/subsites/cpolicy/docs/CPSet/cpsetp3.htm (12.08.205).

- *US Department of Justice*, Horizontal Merger Guidelines, April 8,1997, s. 1, available at: http://www.usdoj.gov/atr/public/guidelines/hmg.htm.
- *United Nations*, Charter of the United Nations, available at: http://www.un.org/aboutun/charter/.
- United States International Antitrust Enforcement Assistance Act of 1994, available at: http://www.ftc.gov/ogc/stat2.htm (21.05.2005).

Table of Cases

European Case Law

Comission decisions

- *Aerospatiale-DeHavilland* [1991] OJ L334/42; [1992] CMLR M2.
- *Boeing/McDonnell Douglas* (Case No IV/M.877) [1997] OJ L336/16.
- *Re the Agreement of Davide-Campari-Milano SpA* [1978] OJ L70/69, [1978] 2 CMLR 397.
- *Soda-Ash-Solvay Case* [1991] OJ L152/21.
- *Schöller Lebensmittel GmbH,* OJ 1993, L 183/1.
- *Polypropylene* [1986] OJ L230/1.
- *Oscar Bronner GmbH & Co. KG* v. *Mediaprint* (Case C-7/97) [1998] ECR I-7791.
- *GE Honeywell,* Case No. COMP/M.2220, 3 July 2001.

Court of First Instance

- *Airtours v. Commission* (Case T-342/99) [2002] OJ C191/24.
- *Bayer AG v. Commission* (Case T-41/96) [1996] 5 CMLR 416.
- *European Night Services v. Commission* (Cases T-374, 375, 384 & 388/94) [1998] ECR II-3141;

- *Gencor v. Commission* (Case T-102/96) [1999] ECR II-7153.
- *Langnese-Iglo GmbH & Co KG & Schöller Lebensmittel v Commission* (Cases T-7/93 and T-9/93) [1995] ECR II-1533.
- *Matra Hachette v. Commission* (Case T-17/93) [1994] ECR II-595.
- *Métropole* (Cases T-528/93, T-543/93 and T-546/93, [1996] ECR II-649.
- *Métropole television (M6) and others v. Commission* (Case T-112/99) [2001] 5 CMLR 1236.
- *Micro Leader* (Case T-198/98) [1998] ECR II-3989.
- *Schneider Electric SA v. Commission* (Case T-310/01) [2003] OJ C55/24.
- *Società Italiana Vetro SpA v. Commission* (Cases T-68 and 77-78/89) [1992] ECR II-1403.
- *Tetra Laval BV. v. Commission* (Case T-5/02) [2003] OJ C19/34.

European Court of Justice

- *AKZO Chemie BV v. Commission* (Case C-62/86) [19991] ECR I-3359, [1993] 5 CMLR 215.
- *Compagnie Maritime Belge Transporst SA v. Commission* (Cases C-395 & 396/96) [2000] 4 CMLR 1076.
- *Consten & Grundig v. Commission* (Case 56&58/64) [1966] ECR 299.
- *Courage* v. *Grehan* (Case C-453/99) [2001] 5 CMLR 28.
- *Delimitis v. Henninger Bräu* (Case C-234/89) [1991] ECR I-935.
- *Extramet Industrie SA.* v. *Council* European Court Reports (Case C-358/89) 1992, I-3813.
- France *v.* Commission & Société Commerciale des Potasses et de l'Azote (SCPA) v. Commission (Cases C-68/94 & C-30/95) [1998] ECR I-1375, [1998] 4 CMLR 829 (Kali).
- *Geraets-Smits v. Stichting Ziekenfonds, Peerboom v. Stichting CZ Groep Zorgverzekeringen* (Case 157/99) [2001] ECR I-5473.

- *Gøttrup -Klim Grovvareforening and Others v. Dansk Landbrugs Grovvareselskab AmbA (DLG)* (Case C-250/92) [1994] ECR I-5641, [1996] 4 CMLR 191.
- *Hocsman v. Ministre de l'Emploi* (Case C-238/98) *[2000] ECR I-6623.*
- *Hüls AG v. Commission* (Case C-199/92P) [1999] 5 CMLR 1016.
- *ICI v. Commission* (Cases 48, 49, 51-7/69*)* [1972] ECR 619.
- *ICI v. Commission (Dyestuffs)* (Case 48/69) [1972] ECR 619, [1972] CMLR 557.
- *Javico International and Javico AG v. Yves Saint Laurent Parfums SA* (Case C-306/96) [1998] ECR I-1983; ECJ in Cases C414-416/99 *Zino Davidoff SA v. A & G Imports Ltd. And Levi Strauss and Co. and Others v. Tesco Stores Ltd. And Others* [2000] ECR I-8691.
- *Langnese-Iglo GmbH* [1993] OJ L183/19.
- *Maria Martinez Sala v. Freistaat Bayern* (Case C-85/96) [1998] ECR I-2691.
- *Metro v. Commission (No 1)* (Case 26/76) [1977] ECR 1875, [1978] 2 CMLR 1,*BPCL/ICI* [1984] OJ L212/1.
- *Nederlandsche Banden-Industrie Michelin v. Commission* (Case 322/81) [1983] ECR 3461 [1985] 1 CMLR 282.
- *RTE&ITP v. Commission (Magill)* (Cases C-241 to 241/91P) [1995] ECR I-743.
- *Rudy Grzelczyk v. Centre Public d'Aide Sociale d'Ottignes-Louvain-la-Neuve (CPAS)* (Case C-184/99) [2001] ECR I-6193.
- *Sebago* (Case C-173/98) [1999] 2 CMLR 1317.
- *SGL Carbon Ltd v. Commission* (Case C-308/04P) [2006] OJ C212/5.
- *Silhouette* (Case C-355/96) [1998] ECR I-4799.
- *Société Technique Minière v. Maschinenbau Ulm GmbH* (Case C-56/65) [1966] ECR 235.
- *Tetra Laval BV. v. Commission* (Case C-12/03 P) [2005] OJ C82/02.
- *Tetra Pak International SA v. Commission (Tetra Pak II)* (Case C-333/94 p) [1996] ECR I-5951, [1997] 4 CMLR 662.
- *Vlassopoulou v. Ministerium für Justiz, Bundes und Europaangelegenheiten Baden-Württemberg* (Case 340/89) [1991] ECR 2357.

- *Völk v. Vervaecke* (Case 5/69) [1969] ECR 295, 302.
- *Wood Pulp Cartel: Ahlström Oy v. Commission (Wood Pulp II)* (Cases C-89, 104, 114, 116-117, 125-129/85) [1993] ECR I-1307.
- *Wood Pulp I,* A. Ahlström Oy *v.* Commission (Cases 89, 104, 114, 116, 117, 125-129/85) [1988] ECR 5193, [1988] 4 CMLR 901.
- *Wouters and Others v. Algemene Raad van de Nederlands Orde van Advocaten* (Case C-309/99) [2002] 4 CMLR 27.

US Case Law

- *Brooke Group Ltd. v. Brown & Wiliamson Tobacco Corp., 509 U.S. 209, 113 S.Ct. 2578, 125 L.Ed.2d 168 (1993).*
- *Chicago Board of Trade v. US,* 246 US 231 (1918).
- *Continental TV Inc v. GTE Slyvania Inc* 433 US 36 (1977).
- *Dr Miles Medical Co v. John D Park & Sons Co.* 220 US 373 (1911).
- *Eastern Railways Presidents Conference v. Noerr Motor Freight, Inc.,* 365 U.S. 127 (1961).
- *Eastman Kodak Co. v. Image Technical Services Inc.,* 504 US 451, 119 L. Ed. 2d 265, 112 S.Ct. 2072 (1992)
- *Empagram SA v. Hoffman-LaRoche,* US Court of Appeal D.C. Circuit, Decision of 17 January 2003, No. 01-7115.
- *F. Hoffman-La Roche Ltd. et. al. v. Empagram S.A.*, June 14, 2004, compare Sandra Rubin, *US Antitrust Reach Shortened,* Financial Post 30.6.2004, FP11, at: http://www.mcmillanbinch.com/Upload/News/JWRowley_USantitrust_reach_063004.pdf
- *Ferrosilicon Case, Investigation No. 751-TA-21-27, US International Trade Commission Publication 3218, Washington, D.C., 1999.*
- *Hartford Fire Insurance Co. v. California*, 509 US 764,113 S Ct. 2891 (1993).
- *Mannington Mills Inc. v. Congoleum Corp.*, 595 F, 2d 1287 (3rd Cir.1979)

- *Timberland Lumber Co. v. Bank of America*, 549 F.2d597 at 613 (9th Cir.1976)

- *United Mine Workers of America v. Pennington*, 381 U.S. 657 (1965).

- *United States v. Aluminum Co. of America*, 389 US 49 (1967).

- *United States v. Arnold Schwinn & Co*, 338 US 365.

- *United States v. General Dynamics Corp.*, 415 US 486 (1974)

- *United States v. Grinnell Corp.*, 384 US 563, 570-71 (1966).

- *United States* v. *Nippon Paper Industries Co.*, 109 F, 3d (1st Cir. 1997).

- *Valey Liquors Inc v. Renfield Importers Ltd*, 678 F.2d 742 (7th Cir. 1982), 745.

GATT Panel Reports

- *Canada – Foreign Investment Review Act (FIRA)*, BISD 30S/140, L/5504, adopted on Feb. 7, 1984.

- *EEC – Payments and Subsidies Paid to Processors and Producers of Oilseeds and Related Animal-Feed Proteins*, 37th Supp. BISD 86, adopted on January 25, 1990.

- *European Communities – Regime for the Importation, Sale and Distribution of Bananas*, DS32/R (3 June 1993) [Bananas I Panel Report], DS38/R (1995) [Bananas II Panel Report].

- Japan – Trade in Semi-Conductors, BISD 36S/345.

WTO Case Law

Panel Reports

- *Argentina – Measures Affecting the Export of Bovine Hides and the Import of Finished Leather*, WTO Doc. WT/DS155/R, adopted on Dec. 19, 2000.

- *EC – Regime for the Importation, Sale and Distribution of Bananas*, WT/DS27/R.

- *Indonesia – Certain Measures affecting the Automotive Industry*, WT/DS54, 55, 59, 64/R, adopted on July 23, 1998.

– *Italian Discrimination against Imported Agricultural Machinery*, BISD 7S/60, L/833, adopted on 23 October 1958.

– *Japan – Measures Affecting Consumer Photographic Film and Paper* (DS44), adopted on April 22, 1998.

– *Korea – Taxes on Alcoholic Beverages*, pp. 171-192, WT/DS75/R.

– Mexico – Measures Affecting Telecommunications Services, (2004) WTO Doc. WT/DS204/R.

Appellate Body Reports

– *European Communities – Measures Affecting Asbestos and Asbestos-Containing Products*, WT/DS135/AB/R (March 12, 2001).

– *European Communities – Regime for the Importation, Sale and Distribution of Bananas*, para. 220, WT/DS27/AB/R.

– *Japan – Taxes on Alcoholic Beverages II*, WT/DS8/AB/R, WT/DS10/AB/R, WT/DS11/AB/R, Nov. 1, 1996.

Völkerrecht, Europarecht und Internationales Wirtschaftsrecht

Herausgegeben von Peter Hilpold und August Reinisch

Band 1 Florian Razesberger: The International Criminal Court. The Principle of Complementarity. 2006.

Band 2 Christian Wimpissinger: Steuerliche Verlustverrechnung nach EG-Recht. 2006.

Band 3 Christina Knahr: Participation of Non-State Actors in the Dispute Settlement System of the WTO: Benefit or Burden? 2007.

Band 4 Daniela Kröll: Toward Multilateral Competition Law? After Cancún: Reevaluating the Case for Additional International Competition Rules Under Special Consideration of the WTO Agreement. 2007.

www.peterlang.de